The decolonization of imagination

The decolonization of imagination

CULTURE, KNOWLEDGE
AND POWER

edited by
Jan Nederveen Pieterse
and Bhikhu Parekh

Zed Books Ltd
LONDON AND NEW JERSEY

The Decolonization of Imagination was first published by
Zed Books Ltd, 7 Cynthia Street,
London N1 9JF, UK, and
165 First Avenue, Atlantic Highlands,
New Jersey 07716, USA, in 1995.

Cover designed by Andrew Corbett.
The publishers have made every effort to trace the
copyright holder of the photograph on the front cover,
but without success. Any information as to the
photographer's identity will be gratefully received by
the publishers, and due credit given in subsequent
editions.
Set in Monotype Garamond by Ewan Smith.
Printed and bound in the United Kingdom
by Biddles Ltd, Guildford and King's Lynn.

A catalogue record for this book is available from
the British Library.

US CIP data is available from the Library of Congress.

ISBN 1 85649 279 6 cased
ISBN 1 85649 280 x limp

Contents

Preface

This volume originates from a conference organized in Amsterdam in 1991. The original idea for the conference was that scholars from various parts of the world would deconstruct the images that had been produced in Europe or the West about these areas, decode and interpret them as Western self-images projected onto others, and so arrive at a negative mirror image of the West. Accordingly one of the working subtitles was 'Europe in Reverse Video' (an earlier subtitle was 'Europe and its Others'). What I had in mind were visual images and stereotypes about Asia, the Middle East and Africa since at the time I was completing work on a book entitled *White on Black: Images of Africa and Blacks in Western Popular Culture*, which dealt with visual materials. The agenda of the scholars invited turned out to be, as conferences go, rather different – more concerned with textual discourse than with images, more complex and much wider, addressing questions such as postcoloniality and multiculturalism.

The contributions have been revised for this volume and in several cases authors' contributions differ from those presented at the conference (Parekh, Takaki, Spivak, Goonatilake). For various reasons a number of conference contributions could not be included, but I would like to thank the participants: Ivan Van Sertima, Mohamed Babu, Cameron Duodu, Ampie Coetzee, Julie Frederikse, Vernon February, Teun van Dijk, Laura Balbo, Manning Marable, Lillian Anthony, Rhoda Reddock, Mohamed Arkoun, Hassan Hanafi, Leila Shahid, Kumkum Sangari, Majid Siddiqi, Oda Makoto, Bernadette Devlin McAliskey, Nawal el Sadaawi, Barney Pityana, Ngugi wa Thiong'o and Raymond Chasle. I would like to express my cordial thanks to the participants and to the institutions and persons whose cooperation made the conference possible: the Transnational Institute in Amsterdam, in particular Laurian Zwart; European Studies and the Centre for Race and Ethnic Studies of the University of Amsterdam, in particular Joep Leerssen and Philomena Essed; the Netherlands Association for Culture and Development, in particular Marjan Rameijer and Cees Hamelink; and Paradiso, in particular Caroline Nevejan. I would also like to express my appreciation to the sponsors who funded the project: the Fondation pour la Coopération Culturelle ACP/CEE in Brussels, UNESCO and, in the Netherlands, the Ministry of Foreign Affairs, the National Commission for Development Information, the Council of Churches, the National UNESCO Commission and the City of Amsterdam. I would like to thank Lisa Chason for her help in editing the volume. I invited Bhikhu Parekh to co-edit this volume and his cooperation made the project a pleasure to work on.

Three chapters have been published before in different versions. We thank *Cultural Anthropology* for permission to reprint that of Raymond Corbey. Earlier versions of Gayatri Spivak's chapter appeared in the *Midwestern Modern Language Association Quarterly*, Spring 1992, and that of Ann Stoler in *Comparative Studies in Society and History*.

Jan Nederveen Pieterse

Contributors

Jan Berting is Professor of Sociology and Research Director at Erasmus University, Rotterdam. His main interests are social inequality and mobility; technology and social change with special interest in risk analysis; international comparative research and human rights. Recent publications include *The Technological Factor* (1992, in Dutch) and *The Role of National Stereotypes in International Relations* (co-edited with Christiane Villain-Gandossi, Erasmus University, 1994).

Patrick Brantlinger is Professor of English at the University of Indiana, Bloomington. He is author of *Bread and Circuses: Theories of Mass Culture as Social Decay* (Cornell University Press, 1983), *Rule of Darkness: British Literature and Imperialism, 1830–1914* (Cornell University Press, 1988) and *Crusoe's Footprints: cultural studies in Britain and America* (Routledge, 1990).

Raymond Corbey, philosopher and anthropologist, lectures philosophy at the University of Tilburg and is Senior Research Fellow at the Department of Prehistory of Leiden University, both in the Netherlands. Much of his research and publications concerns the history and background of changing and conflicting interpretations of human and animal nature. He co-edited *Alterity, Identity, Image* (Rodopi, 1991) and *Ape, Man, Ape-Man: Changing Views since 1600* (Leiden University, 1995).

Susantha Goonatilake is at the Center for the Study of Social Change, New School for Social Research, New York. Among his books are *Aborted Discovery: Science and Creativity in the Third World* (Zed, 1984), *Crippled Minds: An Exploration into Colonial Culture* (Vikas, 1982), *Evolution of Information* (Pinter, 1992) and the edited volume *Technology in the Bed of History: Technological Independence: the Asian Experience* (UN University, 1993).

Jan Nederveen Pieterse is author of *White on Black: Images of Africa and Blacks in Western Popular Culture* (Yale University Press, 1992) and *Empire and Emancipation* (Praeger, 1989; Pluto, 1990), for which he received the 1990 JC Ruigrok Award of the Netherlands Society of the Sciences. His edited volumes include *Christianity and Hegemony* (Berg, 1992) and *Emancipations, Modern and Postmodern* (Sage, 1992). He is at the Institute of Social Studies in The Hague, where he is currently Research Director.

Marion O'Callaghan was Deputy Director of the Division of Human Rights and Peace of UNESCO. The daughter of the well-known Calypsonian 'Chinee Patrick', she has published *Rhodesia: the Conquest Society*, *Namibia: the Effects of Apartheid on Education Science, Culture and Information*, *Racism, Sexism and Apartheid* and, with Colette Guillaumin, *Reply to Lévi Strauss*. She has also published several novels under the name of Marion Patrick Jones. She lives in Trinidad.

Bhikhu Parekh is Professor of Political Theory at the University of Hull. He was Deputy Chairman of the Commission for Racial Equality, UK, between 1985 and 1990. His major publications include *Marx's Theory of Ideology* (Johns Hopkins University Press, 1982), *Contemporary Political Thinkers* (Johns Hopkins University Press, 1982), *Gandhi's Political Philosophy* (Macmillan, 1989) and *Colonialism, Tradition and Reform* (Sage, 1989).

Gayatri Chakravorty Spivak is Avalon Foundation Professor in the Humanities at Columbia University, New York. She is author of *In Other Worlds* (Methuen, 1987), *The Postcolonial Critic* (Routledge, 1990) and *Outside in the Teaching Machine* (1993).

Ann Stoler is Associate Professor of Anthropology and History at the University of Michigan. She has published widely on the cultural contours of power and hierarchy in colonial and contemporary Indonesia. Her works include *Capitalism and Confrontation in Sumatra's Plantation Belt, 1870–1979* (Yale University Press, 1985), for which she received the 1992 Harry Benda Prize in Southeast Asian Studies; *Racial Transgressions and the Education of Desire: A Colonial Reading of Foucault's History of Sexuality* (Duke University Press, 1995); and *Carnal Knowledge and Imperial Power: Bourgeois Civility and the Cultures of Whiteness in Colonial Southeast Asia* (University of California Press, forthcoming). She is on the editorial boards of the *Journal of Peasant Studies*, *American Ethnologist*, *Bijdragen* and the *Journal of the History of Sexuality*.

Ronald Takaki is Professor of Ethnic Studies, University of California, Berkeley. His books include *A Pro-Slavery Crusade*, *Violence in the Black Imagination*, *Pau Hana: Plantation Life and Labor in Hawaii*, *Iron Cages: Race and Culture in 19th Century America* (Athlone, 1979), *Strangers from a Different Shore: A History of Asian Americans* (Little, Brown and Company, and nominated for a Pulitzer Prize) and *A Different Mirror: The Making of Multicultural America* (Little, Brown and Company).

Toine van Teeffelen is Visiting Professor in Discourse Analysis at Birzeit University, West Bank. His books include *At the Edge of the Wilderness: Popular Fiction and the Palestinian–Israeli Conflict* (Amsterdam University, 1993) and *Soemoed: Palestinians under Occupation* (1986, in Dutch), and he has published articles on the ideological implications of Israeli anthropology and on media representations of the Palestinian–Israeli conflict.

Hiroshi Yoshioka is Associate Professor in Aesthetics at Konan University, Kobe. He studied philosophy and aesthetics at Kyoto University. He has published articles in Japanese on critical theory, poststructuralism and contemporary culture.

Sol Yurick is author of several novels including *Warriors*, *The Bag*, *Fertig* and *Richard A* and essays such as 'Behold Metatron the recording angel' (*Semiotext[e]*, 1985). He lives in Brooklyn, New York.

Shifting imaginaries: decolonization, internal decolonization, postcoloniality

Jan Nederveen Pieterse and Bhikhu Parekh

Conquest and domination may have been perennial in human history, but Western imperialism differs from other episodes of domination in that it involved a different mode of production (capitalism) and technology (industrialism), and took on a virtually global scope. This makes Western imperialism a much more complex and far-reaching process than any previous mode of domination. Universal features of Western hegemony in such spheres as science and technology, production and politics, have been inextricably interwoven with European or Western particularities and, in addition, with the peculiarities of colonial domination itself. All the faces of Western hegemony carry the multiple character of being both a contribution to the collective human repertoire (as well as being its manifestation in that their lineages were not exclusively European or Western) and an expression of imperial domination, suffused with the effect of power. The effect of power has been built into the notions of race, progress, evolution, modernity and development as hierarchies extending in time and space. Hence the profound complexity and extraordinary ramifications of the Western impact: a constellation of contributions that cannot be ignored, but that need to be extricated from the pervasive effect of power. Another difference to reckon with is that between the imagined and the actual impact of colonialism.

Although colonialism ended in India, the largest of the European colonies, nearly half a century ago and in most of the rest of the world about two decades ago, we still await a satisfactory analysis of its nature and its impact on both the metropolitan countries and the colonies. Even the economic balance sheet, which should have been the easiest to prepare, has not yet been worked out, and we do not know how exploitative colonial rule was, in what areas, with what consequences, and whether the new economic impulses and energies it generated partially compensated for its evils. The cultural impact of colonialism raises even more complex issues. It is widely argued by both colonial and metropolitan intellectuals that colonial rule brought with it modern ideas and values. Although these values are not clearly specified, they are generally taken to include those associated with liberal individualism, industrialization and the centralized nation-state.

If one probes deeper, the picture becomes complex, and the prevailing view needs radical revision. First, it is not entirely correct to say that colonial rule introduced modern values. Colonial rulers were primarily concerned with creating and maintaining the basic conditions of their rule. Since they justified their rule in civilizational terms they needed to introduce some of the European values and institutions. However, the continuity of colonial rule required that the prevailing values and institutions should not be too much disturbed, and that modern values, which were ultimately subversive of colonial rule, should be introduced partially and half-heartedly. This means that colonial rule both introduced and arrested the flow of new values and institutions, and also that it both changed and froze their traditional counterparts. To say that it only subverted or froze the precolonial society is to be guilty of half-truths.

Second, values and institutions introduced by colonial rule could not last or even be understood unless they were grafted onto their hospitable traditional analogues. Both the colonial and metropolitan intellectuals therefore needed to interpret the inherited institutions and practices of colonial societies. Their interpretations often differed and led to much debate, and although some of them became more influential, others were never totally defeated. Colonial rule forced the colonized intellectuals to ask questions about themselves, their society and their history which they never had asked before, and generated an unprecedented level of self-consciousness. The new values and institutions introduced by colonial rule worked their way not directly but through the medium of this self-consciousness. Colonial intellectuals and leaders dug deep into their past, reinterpreted their resources, and formulated a range of responses to the colonial cultural legacy. They played as vital a role as the colonial masters in structuring and shaping the influence of colonial rule.

Third, colonial rule did not represent as drastic a rupture in the history of colonial societies as is often made out. Some countries, such as India, had long been used to foreign invasions, and knew how to take them in their stride. No doubt European rule had an unprecedented reach and penetration, but it also had its inherent limitations, derived partly from the fact that the new rulers, intuitively perceived as racially and culturally different, lacked the accessibility and relative familiarity of their predecessors. Even so far as the societies with no previous experience of foreign rule were concerned, colonial rule remained limited in its impact. Barely 5 per cent of their people ever cared to learn their masters' language, and even fewer came into close contact with them. The fact that colonial rulers often did not disrupt local traditions and institutions further restricted their influence. All this means that colonialism introduced no more than one new idiom, one new strand, in the complex mosaic of the societies subjected to it. To talk of the disruption of traditional identities, of the need to cope with the schizophrenia induced by the dramatic conflict between traditional and modern identities, is wholly to misunderstand the situation.

Since colonization was a highly complex process, decolonization lacks a clear focus and target. It may be easy to resent and attack foreign rulers or capital, but it is extremely difficult to identify what values, institutions and identities are foreign and part of the colonial legacy. And if one succeeds in identifying some of them, they are sometimes too deeply intertwined with their endogenous analogues to be clearly separated from them. Even if one manages to isolate some of them, one is sometimes so deeply shaped and moulded by them as to be unable to reject them without rejecting parts of oneself. Even as colonialism did not involve the imposition of something entirely new and foreign, decolonization cannot consist in discarding what is deemed to be alien. Colonialism evolved a new consciousness out of a subtle mixture of the old and new; decolonization has to follow the same route. It requires not the restoration of a historically continuous and allegedly pure precolonial heritage, but an imaginative creation of a new form of consciousness and way of life.

The decolonization of imagination involves both the colonizers and the colonized. The decolonization of the *Western* imagination means reviewing Western horizons in the light of the collusion with empire and colonialism, and with the ongoing asymmetries of global power. In the South, decolonization has often been viewed in narrowly political (national liberation) or economic terms (as in dependency theory), while as a cultural politics it means engaging the imaginaries that guide 'development'.

This is not merely a matter of disentangling the effect of power (as if it were possible to separate the wheat from the chaff), but of understanding the interweaving of progress and power, and to reflect on the role of power in history. Engaging the collective record requires confronting both the universal and the particularist dimensions of empire. This includes the universal scope of the effect of power, for the mimesis in the course and aftermath of colonialism also extended to the model of power, the imperial model. Thus the nation-state form, to mention a familiar point, has been universally adopted in the wake of the colonial epoch. The West also taught lessons of power, and societies and horizons in the West and in the colonized, or otherwise imperially affected, world have been bent and shaped along the lines of colonial imaginaries. This problematic means transcending the battle lines drawn by colonialism as well as by anticolonialism. It involves an engagement with global times that is no longer premised either on Eurocentrism, modernization theory or other forms of Western ethnocentrism passing for universalism, or on Third Worldism, nativism and parochially anti-Western views.

In these reflections, 'decolonization' is taken both in a historical and in a wider metaphorical sense. In the historical sense, it refers to the momentum of political decolonization, a process that has largely been completed. In an economic sense it has been on the agenda for almost as long, under the blanket heading of 'development'. A process of intellectual decolonization has also been under way, in the sense that critical perspectives on colonialism have become more and more common, also in the West. It is only in recent years that cultural decolonization has been recognized as a concern, also in the sense of retracing the culture of colonialism in the Western world.

> [D]ecolonization comes to be understood as an act of exorcism for both the colonizer and the colonized. For both parties it must be a process of liberation: from dependency, in the case of the colonized, and from imperialist, racist perceptions, representations, and institutions ... in the case of the colonizer (Mehrez 1991: 258).

The legacy of 500 years of Western expansion, including 200 years of Western hegemony, reflected in racism and exotism, continues to be recycled in Western cultures in the form of stereotypical images of 'non-Western' cultures. Moreover, neocolonial culture in the West is mirrored in the prevalence of neocolonial culture in the South. The adoption of Western stereotypes about the South in the South carries consequences for policy-making, e.g. in the adoption of Western development models, and for South–South relations. For instance, Western stereotypes about Africa and blacks have been common in Japan and Asian countries (cf. Nederveen Pieterse 1992).

To what extent is this situation in a state of flux, now that we experience a transition from an era of Western hegemony towards polycentrism in a context of high interaction? Only to a limited extent, considering that most centres of power and influence in the multipolar world – from Tokyo to Buenos Aires – largely operate within an occidental orbit. The main, partial, exceptions are several of the ASEAN countries, Islamist theocracies and a diverse range of indigenous peoples.

There are as many different modes of decolonization as there are modes of colonization and ways of conceptualizing them. In a historical framework, colonialism and imperialism are countered by anticolonialism. The wider question of culture and imperialism has been addressed by critiques of orientalism. Interestingly the notion of colonialism has taken on a wider, metaphorical meaning in the West to describe modes of domination and control within the West, for instance in Jürgen Habermas's concept of the 'colonization of the life-world' to describe the impact of the spread and deepening of capitalist relations. In fact one might as well speak 'of any number of methaphorical "colonisations" having to do with region, class, race and gender' (Shohat and Stam 1985: 53).

On a general level what is at issue in decolonizing the imagination is the relationship between power and culture, domination and the imaginary. Overall questions of culture, language and power are taken up in discourse analysis, while popular culture and media are a subject of inquiry in cultural studies. More specifically, power and the imaginary are addressed in a variety of theoretical frameworks – inspired by phenomenology, by Durkheim, and by Lacan's work on the imaginary.

Western iconoclasm has found an expression in the critique of the spectacle by the Situationists in the 1960s; a line of thinking that is extended in Baudrillard's views on the simulacrum and hyperreality, and his concern with power as seduction. Part of this preoccupation is that, as Michel Maffesoli remarks, 'in the tracks of western iconoclasm, contemporary radical thought finds it difficult to integrate everything which belongs to the non-conscious, the non-rational or to the vast domain of non-verbal communication' (1993: 3). Current work on the imaginary takes a different position. In Lacan's work, which has been particularly influential in feminist writing, the imaginary represents an early, pre-Oedipal form of subjectivity which is contrasted to the symbolic (understood as the level of culture, language and the law) (Grosz 1990). The phenomenological and Durkheimian approaches arrive via different routes at a similar assessment. Moscovici on social representation (1993) and Bourdieu's work on reproduction and symbolic violence are instances of a line of inquiry inspired by phenomenology. Durkheim's notions of conscience collective and communion of consciousness have generated a different sociological appraisal (Maffesoli 1993). Paraphrasing the physicist David Bohm, Gilbert Durand refers to the imaginary as 'the "implicate order" through which all understanding necessarily passes' (Durand 1993: 17). The imaginary is viewed as crucial to the process of social representation and as the basis of a social aesthetics (Tacussel 1993). 'The image becomes a vector of communion' (Maffesoli 1993: 3). In the case of 'sports, musical concerts, patriotic assemblies or even gatherings for the purposes of consumption' ... 'the "binding" process takes place around images which one shares with others' (Maffesoli 1993: 4; cf. 1988). This kind of interest in the imaginary is quite different from the concern with image-breaking which links rationalists, positivists and some forms of radical critique: it posits instead the imaginary as constitutive of community and society. It follows that the analysis of discourse as constitutive of politics, crucial as it is, is not enough, for it addresses only the symbolic level. The imaginary is also a vector of political analysis (Laclau and Mouffe 1988) and is thematized in various historical studies (e.g. Le Goff 1986, Comaroff and Comaroff 1992).

Also in the context of imperialism and colonialism, different lines of inquiry converge on the theme of imagination. On the one hand, in the sceptical tradition, there is the theme of image versus reality, or the false imagery of domination, such as stereotypes, othering, orientalism, narcissism. There is a wide stream of studies of Western 'images of' – the Middle East, Islam, Africa, Asia, China, India, the Pacific, Tahiti, Maoris, native Americans, etc. This has also generated studies of imagery in reverse, such as 'Barbarians in Arab eyes' (Al-Azmeh 1992). A different take on the imaginary of power is concerned with the ways in which images, regardless of whether they are true or false, are constitutive of social relations and realities. Said's *Orientalism*, and that is part of the strength of this work, features both elements: the critique of orientalism as a false imaginary, and the acknowledgement of this imaginary, whether false or true, constituting certain practices and institutions. Images function as signals and markers in constituting boundaries between self and other, us and them, normal and abnormal, etc. (e.g. Gilman 1985, Downing and

Bazargan 1991). Salient boundaries are richly flagged by clusters or chains of images – as indicated in works such as 'Frankenstein's monster and images of race in nineteenth-century Britain' (Malchow 1993).

Decolonization: nationalism and nativism

The observation made in the context of anticolonial struggles – that liberation requires psychological liberation for its precondition – holds true generally. 'Freeing the imagination' has been a recurrent theme in movements of reorientation, renaissance, reform or revolution through history and across cultures, hence their iconoclastic nature. If, however, we view images as, in the words of Maffesoli, 'vectors of communion', it follows that liberation means the substitution of one vector of communion – imported and imposed by the colonial power – by other, presumably self-generated vectors. Emancipation involves communion, and communion cannot exist without binding images. The distinction between image and reality, falsity and truth, merges, then, with the boundary between dominator and subaltern, and, in turn, with other and self. In the process, the other of colonialism becomes the self of decolonization: the roles are reversed, but the logic of image and power, which is also the power of communion, has not necessarily changed.

Cultural decolonization anticipated and paved the way for political decolonization, accompanied it, and follows independence. In the engagement with colonial imaginaries we can identify several episodes and currents: decolonization, internal decolonization and postcoloniality. In a schematic fashion, these represent the mainstream pattern of cultural decolonization.

The anticolonial movements, just like Third Worldism later on, carried cultural components all along, reinvoking and reworking indigenous resources to mobilize for decolonization. Often these figured as part of the momentum of the nationalist movement or, over time, were subsumed within its stream. Often the first nuclei of what were to become movements for national independence were movements we would now term cultural, such as Sarekat Islam in Indonesia, or the Buddhist revival movement in nineteenth-century Ceylon. Indeed, religion has been a major ground for popular mobilization. Gandhi's movement for *swaraj* (self-rule) built on local resources in its methods, such as *satyagraha* (non-violent resistance), its symbolism, such as the home-spun cotton peasant dress, and its vision of the future India. At the same time Gandhi also drew inspiration from his experiences in England and South Africa, and his readings of Western authors such as Tolstoy and Emerson.

Cultural reorientations during the colonial era range from reorientations in a religious framework (such as the *Nahda*, renewal or reawakening, in the Middle East, religious revival and humanism in Asia) to the 'Pan-' movements of the turn of the century that were avowedly 'cultural', sometimes with religious, at other times with biological-racist, overtones.

Ethiopianism and Pan-Turkism belong to the earlier expression, and the momentum of Pan-Europeanism, Pan-Islam, Pan-Arabism, Pan-Africanism, and *indigenismo* and *mestizaje* in Latin America still lives on in different guises. The common denominator is the mobilization of the cultural resources of civilizational areas, supplementing, amplifying and superseding nationalism.

In the wide array of cultural decolonizing gestures, one of the earliest with respect to Africa was *négritude* or the philosophy of an authentic African otherness and humanity, advanced by Léopold Senghor, Aimé Césaire and others in Paris in the 1930s. Negritude lives on in African historical revisionism, as in the work of Cheikh Anta Diop (1991) and his claim that ancient Egypt was an African project, and in philosophies of *Africanité* and African authenticity. As such it formed part of the early ideas of African nationalism, African socialism and Pan-Africanism. In Kwame Nkrumah we find a combination of various anti-imperialist imaginaries and politics, a convergence of nationalism, socialism and Pan-Africanism. Afrocentrism has a double career, in Africa and among the African diaspora, in the West Indies and the USA in particular.

Various dimensions of colonialism evoked different responses. *Négritude* was a response to colonial racism. The discourses of authenticity, *Africanité* and Afrocentrism all follow the logic of nativism. Nationalism was embedded in a wider civilizational project, just as politically it was often embedded in movements of regional solidarity or hegemony, such as Pan-Africanism or Pan-Arabism. This too reflected imperial imaginaries: the classification of 'races' matching civilizational areas, turned into political projects.

The discourse of civilizational areas has not vanished but is being put to new use. Among Indian intellectuals the notion of an 'Indic civilization' remains an influential idiom because it provides distance from the colonial legacy ('India') and the state, and room for manoeuvre in relation to the multicultural nation. In East Asia, neo-Confucianism and the 'Confucian ethic' serves as an ideology to explain the economic success of the East Asian Newly Industrialized Countries, as an Asian equivalent to Weber's Protestant ethic as the spirit of modern capitalism. Promoted from Singapore to Japan, it serves well as a state ideology of civil obedience and collective conformity in the name of economic prosperity.

Internal decolonization: critiques of nationalism and nativism

The cynical popular reading of decolonization went: once white sahib, now brown sahib. This sentiment is part of what we may term 'internal decolonization'. Social forces who earlier followed the nationalist flag, or whose voice was not registered in the anticolonialist confrontations, may challenge the nationalist project in the name of class, gender, ethnicity, region or religion.

If the nationalist project was hegemonized by the middle class, popular sectors of workers and peasants may initiate a rejection of the state, the bureaucracy, its centralization, its policies and official culture. Third World nationalism, although liberating in being anti-imperialist, may be another form of elitism. Early on, Third World nationalism had already been criticized for its lack of social consciousness, for instance by Frantz Fanon (1967). In India, the school of Subaltern Studies (e.g. Guha and Spivak 1988) has undertaken a review of official, nationalist history of de-colonization from the point of view of subaltern social forces – the term subaltern is a reference to Gramsci's terminology for the popular strata.

Gender is another avenue of 'internal decolonization': women have criticized the gendered, masculinist character of nationalism (e.g. Kandyoti 1991; Enloe 1990). Third World nationalism has also been criticized from within for its inclination towards 'internal colonialism', on regional or ethnic grounds, on the grounds of language or religion, by minorities or indigenous peoples. Third World nationalism has been analysed as a derivative discourse (Chatterjee 1986) and Third World states have been criticized as 'inheritor states', inheriting the colonial administrative struc-tures. Accordingly Ernest Wamba-dia-Wamba (cited in Tadesse 1992) calls for the 'de-imperialization of the state' in Africa. As a cultural politics, Third World nationalism may take the form of state culture, along with a cultural variation on dependency theory and policies of cultural pro-tectionism. It subjects the autonomy of culture and literature to the politics of official nationalism and dominant parties (Harlow 1987).

The critiques of nationalism from popular, gender and ethnic points of view also extend to nativism. Thus, *négritude* as a movement foundered in the course of time for a number of reasons. It was criticized as 'idealist' by 'materialist' critics because Léopold Senghor subordinated economic and social liberation to spiritual and cultural liberation (Hymans 1971: 154). It was criticized because of its romanticization of the African past as 'pastoral idyllism' (Arnold 1981: 122). Wole Soyinka ridiculed it as 'tigritude': 'I don't think a tiger has to go around proclaiming his tigritude' (quoted in Jahn 1968: 265). Besides, in the words of Madubuike, 'When a nigger kicks a nigger/Where is the negritude?' (cited in Chinweizu et al. 1983: 258).

The discourses of nativism, such as *indigenismo* in Latin America and *Africanité* in Africa, are no longer as persuasive as they used to be. The discourse of authenticity has been inherited as a see-through ideology ventriloquated by the likes of Mobutu sese Seko. As political movements began to lose the niche provided by the Cold War they adopted the discourse of authenticity. Now that railing against communism no longer pays, Unita in Angola and Inkatha in South Africa opt for cultural authen-ticity, which in local vernacular means: ethnicity. The very discourse of cultural cohesion has become a discourse of ethnic fragmentation. The Ghanaian philosopher Kwame Appiah observes: 'nativism in theory is unlikely to lead us away from where we already are. Time and again, cultural nationalism has followed the route of alternate genealogizing. We end up always in the same place; the achievement is to have invented a different past for it' (1992: 68). He concludes: 'We run the risk of ersatz exoticism, like the tourist trinkets in the Gift Shops of Lagos and Nairobi' (1992: 72).

As oppositional discourses nationalism and nativism tend to reproduce the underlying logic of the colonial project and imaginary: adjusting to the overall power structure they find a niche within it. The logic is that of indigenization and this process of mimesis may involve the essentialization of difference – according to a logic not unlike that of colonial racism, except that the other has become the self and the values are reversed. Discourses of difference, such as Africanity, etc., play on the same themes as right-wing discourse in the West – white supremacism, white power, the National Front. For those Africans, Asians and Latin Americans living in the West, this game of mirrors and discourse of incommensurable authenticity may have uncomfortable consequences, although Afrocentrism also serves as an affirmative discourse under pressure. Criticisms of Afrocentrism acknowledge the importance of self-affirmation but argue that it reproduces the structure of colonialist thought and epistemology, in replicating its racist categories (e.g. West 1992). The consequence of this view has been referred to as 'universal otherhood', that is, the world as an archipelago of particularisms which can intercommunicate only on the basis of difference.

Hence another move, beyond nationalism and nativism, has been to opt for *syncretism*, for some form of synthesis between Western and local culture. But at times the difference between this and nationalism is not quite clear. In their book *Toward the Decolonization of African Literature*, Chinweizu and his co-authors state their task as follows:

> on the one hand, our culture has to destroy all encrustations of colonial men-
> tality, and on the other hand, has to map out new foundations for an African
> modernity. This cultural task demands a deliberate and calculated process of
> syncretism: one which, above all, emphasizes valuable continuities with our pre-
> colonial culture, welcomes vitalizing contributions from other cultures, and
> exercises inventive genius in making a healthy and distinguished synthesis from
> them all (1983: 239).

Such a synthesis, they insist, 'must be within the parameters of the African tradition'. They characterize their project as 'traditionalist', i.e. 'experimentation for the purpose of modernizing and revitalizing the tradition' (1983: 239). 'Tradition' as a vector of communion is an image that, apparently, it is difficult to do without. Interestingly, their terminology closely matches that of Philip Curtin's (1972) analysis of African modes of decolonization. They do qualify their position by arguing that tradition must not be romanticized, for a 'mythical portrait of traditional Africa can prove to be a new prison' (1983: 257).

Postcolonial boundary crossings

In studies on the cultural dimensions of colonialism, Eurocentrism has been the focal point of criticism. Critiques of colonial imaginaries have targeted orientalism (Said 1978), Victorian anthropology (Fabian 1983), anthropology's connection to imperialism, modernization theory (Banuri 1990), etc. The theme of cultural imperialism has found expression in concerns with domination by Western discourses on modernity and development, Western historiography, media conglomerates and consumption patterns. It has led to debates on the reception of Western culture in the South, on multiple paths of modernization, 'orientalism-in-reverse', post-orientalism, occidentalism, and 'Westoxification'.

Diverse streams mingle in the critiques of Eurocentrism, fed both by the postcolonial world and by the diasporas in Western countries. This involves the tradition of revisionist history in postcolonial countries engaged in building and rebuilding the profile of national identity – along multiple frontiers, from 'nativism' and 'modernity' to hybridity. It also involves the tradition of critique on the part of emancipatory diasporas, concerned with questions of racism and stereotyping, engaging multiple fronts of anti-racism and racism-in-reverse, identity and cultural pluralism. Historically these currents have often met and converged, just as the anticolonial movements were fed both from within the colonial countries and the diasporas of exiles, students and *émigré* communities in the metropolitan centres.

The rejection of Eurocentrism opens the way to polycentrism and, next, to a more radical claim for the decentralization of knowledge (Banuri 1990). Polycentrism in a context of high interaction generates boundary crossings. Colonialism meant the imposition of boundaries, and decolonization consisted in their appropriation. Postcoloniality – arguably, a condition as well as a diffuse array of perspectives – brackets these boundaries, leaves them behind, and questions cultural nationalism and statist decolonization, in the name of multiple identity, travelling theory, migration, diaspora, cultural synthesis and mutation. For instance, popular culture is a hybrid mode that cannot be contained in 'national culture'. Post-structuralism, deconstruction, new historicism and postmodernism are among the theoretical currents informing various reassessments of the postcolonial condition.

Postcoloniality has been the latest platform for addressing questions of culture and power. In literature studies, where the term originates, it simply refers to the literature of former colonial countries. By now the term is used almost as often as it is maligned. It is criticized for disguising the ongoing asymmetries of global power (Shohat 1992, Dirlik 1994), and hence a better term would be neocoloniality. It is criticized for invoking the illusion of a 'colonial past, liberal present' and seen as fraudulent in view of the persistence of primitivist constructions of aboriginal 'others' (Thomas 1994: 17, 30). Furthermore, the term postcolonial 'is haunted by the very figure of linear "development" that it sets out to dismantle' (McClintock 1993: 292). The notion of the postcolonial involves several nuances – colonialism and anticolonialism are past, but the colonial legacy remains relevant. Sometimes a distinction is made between the postcolonial, i.e. the former colonial countries, and the post-imperial, i.e. the former imperial countries.

The epoch of decolonization is enframed by contradiction and by the oppositional mode of anticolonialism; a binary, dichotomizing approach predominates, contrasting colonial culture to national culture, cultural imperialism to cultural resistance, Pan-Europeanism to Pan-Arabism, Pan-Africanism (etc.), Eurocentrism to Afrocentrism (etc.), CocaColonization to 'Westoxification', and so on. Decolonization is a process of emancipation through mirroring, a mix of defiance and mimesis. Like colonialism itself, it is deeply preoccupied with boundaries – boundaries of territory and identity, borders of nation and state. The dynamics of internal de-colonization displace opposition from without to within, carried by popular social forces, women and ethnic groups, in the name of equal rights, or possibly autonomy to the point of secession. The latter starts a new cycle of micro-nationalism and decolonization.

The postcolonial is an open-ended field of discursive practices character-ized by boundary and border crossings. At this stage, bicultural and bilingual social forces – typically migrants, diasporas, exiles, returnees – come to the foreground. Keynotes of the postcolonial sensibility are reflexivity and play. Reflexivity also in the sense of self-questioning – decolonization and internal decolonization have been so preoccupied with animosities and enemy forces that little room remained for questioning one's own position. Play because the postcolonial world is more fluid, less rigid than the space of confrontation and re-conquest; boundaries, to those who have experience crossing them, become a matter of play rather than an obsession. The element of play opens possibilities for innovation beyond the logic of opposition-through-imitation. The postcolonial over-laps with other 'post' sensibilities. Thus, the response to orientalism is no longer 'orientalism-in-reverse' (denounce the Occident, embrace the Orient), nor occidentalism (study the West like the West studied the East), but post-orientalism (Prakash 1990). Post-nationalism emerges on the horizon once the political kingdom of independence and, next, human rights within it have been gained and aspirations sprawl and spill over to further targets and opportunities. Post-nativist imaginaries of decolon-ization have highlighted syncretism or hybridity (e.g. Said 1993, Bhabha 1994, Nederveen Pieterse 1994). Postmodernity emerges as a field of unexplored possibilities once the constraints and ecological costs of modernity have become apparent. Kwame Appiah (1992) in 'Is the post-in postmodernism the post- in postcolonial?', notes that the similarity between the postcolonial and the postmodern lies in that they are both 'space-clearing gestures.' A brief, schematic account of the three modes of engaging colonial imaginaries may run as follows:

Decolonization: nationalism, nativism

From:	*To:*
Other	Self
Self	Other
Cultural imperialism	Cultural resistance
Colonial culture	National culture
Colonial racism	Négritude
Orientalism	Orientalism-in-reverse
Pan-Europeanism	Pan-Arabism, etc.
Eurocentrism	Afrocentrism, etc.
CocaColonization	Westoxification
McDonaldization	Self-reliance

Internal decolonization

National elite	Popular sectors
Masculinism	Women
Monocultural régime	Minorities, indigenous peoples
Nationalism	Ethnicity

Postcoloniality

National culture	Popular culture
Nativism	Post-nativism
Indigenization	Migrants, diasporas
Authenticity	Mix, syncretism, hybridity
Borders	Border crossings

Postcolonial studies are influenced by post-structuralism and deconstruction, specifically the departure from essentialism and dichotomic thinking or binarism. To a certain extent, the post-structuralist and deconstructionist turn in Western thinking has been influenced by the impetus of the anticolonial movements. Roland Barthes' seminal book *Mythologies* (1956) was a work of anthropology-in-reverse: applying to the West the categories of anthropological inquiry previously, in the era of imperialism triumphant, reserved for the study of 'primitive peoples'. Over time the critique of dominant imaginaries in the West and in the postcolonial world has mingled, merged, separated again and reconverged. Nietzsche's diatribes against European philistinism echo in Foucault's 'regime of truth', discourse as normalizing power, and his history of disciplinary power embedded in Western institutions. Edward Said applied and reworked Foucault's methodology of analysing power as discourse to the discourse of orientalism.

Since the publication of *Orientalism* there has been a widening stream of literature on culture and postcolonialism. First this focused on the question of representation. The two key modes of representation under investigation were anthropology and literature, as obvious avenues for representing the colonized, and this was extended to adjacent terrains such as philosophy, history and religious studies, and later supplemented with studies of photography, film and other media. Representation and the 'question of the Other' became keynotes of reflexive social science. In anthropology this led to questioning the authority of the ethnographic text (Clifford and Marcus 1986) and to an increasingly self-questioning body of work on representing others.

This mode of questioning has been informed by methodologies derived primarily from literature criticism. The critique of colonial imaginaries often concentrates on the role of literature and language, as in Ngugi wa Thiong'o's *Decolonising the Mind* (1986) and *Moving the Centre* (1993). This trend continues in postcolonial studies which primarily, but by no means solely, concern literature. The central terrain and approach in studies such as *The Empire Writes Back*, *Past the Last Post* and *Colonial Discourse and Post-colonial Theory* are literature and literature criticism. That this should be so is altogether meaningful in the context of the general linguistic and cultural turn in social science and philosophy. It also matches the career of Third World intelligentsia who find a voice first through literary writing. But this focus, this definition of the terrain and methodological range of approaches, also involves omissions. For instance, political economy is neglected. To a certain extent this makes up for the earlier monocentric emphasis on political economy, but it also veers in the opposite direction: as if the determinism of Marxism has made place for 'discursivism' *à la* Foucault, i.e. either material conditions are seen as all-determining, or discourse is treated as the all-embracing universe of reality. Politics tends to be brought in as a background variable, or, more often, it is discussed in a generalized and unreflexive way. Edward Said, in the closing chapter of *Culture and Imperialism* (1993) on the continuities of imperialism in contemporary US foreign policy, uncritically recycles Noam Chomsky's ideas.

As William Roseberry notes:

> The words 'colonialism', 'postcolonialism', 'power', and 'the state' are among the most popular and frequently occurring in recent titles. One is often struck, however, by how little the authors actually have to *say* about colonialism or the state ... There is no attempt to conceive of capitalism (or colonialism) in active and particular terms – particular problems or periods, particular policies or powers, particular capitals or states – in specific relation to processes of social and cultural formation (1992: 850–1).

Just as the political economy approach in its prime ignored other fields of inquiry, a certain cognitive insularity also prevails in the 'discursivist' approach. Other avenues of inquiry remain unexplored or relatively unconnected to the main textual thrust of postcolonial inquiry. If the distinctive features of Western imperialism have been a mode of production, capitalism, a technology, industrialism, particular political forms, and a global scope, we would expect these dimensions to be highlighted also in cultural analyses of empire and its aftermath. Thus, studies of globalization, economic, political and otherwise, of comparative politics, development studies and critiques of mainstream developmentalism (Marglin 1990, Nederveen Pieterse 1991), and questions of culture and development, are all pertinent avenues of inquiry which are underrepresented given the literary preoccupations of postcolonial studies.

The linguistic turn, on the other hand, has also provided epistemological and methodological gains. For instance, a theoretical cleavage in the debate used to run between structuralism and culturalism. The structuralists hold that economic and political structures shape cultural development, while the culturalist argument focuses on the autonomy of cultural expressions. This broadly parallels an ideological cleavage between, on the one hand, socialists and Marxists and, on the other, nationalists. However, in approaches influenced by post-structuralism the distinction between structure and culture (as in base and superstructure) is no longer accepted and regarded as superficial. Thus, in discourse analysis, discourse is viewed as both a mode of expression and a set of practices and institutions – as in orientalism.

Globalization and cultural pluralism

Empire and colonialism can be viewed as monocultural regimes amplified globally – as in *mission civilisatrice*, White Man's Burden, and modernization as Westernization. Ultimately, then, a key issue is the acknowledgement and revalorization of cultural plurality – not as the stratified multiplication of ghettos, as in colonial 'plural society', contemporary 'multiculturalism', or global pillarization, but as a working agenda of democratization in national, civilizational and global cultural politics.

Many current discussions of global cultural politics, however, are far removed from this agenda. Often 'the West' itself is represented in one-dimensional terms, for instance in terms of 'McDonaldization' (Ritzer 1993). Popular Western media thrive on representing the non-Western world as a collection of fanatics, drug traffickers and terrorists (Link 1991). Relations between the West and the 'others' are, likewise, represented in Manichaean terms, as an inevitable 'clash of civilizations' (Huntington 1993) or as *'jihad* versus McWorld'.

Cultural imperialism in this rigid context is attributed a unitary logic similar to that of capitalism, which is in turn equated with imperialism (Petras 1993). This one-dimensional view is contested notably by Tomlinson (1991) who makes the case that the era of imperialism has made place for that of globalization: while imperialism was state-centred, globalization lacks a single centre and a state-orchestrated character. It is against this backdrop that a different set of stories unfold: stories under the sign of diaspora, hybridity, global *mélange* – signposts of a different horizon. Diaspora has become topos straddling the postcolonial and post-imperial worlds through *métissage*, migration, exile and travel. This also belongs to the epoch of imperialism, for bicultural intellectuals have played a leading part in decolonization, politically and culturally, as part of the dialectics of empire and emancipation (Nederveen Pieterse 1989, Said 1993).

If the story of decolonization does not end with nationalism/nativism, then where does it lead? The critique of Western universalism as Euro-centrism, false claims of a universal subject, can lead to fragmentation, to archipelagos of particularisms – as in identity politics, neo-traditionalist religious movements and ethnicity. Polycentrism is one of the alternatives (Amin 1990), but this replicates the logic of centrism.

Does this add up to a new universalism? The key question that emerges is: what are the points of reference for a 'new' universalism that accommodates cultural pluralism? The concerns are epistemological: the communication of knowledges, or towards a Rainbow epistemology; as well as political: a politics of global cohabitation, or towards a global Rainbow democracy.

Métis or multiple identities can be viewed from several perspectives. One perspective is to view *métis* identities not as tragic misfortunes, as in nineteenth-century racist views (the half-caste as a misfit in whom different tendencies are ever at war, or the topos of the 'tragic mulatto'), which live on in some notions of exile and diaspora, but in terms of intercultural synthesis. The perspective of the mulatto as victim follows from first taking seriously a dichotomic or Manichaean view dividing the races and the colonizer and the native. The *métis*, half-caste, then occupies an indeterminate status, squeezed thin betwixt the camps of overwhelming conflicting political and cultural identities. Racist views could only place the *métis* as someone without place, who did not belong, failing in terms of racial purity, or, in twentieth-century terms, failing in authenticity. A decolonization discourse that remains within the framework of binary opposition (Westernization/orientalization, white/black, etc.) without room for the interstices, lacks the resources for imagining the mixed and betwixt as a creative jostling space, of home-making in multiple worlds. This is a matter of viewing cultural pluralism not as a 'social problem', from the point of view of a static 'national culture', nor as a transitional stage towards some other end state (as in 'melting pot'), but as a condition in itself of complex multiple identities – a situation which increasingly reflects the global human condition. This means taking a forward perspective beyond victimhood – either the victimhood of North–South domination, or of the Orient and Occident as unbridgeable habitus.

Hybridization as a thematic and perspective differs from previous imageries of intercultural mixing. *Mestizaje* in Latin America had a cultural centre of gravity and served in fact as an ideology of whitening or Europeanization, a cultural politics that accompanied modernization. Hybridization does not have such a cultural centre of gravity.

In the end the problematic of the decolonization of imagination merges with wider questions: the scrutiny of Western ideologies that have become part of the 'operating system' of global politics, in particular liberalism and liberal democracy (see Parekh 1993 and this volume). The notion of global civil society is part of the question of global democratization.

Introduction to the book

Decolonization is as complex a process as colonization, generating extremely varied responses. Rather than impose an artificial unity or select only one range of responses, we feel that the volume should alert readers to the complexity and eclectic character of the debate. In the debate on decolonization there cannot be a consensus, and the subsequent chapters are to be seen in this light.

Part one, 'Imaginaries of domination', consists of reflections on colonial imaginaries, from classical episodes of colonialism to Japan and contemporary Western images of the Middle East. Keynotes of this section are unpacking imageries and discourses of domination, while showing that colonial imagery is not merely of the past nor confined to the West.

Marion O'Callaghan opens with an overview discussion of the terrain of decolonization of imagination, problematizing decolonization as well as 'imagination' and taking issue with the tendency towards 'culturalism' as well as the nativist proclivity towards reverse discourse and racism in-reverse. Patrick Brantlinger takes a close look at nineteenth-century evolutionism and the Darwinist thesis of the 'inevitable extinction of the weaker races', specifically with regard to the 'last Tasmanians'. Raymond Corbey reviews the exhibitions of colonial Africa in the West as displays of evolutionism and the panoptic adage that 'to see is to know'. Bhikhu Parekh engages the cultural particularism embedded in the theories of liberalism of Locke and Mill, reread in the context of empire and colonialism.

These are engagements with various aspects of colonial imaginaries in their classical European and Western forms. Two further contributions in this section expand this reflection beyond the West and into the present. Hiroshi Yoshioka explores the notion of Japan's 'self-colonization', arguing that in the absence of colonialism from without, Japan, since the Meiji restoration, colonized itself, using samurai imagery as a framework of 'conservative modernization' and later as a form of collective self-stereo-typing, in which intensive industrialization and industrial exports merge with a masculinist imagery of technology. Toine van Teeffelen makes a case for discourse analysis as an instrument for cognitive decolonization by examining the discourses of 'crisis' and 'explosion' commonly used in Western media in relation to the Gaza Strip and the Middle East.

In Part two, 'Imaginaries of cultural pluralism', the theme of *métissage* under colonialism bridges the colonial situation and postcolonial and post-imperial situations of multicultural societies in the United States and Europe. Ann Stoler treats *métissage* as a subtext of colonialism, in a rereading of colonial history's exterior and interior frontiers, situated in nineteenth-century French and Dutch colonial Southeast Asia. Jan Berting examines the interplays of nation, class, ethnicity and gender in European patterns of marginalization in the nineteenth and twentieth centuries, thus scrutinizing Europe's interior frontiers from within. Ronald Takaki takes this question across the Atlantic and into the present by reflecting on the 'culture wars' across the United States' interior frontiers in the wake of the Los Angeles riots. Gayatri Spivak, in the same setting, queries the academic agenda of teaching the multicultural curriculum in the United States, arguing that multiculturalism represents an 'emerging dominant' and an ongoing shift of hegemony.

Part three, 'Global imaginaries', consists of assessments of contemporary globality, engaging the questions of culture/power and cultural plurality in the global context. Sol Yurick evokes an emerging capital-driven metastate in conjunction with processes of 'Lebanonization' driven by local cultures, an evocation that converges on the need for a total rethinking of culture, technology, development. Susantha Goonatilake reflects on the paradox of separatist movements in the Third World in today's transborder world in communications, technology, production and finance. In order to achieve their separate status separatist movements have to participate in global networks. The 'jostling' relationship between cultures – as in parts of the USA and India – serves to illustrate the interpenetration of cultures on the ground, an ongoing process in which, it is argued, also the weakest cultures can achieve a share of globality.

References

Al-Azmeh, Aziz 1992 'Barbarians in Arab Eyes', *Past & Present* 134: 3–18.

Amin, Samir 1990 *Delinking: Towards a Polycentric World,* London, Zed (original French edn 1985).

Appiah, Kwame A. 1992 *In my Father's House,* New York, Oxford University Press.

Arnold, A.J. 1981 *Modernism and Negritude: The Poetry and Poetics of Aimé Césaire* Cambridge, MA, Harvard University Press.

Ashcroft, B., G. Griffiths and H. Tiffin 1989 *The Empire Writes Back: Theory and Practice in Post-colonial Literatures,* London, Routledge.

Banuri, Tariq 1990 'Modernization and its discontents: a cultural perspective on theories of development', in F. Apffel Marglin and S.A. Marglin (eds), *Dominating Knowledge: Development, Culture, and Resistance,* Oxford, Clarendon, pp. 73–101.

Barthes, Roland 1956 *Mythologies,* Paris, Seuil.

Bhabha, Homi K. 1994 *The Location of Culture,* London, Routledge.

Chatterjee, Partha 1986 *Nationalist Thought and the Colonial World: A Derivative Discourse,* London, Zed/UN University.

Chinweizu, Onwuchekwa Jemise and Ihechukwu Madubuike 1983 *Toward the Decolonization of African Literature,* Vol. 1, Washington, DC, Howard University Press.

Clifford, J. and G.E. Marcus (eds) 1986 *Writing Culture: The Poetics and the Politics of Ethnography,* Berkeley, University of California Press.

Comaroff, John and Jean Comaroff 1992 *Ethnography and the Historical Imagination* Boulder, Westview.

Curtin, Philip D. (ed.) 1972 *Africa and the West: Intellectual Responses to European Culture,* Madison, WI, University of Wisconsin Press.

Diop, Cheikh Anta 1991 *Civilization or Barbarism: An Authentic Anthropology,* New York, Lawrence Hill (original French edn 1981).

Dirlik, Arif 1994 'The postcolonial aura: Third World criticism in the age of global capitalism', *Critical Inquiry*, 20: 328–56.

Downing, D.B. and S. Bazargan (eds) 1991 *Image and Ideology in Modern/Postmodern Discourse*, Albany, NY, State University of New York Press.

Durand, G. 1993 'The implication of the imaginary and societies', *Current Sociology*, 41 (2): 17–32.

Enloe, Cynthia 1990 *Bananas Beaches and Bases: Making Feminist Sense of International Politics*, Berkeley, University of California Press.

Fabian, J. 1983 *Time and the Other: How Anthropology Makes its Object*, New York, Columbia University Press.

Fanon, F. 1967 *The Wretched of the Earth*, Harmondsworth, Penguin (original French edn 1961).

Gidley, M. (ed.) 1992 *Representing Others: White Views of Indigenous Peoples*, Exeter, University of Exeter Press.

Gilman, Sander 1985 *Difference and Pathology: Stereotypes of Sexuality, Race, and Madness*, Ithaca, Cornell University Press.

Grosz, Elizabeth 1990 *Jacques Lacan: A Feminist Introduction*, London, Routledge.

Guha, R. and G.C. Spivak (eds) 1988 *Selected Subaltern Studies*, Oxford, Oxford University Press.

Harlow, Barbara 1987 *Resistance Literature*, New York, Methuen.

Huntington, Samuel 1993 'The clash of civilizations?', *Foreign Affairs*, Summer: 22–49.

Hymans, J.L. 1971 *Léopold Sédar Senghor: An Intellectual Biography*, Edinburgh, Edinburgh University Press.

Jahn, J. 1968 *Neo-African Literature*, New York, Grove Press.

Kaplan, M. and D.E. Pease (eds) 1993 *Cultures of United States Imperialism*, Durham, NC, Duke University Press.

Le Goff, J. et al. 1986 *Histoire et imaginaire*, Paris, Radio France/Poiesis.

Link, Jürgen 1991 'Fanatics, fundamentalists, lunatics, and drug traffickers – the new Southern enemy image', *Cultural Critique*, 19: 33–54.

McClintock, Anne 1993 'The angel of progress: pitfalls of the term "post-colonialism"', in P. Williams and L. Chrisman (eds), *Colonial Discourse and Post-colonial Theory*, New York, Harvester Wheatsheaf, pp. 291–304.

Maffesoli, M. 1993 'The imaginary and the sacred in Durkheim's sociology', *Current Sociology*, 41 (2): 59–68.

Maffesoli, M. 1993 'Introduction', *Current Sociology*, 41 (2): 1–6.

Maffesoli, M. 1988 *Le temps des tribus*, Paris, Klincksieck.

Malchow, H.L. 1993 'Frankenstein's monster and images of race in nineteenth-century Britain', *Past & Present*, 139: 91–130.

Marglin, S.A. 1990 'Towards the decolonization of the mind', in F. Apffel Marglin and S.A. Marglin (eds), *Dominating Knowledge: Development, Culture, and Resistance*, Oxford, Clarendon, pp. 1–28.

Mehrez, Samia 1991 'The subversive poetics of radical bilingualism: postcolonial francophone North African literature', in D. Lacapra (ed.), *The bounds of race*, Ithaca, Cornell University Press, pp. 255–77.

Miller, C.L. 1990 *Theories of Africans: Francophone Literature and Anthropology in Africa*, Chicago, University of Chicago Press.

Moscovici, Serge 1993 *The Invention of Society*, Cambridge, Polity (original French edn 1988).

Nederveen Pieterse, Jan 1989 *Empire and Emancipation*, New York, Praeger.

Nederveen Pieterse, Jan 1992 *White on Black: Images of Africa and Blacks in Western Popular Culture*, New Haven and London, Yale University Press.

Nederveen Pieterse, Jan 1994 'Globalisation as hybridisation', *International Sociology*, 9 (2): 161–84.

Parekh, Bhikhu 1993 'The cultural particularity of liberal democracy', in D. Held (ed.), *Prospects for Democracy*, Cambridge, Polity, pp. 156–75.

Petras, James 1993 'Cultural imperialism in the late 20th century', *Journal of Contemporary Asia*, 23 (2): 139–48.

Prakash, Gyan 1990 'Writing post-orientalist histories of the Third World: perspectives from Indian historiography', *Comparative Studies in Society and History*, 32 (2): 383–408.

Ritzer, George 1993 *The McDonaldization of Society*, Newbury Park, CA, Pine Forge.

Roseberry, W. 1992 'Multiculturalism and the challenge of anthropology', *Social Research*, 59 (4): 841–58.

Said, E.W. 1978 *Orientalism*, Harmondsworth, Penguin.

Said, E.W. 1993 *Culture and Imperialism*, New York, Alfred Knopf.

Shohat, Ella 1992 'Notes on the "post-colonial"', *Social Text*, 31/32: 99–113.

Shohat, Ella and Robert Stam 1985 'The cinema after Babel: language, difference, power', *Screen*, 26 (3–4): 35–58.

Shohat, Ella and Robert Stam 1994 *Unthinking Eurocentrism*, New York, Routledge.

Schweder, R.A. 1993 '"Why do men barbecue?" and other postmodern ironies of growing up in the decade of ethnicity', *Daedalus*, 122 (1): 279–308.

Tacussel, Patrick 1993 'The epistemological propinquity of social aesthetics and the imaginary', *Current Sociology*, 41 (2): 33–42.

Tadesse, Z. 1992 'African debates on social movements and the democratic process', *Development*, 3: 34–7.

Thiong'o, Ngugi wa 1986 *Decolonising the Mind: The Politics of Language in African Literature*, London/Nairobi/Portsmouth, James Currey/Heinemann.

Thiong'o, Ngugi wa 1993 *Moving the Centre: The Struggle for Cultural Freedoms*, London/Nairobi/Portsmouth, James Currey/Heinemann.

Thomas, N. 1994 *Colonialism's Culture: Anthropology, Travel and Government*, Cambridge, Polity.

Tomlinson, J. 1991 *Cultural Imperialism*, Baltimore, Johns Hopkins University Press.

West, Cornel 1992 'The postmodern crisis of the black intellectuals', in L. Grossberg, C. Nelson and P. Treichler (eds), *Cultural Studies*, New York, Routledge, pp. 689–705.

Williams, P. and L. Chrisman (eds) 1993 *Colonial Discourse and Post-colonial Theory*, New York, Harvester Wheatsheaf.

Imaginaries of domination

2

Continuities in imagination

Marion O'Callaghan

Decolonization and imagination

The words 'decolonization' and 'imagination' raise fundamental issues, whilst their combination in the same phrase poses theoretical questions that cannot easily be swept aside. 'Decolonization' seems to mean a precise event: the end of colonial rule and the coming into being of independent nation-states. 'Imagination' seems to pitch the final stage of decolonization in the realm of what has been called attitude change.

Colonization, however, was not a simple phenomenon. It varied over periods. It differed in the ways it operated, it differed in the ways political independence was achieved, granted or withheld. These variations depended on the colonial power and on its arrangements with groups within specific colonies. Colonization was also affected by the extent and nature of rivalries among colonial powers on the one hand and colonies on the other. In other words colonization, like its corollary decolonization, was a complex process influenced by the internal context and modified by internal structures, accommodations and conflicts of both the colonizing power and the colony.

Imagination is the selecting out and rearrangement of 'facts' in order to provide coherence, framework and seeming unity between ideas and action, or more precisely to provide a basis for the direction of social relationships and the social creation of categories. It is what is imagined that posits the 'natural', that is, the normal, the fixed and unchanging. Seeming to exist in a historical forever, this is nevertheless framed by the present. To put it in another way, imagination is socially created and follows, not precedes, the structure of social relations. Because of this, 'knowledge' is not necessarily affected by access to information, since information is placed within a particular framework that is hardly ever explicit. This is not to say that it is not understood. Social significance is shared, but not openly acknowledged. Nor indeed challenged. The decolonization of the imagination, then, is closely linked to structural change, at a level at which, no matter the seeming historical or cultural continuity, new types of legitimation and, therefore, 'imagination' occur. It is this structural change that has not happened in spite of the end of direct colonial rule.

If colonization is to be correctly analysed I suggest that the time span to be examined should be the period dating from the discovery – so-called – of the Americas. Even then, the period before this is not without interest as to how colonization proceeds. Colonization can in no way be separated from the formation and consolidation of European nation-states. This formation proceeded on the basis of the fiction of homogeneity, of a quasi-sacred unity of the state and values and the sacralization of the state symbolized by the monarch. The latter becomes the intermediary between the temporal and the spiritual kingdoms. The legitimacy of European nation-states therefore is guaranteed by religion. This development is accompanied by key changes in social relationships that are not without an impact on the direction of European expansion.

The same is true of certain so-called Third World countries. The emergence of what is called the 'state' is accompanied by new types of social and economic incorporation, by changes in the nature of political rule and by changes in the nature of power and of its legitimation. These changes everywhere include the transformation of the manner and extent of capital accumulation, as well as of the extraction and distribution of surplus.

It is therefore more useful to conceive of the colonial period, if taken to start only on the date at which rule from the metropolitan countries is formally established in Africa and most of Asia, as only a stage in a continuum that begins before this and which has in no way ended. This continuum is one of the establishment of complex relationships of domination maintained in the final analysis by the use or threat of overwhelming military force.

I have deliberately included Third World countries with regard to both social relations and the extraction and distribution of surplus. The expansion of Europe triggered off in some areas the beginnings of modern nation-state formation, the transformation of proto-states, changes in the nature of commerce, and facilitated the rise or continued hegemony of specific dominant groups within Third World countries. Dominance was more profoundly and structurally linked than has been supposed or admitted. This is in no way to suggest that there were not within this linked dominance conflicts of interest between dominant groups. Indeed these conflicts could be sharp enough to appear under certain conditions as the primary lines of cleavage. Neither do I share the view that there was an identity of class interests within colonial countries, or the view that dominated groups acted according to an automatic class-consciousness. I would argue for more complex linkages, for shifting alliances, and I would argue also that under certain conditions category and closure could be reshuffled while seemingly maintaining continuity. It is this reshuffling of alliances that permits both the maintenance of dominance and the incorporation into dominance of formerly dominated groups or fractions. It is the mystification of the automatic nature of group interests – nation, race, gender, culture, class-consciousness – that permits the maintenance of social boundaries and structures the ways in which the imagination both selects and ranks and legitimation operates. Outside of a more detailed examination of economic sectors, of the insertion of specific population segments into the economy both at an international and a national level, and of the articulation between these and the operation of social institutions, neither dominance nor power can easily be located. It is insertion into the international level rather than the emergence of capital accumulation that differentiates colonialism from former conquests. Every society is affected by it. The 'dual economy' exists only for short unsustainable periods, as do parallel markets.

The phrase 'Europe and its others' requires the same questioning. The imagination that fractures something called Europe from something called 'its others' serves to hide the interlocking that exists and fabricates both a unity and a rupture that are in no way evident. For, in everyday relationships 'its others' are known. They are not those 'others' of white North America, or of Australia. The 'others' are those whose perfectly valid cheques are not accepted, whose perfectly in order credit card is automatically supposed to be stolen, who are never ordinary tourists but are in an intrigue, a subterfuge to enter illegally a Europe never more 'European'. The 'others' are never European even if sharing that now most coveted of all things, citizenship; they remain 'outside the European community'. 'Citizenship' is the new word not for the extension of rights but for their limitation − whilst citizenship itself turns out to be linked not to passports, but to the perception of race as equalling 'European'. This usage is being borrowed outside of Western Europe, where citizenship has become a shorthand nomenclature for race, religion or the like.

That this is more likely to be so at the level of the petty bourgeoisie or the working class shows the extent of this 'imagination' that roots itself, not in a past, but in the very present. It is this present with its crises and its deliberate ambiguities that resurrects nostalgia for a past that, for most, never existed and for all is, at least in part, more fictitious than fiction − as anyone who has seen Van Gogh's potato eaters well knows.

European settlers

Colonialism occurs as a phase within capitalism. I will not here enter the debate as to when capitalism began except to suggest that its beginnings may well not have been a purely European phenomenon and to question as others have done before me assumptions as to the static nature of other-than-European societies. I also question the 'stages' sometimes evoked, through which capital development or class formation is said to proceed, while acknowledging the crucial change introduced by the Industrial Revolution.

This is not to say that fifthteenth- or sixteenth-century Europe did not experience relatively rapid social change. The nature of the Spanish conquest, colonization and settlement of Latin America cannot be dissociated from the consolidation of the Spanish state, and the final annihilation of the threat of 'Moorish' domination. The final legitimation of 'usury' was in part a function of the Spanish Inquisition and of the rise of Protestantism. In the same way the nature of Dutch colonization cannot be dissociated from the formation of the United Provinces as a state, or from the conversion of Hanseatic trade into the establishment of burgher trading stations.

The juxtaposition of 'Europe' and its 'others', where the 'others' for the settlers in South and North America were societies classified under a single non-complex category of 'Indians', posits a dualism that I would question. These 'others' were a fundamental part of European development at all levels. Europe was a fundamental part of attempts at hegemony and cacicism within the conquered or penetrated territories. Resistance there was: indeed the advanced military technology of Europe permitted not only conquest. The attempt by some countries to maintain dominance or independence by securing firearms through arrangements with this or that European power could be manipulated through forms of protection.

In no situation was culture the main component of the maintenance of independence or the main determinant of how the conquered were treated. The accepted complexity of Aztec culture was not enough to arrest the march of Cortés nor yet to secure for later Mexican Indians equality of political or economic incorporation into Mexican society. Aristotle entered Catholicism via a Thomas Aquinas heavily influenced by Islamic thinking. This influence extended to the Italian Renaissance. This, continually portrayed as a European 'miracle', flourished partly because of European social conditions and methods of patronage. However, the cultural production that emerged owed much to Islam as Islam owed much, not to some fundamental essence of Islam, but to trade and conquest. The knowledge of Islamic contributions or capacities did nothing to change settlement or colonization in North Africa.

Europe's 'others' were also within Europe. The Cromwellian conquest of Ireland in the seventeenth century – the alienation of Irish lands, the elaboration of settler–planter societies and the attempt (which in Ireland partly failed) to break the ideological cement of an otherwise clan-fragmented Irish society – was part of the same process that succeeded more powerfully in Mexico or Peru. The failure in Ireland, as the failure among the Mapuche in Chile, may well have had to do with the segmentary nature of both societies. Weak and contested kingship did not easily permit arrangements between dominant groups to be recognized among the entire population, whether these arrangements were through treaty, intermarriage or admission of conquest. Indeed, the nature of the continuing revolts in Ireland, as among the Mapuche, sharpens the question as to the role of internal centralized dominance in colonial rule and makes sense of the frantic colonial attempts to establish tribes where there were none, to maintain and fabricate chiefs, or to 'respect' so-called traditions.

European settler societies were demarcated from former movements of peoples in two major ways. European settlers remained part of the former exporting country both in terms of the tracing of ancestry and of being brokers in the extraction and exportation of surplus. I have used the words 'tracing of ancestry', since settlement did not necessarily preclude intermarriage and concubinage. These, whether it concerns the Spaniards and Portuguese in Latin America, or the Dutch in South Africa, proceeded, permitting property and trading alliances to be established. Descent within dominance was, however, traced to Europe. This was different from the fabricated ancestry that permitted entry into dominance in precolonial India, the absorption of foreign conquerors into the imperial traditions of China, the mythical tracing of ancestry in pre-Hispanic conquered Mexico, or the mythical Arabization of North Africa. Tribute would continue as a parallel and a mixed method of extracting surplus; however, surplus was more likely to be directly obtained through the ownership of property and labour. It is the existence of tribute – posed in terms of 'taxation without representation' – that led to the breakaway of the American colonies from Britain. Tribute was an important part of the British colonization of India and the European semi-colonization of China.

Settlers are nowhere perceived as either extractors of tribute or as part of a systematic booty or plunder economy. Settlement is posed in terms of values: the spreading of Catholicism in Hispanic America, the quest for religious freedom in Anglophone North America. Both legitimize conquest abroad and the contestation of power within Europe through the assumption of perennial cultural values. This evokes, on the one hand, ancient Rome, on the other, ancient Greece. Rome evokes the continuity of the political–cultural–religious space of the Holy Roman Empire. Democratic traditions, however, are as perennial, anchored in Greek Platonic or Aristotelian traditions. This 'new' Europe is the secularized equivalent of the 'old' Europe. There are already, then, the dual myths of Greece or Rome. These myths are not imagination. They mark real conflict. Nor is it at all certain that, in the new 'new' Europe supposedly in the making today, there is agreement on the myth that will be used to mark its foundation. This perennial Europe, Greek or Roman, permits the incorporation of settlers not only into a linked economy, not only into a system of descent, but also into an ideological framework, even if these last two are in no way givens, while the first is fraught with conflict. Indeed, Europe's 'others' are socially created since Europe itself is a social creation. Its historical delineation is based on a entirely created geographical and cultural entity. For there is nothing to indicate that either Rome or Greece saw themselves as European or considered the then 'barbarians' as within their traditions rather than within their possible domination. Those 'others' with their 'other' religions and traditions not only permitted the myth of a single European culture, they permitted an external level of exploitation that, while perhaps as desired internally in Europe as externally among its 'others', was nevertheless subject to some internal constraints. Where these constraints were absent, as for example in Ireland, or weakened as in the ceding of Gibraltar to Britain, the 'others' could be constructed in terms of religion or race then, in terms of ethnicity or as unassimilable 'immigrants' today.

The limitations of this common Europeanness are seen in the hierarchy of 'whiteness' within the USA and the differences within the white community of Americans and hyphenated Americans. In Canada, French Canadians are separated not only by language or religion but by a more tangible discrimination in access to credit, jobs, the siting of industry, and the way that separate education was used.

The 'others' masked not only from Europeans but also from the majority of these 'others' the interlocking nature of the system being established and the roles of the 'others'' dominant groups.

Slave trade

If North Africa was already being impoverished and its trade sent into decline, nevertheless certain Arab groups were important in the evolution of the Portuguese slave trade, in the pressure that weakened Zimbabwe and in the way East Africa could be 'opened'.

West Africa was the source of a slavery that was to mark extreme 'otherness' – not without the collaboration, however, of the powerful African kingdoms that were emerging. The same process was happening in East Asia. Indeed, in the sixteenth and seventeenth centuries, the conditions for capitalist development existed in a number of countries. In a number of areas, states were emerging. However, it was the already advanced military technology that affected the nature of state formation outside Europe as it affected it, in a complex and differentiated way, within Europe.

It was the strength of a certain European technological advantage that required the retention of the non-rational in a Weberian sense or the Asian mode of production in the Marxist sense among its 'others'.

European commerce, protection or colonization was already laying foundations in Africa, Asia and the Middle East for the political structures and economic development of today. The African slave trade presupposed the tyranny of the slave plantation, the concentration camp in the slave stations and the establishment of tightly hierarchically arranged military states in key West African countries, capable of delivering the quota of commercial goods, namely slaves. It was the slave trade that was the source of dominant wealth in West Africa as in much of Europe, North America and the Caribbean. It was not by chance that the abolitionist lobby in England had ranged against it not only slavers and slave owners but also certain African chiefs who complained quite rightly that their source of income would be affected by the cessation of the human trade on which their empires were built.

The slave economy structured and maintained the preference for young male slaves for the Atlantic slave trade. This in turn accentuated the use of female slaves and semi-slave female agricultural labour within Africa, profoundly affecting gender relations on both sides of the Atlantic, while at the same time deflecting the agricultural revolution within Africa and with it both industrial development and the effective internal contestation necessary for the internal political change associated with modern development and scientific enquiry.

Europe was not without its 'others' ranked within Europe. Not only was there Ireland, that area of colonial experimentation within Europe. Spain and Portugal were slotted into an intermediate category which permitted the mining exploitation of Latin America and its settlement, while at the same time restraining industrial development and with it modern political development in the Iberian peninsula. Whatever the independence of Latin American states, the economic transformation within Latin America never equalled that of the British settler colony of North America. The latifundium is not the plantation of the Southern states – the cotton gin is not repeated. Nor is it the feudal estate – reciprocal relationships are weak in conquest and slave societies, whilst client relationships are accentuated. Nor did Latin America or Spain benefit from the lucrative sugar trade. Indeed the emergence of Cuba as a sugar producer was marked by sharp Spanish–US conflicts, which had to do less with the then fashionable morality of 'independence' than with the evolution of the Cuban plantation as a probable sugar competitor.

If the Ottoman Empire was allowed to continue, it was because its backwardness was no block to 'European' ambitions, but rather its method of segmentary rule contained a variety of peoples, whether Muslim or Christian, contained Arab ambitions, and partly contained the expansion of Russia and its possible entry into the modern system of trade. That the supposed heartland of secular Europe–Greece – was easily sacrificed to Turkey, that the romance of the Christian kingdom of Prester John in today's Ethiopia together with Jerusalem are forgotten, indicates the uses and limits of myths. With the opening of the Suez Canal in 1896 following the consolidation of British rule in India in 1857, it was securing the complicity of the King of Egypt that mattered. The rest followed. The establishment of direct colonial rule in India occurred at the same time as the emancipation of British slaves. In the same period there was the disastrous Irish famine with its resulting coffin ships, while England and France disputed dominance within Europe and outside. The triumph in India was directed as much against Dutch traders as against Indians. This time saw the final demise of Spain and the growing internal settler colonization of the Americas with its attendant genocides and reservations. Nor should we forget what was happening with the working class within Europe, those 'others' of the new factories, always oscillating between Europeanness and some genetic incapacity – that of 'others'.

Free trade demanded markets and raw materials, selling dear and buying cheap. Both undermined the need for direct slave labour in the British Empire, while the ideology of freedom undermined the re-establishment of Napoleonic France's slave colonies and the emerging slave plantations in Brazil or Cuba. Moreover, the experience in both Britain and France indicated that the development of a working class did not necessarily lead to undue risk. The production and reproduction of labour could be managed, as could the mobility of the labour force. What did matter was the nature of the alliances struck, not outside the bourgeoisie but with factions within it. Indeed the possibility of migration to settler colonies was an important part of the management of internal peasant or worker revolts.

Christian moral Europe

The tolerance of the French Revolution was principally a religious compromise between Catholic and Protestant. Britain effected a similar compromise between Anglicans and Nonconformists, while the Irish famine marked the beginning of the emergence of an Irish Catholic commercial and agricultural bourgeoisie out of the land grabbing and depopulation, which were the real transformations of Irish society in spite of continuing myths to the contrary. This agricultural bourgeoisie could coexist with Protestant control in the North and what was increasingly its racial–religious configuration. This was not a simple feature of class. Indeed it depended on both a Protestant ruling class and the presence of a Protestant working class and Protestant poor farmers.

Colonization, increasingly posed in moral terms within Europe, could coexist with 'indirect rule', forced or semi-forced labour (through the poll tax), or in key areas combined with direct settlement and a dual economy. The moral terms were precisely those of freedom from 'tyrants', a civilizing 'mission', the assumption of a 'white man's burden', or the 'protection' of Christians.

The founding dates of missionary societies, bible societies, missionary congregations are in themselves eloquent as is the conversion of congregations formed to fight the evils of the French Revolution into congregations vowed to spread the good news. Indeed, the period from 1835 to 1895 is crucial for understanding the world of today. It is within those sixty years that 'Europe' takes on a particular sense, while otherness becomes more closely defined. This 'Europe' is in no way cultural; it involves important structural changes which mark the emergence of a single market which destroys frontiers at the same time that it erects them.

This Christian moral Europe was not without internal ramifications. With the decline of the European domestic economy, women lost their base of economic power, even if this was always unequal. The near total triumph of property transmission through males and the near impossibility of converting dowry into capital governed by female spouses, was matched by the increasing elimination of monasteries as dominant land holders. Women lost the ritual power they had to some extent held. They were, however, given a special place in the 'new' nineteenth-century order: as upholders of morality and virtue and the transmitters of ideology. The family was to be the cornerstone of society. This too was myth. Joe Lee has pointed out that the Irish family was being extolled at the same time that the social conditions were being elaborated for the separation of its members through massive emigration and that the emerging Catholic bourgeoisie was consolidating property through the encouragement of a high degree of celibacy. Victorian morality existed side by side with exploitative working-class female prostitution. The real preparation of the children of the bourgeoisie was in the hands of paid governesses and the public boarding schools. Homosexuality, banned by laws and in polite conversation, was endemic at the highest echelons of society.

That gender relations are social relations and neither natural nor inevitably posed as male dominance, was most clearly seen in plantation gender relationships. Where, as in slavery, enslaved men failed to achieve even the limited autonomy of the working class, they became marginal within the family which reproduced itself in a quite different way, reflecting not the naturalness of male dominance, but the real possibility of some female earnings by higgling (as in the Caribbean), domestic service or sex work (in all plantation societies).

The advance of science and technology, the search for seeming coherence and rationality in a social order no longer acceptable to all in religious terms, contributed to the emergence of 'others' as races, that is, as genetically different. It was this genetic difference that explained dominance and ranking, but which also permitted certain categories to be excluded from the political power that followed from internal European compromises. The Dreyfus affair tested the extent of the French religious compromise. It should be noted that neither perception nor culture are integral in themselves to 'race'. Indeed, perception itself is subject to already elaborated categories, while what is integration and who is integrated can be as easily controlled as separation can be structurally achieved. The ranking of race is reproduced at all levels. Victoria is Queen of Great Britain and Ireland but Empress of India. India is governed by a viceroy, Ireland is governed by a lieutenant, while governors abound in the lesser territories.

Indeed the acceptance of the 'naturalness' of race enters popular culture precisely because it sorts with what is perceived as popular experience. It is where popular expectation flowing from this perceived 'experience' differs from real achievement that endemic racism becomes crisis racism or becomes the basis for working-class racism. It is the latter that requires the elaboration of apartheid South Africa, Nazi Germany, the Orange establishment of Northern Ireland, the 'ethnic cleansing' of Yugoslavia, or the popular perception of 'others' in today's Europe – not that this is in any way equal to South Africa, Nazi Germany or Northern Ireland.

Independence – the new compromise

The 1940s and 1950s saw the last stage in the struggle for independence – a struggle that had in fact never abated, even if alliances and coalitions within the struggle had shifted and changed. The struggle in the 1940s and 1950s, however, differed from the struggles of nineteenth-century Latin America. These had taken place not only against a weakened Spain, but within the framework of white or mestizo societies seeking the same internal expansion North America had achieved and within the context of an accentuation of the search for markets by the USA as against European industrialized countries. The very underdeveloped industrialization of Spain, in spite of its cultural heritage, made it impossible for Spain to convert colony into commonwealth or, in later times, to supplant the dominance of the USA, whatever the strength of language, religion or sentiment. In the 1940s and 1950s, native dominant groups within the colonies faced, not a difference in relationships between Europe and North America, but both the economic hegemony of the United States following the Second World War and the key role of the US both in the Marshall Plan and in NATO. Nor was internal expansion through massive direct land alienation possible.

The compromise struck therefore was both religious – a secular India – and a compromise with working class and peasantry. This period ends with the triumph of the Algerian revolution, although it limps through the Vietnamese conflict. Henceforth, dominance was assured through the granting of independence. Independence was granted as Europe recovered and was aimed at ensuring that the compromise struck before was not repeated: the protection of local dominance was exchanged for the protection of colonial interests. But this independence was also directed against the United States. The latter's *de facto* economic hegemony was contained by the strength of popular movements within European countries, as the total exercise of the specifically US – if in fact never accurate – interpretation of human rights as excluding state ownership or management was contained by the strength of postwar European popular expectations. The first period of independence therefore was not simply an affair of Europe's 'others'. It was closely related to pressures within Europe to end poverty, to establish equality of opportunity, and to create a welfare state. This was done under the pressure of the increased power of organized labour, the political use of this power and a strand of liberal opinion (always nevertheless in the minority) vaguely sympathetic to independence demands and against colonial wars. This was true to a certain extent also for the United States and the heritage of Roosevelt's four freedoms. Decolonization, then, is part of a total movement even if the struggles seem isolated and particular.

The new compromise satisfied internal European disquiet over colonialism and colonial rule, while the coming to power of parties with a working-class base in the absence of international structural change made – and makes – those parties as ferocious in their defence of European national interests as were conservatives. Indeed it is the re-establishment of markets and continuing control of primary products that are seen as the factors able to ensure continued internal wealth and guarantee its distribution. It is not by chance that postwar working-class intellectuals were preoccupied with the legitimation of working-class culture or with the equality of opportunity that the implementation of the Beveridge Report was supposed to achieve. This would largely be accepted by the British Labour Party. Immigration was another issue, as was the North of Ireland. Both raised problems beyond acceptable cooption. Indeed cultural Marxists could respond to the growing racism within Britain only by extolling Rasta-farianism as black revolt, or by wishful thinking that unions and the Labour Party could represent immigrant interests. In the same way Protestant workers in Northern Ireland, the most ferocious opponents of Catholics, were somehow affected by 'working-class consciousness'. In the same way France's 1968 would end, not in imagination taking over, but in the beginning of the debacle of the left, the rise of the new philosphers of the right and the environmentalization of economic issues.

The Cold War in this period was aimed at stopping an expansion of Soviet influence which a weakened Europe had been obliged to accept under the Yalta agreement. Internal peace would be achieved by assuring the direction of working-class protest through an inter-class compromise of the same nature as Protestant–Catholic intra-bourgeoisie compromise. To this end the former evil of paganism was replaced by a new evil: communism. The spearhead of communism, the Soviet Union, was in fact a collection of states where in the absence of advanced capitalism, primitive capital accumulation occurred via state capital. In the absence of either a viable internal market or the technology for rapid distribution there were considerable blockages to the expressed aims of redistribution and of development. Internal expansion in the absence of classic colonial expansion was only a modified form of the internal expansion in the Americas hidden by the maintenance, within the Soviet Union, of idealist philosophy within what was explicitly a society vowed to Marxist materialism. The demands of a primitive accumulation of capital required what was euphem-istically called democratic centralism but which was directed towards eliminating the scientific analysis of society and towards consolidating an emergency petty bourgeoisie.

The fear outside the Soviet Union, however, was not simply the spread of communism. Communist parties in Europe were weak except in France and Italy. The issue was the possibility of a parallel and alternative inter-national economy creating a threat that there would indeed be 'others'. It is noteworthy that while Soviet repression or atheism was an issue before 1964, it was only in 1964 that 'human rights' began – and only tentatively – as a criterion of judgement. Indeed the first meeting on human rights occurred at UNESCO in 1965, and then directed not towards Eastern Europe but towards the 'newly' independent countries. This fear of a parallel market was increased by the emergence of the Non-Aligned Movement which threatened, even if only for a short period, to establish not a bipolar world, but a tripolar world that would affect both military alliances and in the long run the direction of trade.

Négritude and neo-*négritude*

The post-1963 (approximately) colonial compromise between metropolitan and colonial dominant groups in the new phase of decolonization was most widespread in Africa. Here, it was not the 'artificial' boundaries but the lack of that imperative of state formation – transport infrastructure – that prevented the process that made India, itself a collection of communities and states, India. The much-vaunted problem of 'tribalism' was, and is, only competition between factions of the emerging bourgeoisie for the control of the only way through which accumulation of capital could be rapidly assured and client relationships maintained: state power. The ease of military takeovers bears witness to the centrality of weaponry in state formation. The second phase of decolonization saw the consolidation of internal dominance. It is not surprising that this is marked by the emergence of *négritude*. Supposedly a glorification of Africa, this was based not on African thought but on Gobineau, Lévy-Bruhl and Teilhard de Chardin. One of its principal exponents, Léopold Senghor, harkened after not Africa but Greece, while one of his mentors, Teilhard de Chardin, refused to sign a UNESCO declaration that posits racial equality, visited an impoverished and fomenting Trinidad in the 1930s and saw only the beauty of a humming bird, managed to stay in South Africa without seeing the obscenity of the rise to power of the National Party, and persisted in his belief in differing evolutions in spite of all the scientific proof to the contrary. African culture came into vogue.

As in the case of the Aztecs, *négritude* changed nothing. For the real changes were elsewhere. In a quiet agricultural revolution the United States could, by 1964, dump more grapefruit than the entire Caribbean could produce. The transistor brought not information alone but news of consumer production. Mega-agriculture threatened agricultural production not only in the Third World but in Europe, and accentuated the chronic food production crisis in the Soviet Union. Indeed, capital moves more easily across the borders of independent states than colonial states, while independence favours and certainly does not obstruct the growth of consumerism as an index of status. Nasser turned out to be a simple interlude in Egyptian history and the defeat of Suez only one of a series of lessons on the importance of preparing a population for war. Indeed, by the end of the 1960s most of the historic figures of the anticolonial war had died or been deported, while with the exception of Southern Africa colonial wars were replaced by internal conflicts.

In the United States the election of Kennedy marked the entrance of the Irish into dominance and followed, not St Patrick's Day parades with green Guinness, but the control of important components of the Democrats, sections of the trade unions and the achievement of equality in university education and entry into control of capital. The Israeli–Arab war of 1967 would mark as much the victory of Israel as the recognition within the United States of the entry of Jewish Americans into dominance. It was precisely over this entry that Irish–Black and Jewish–Black relationships became conflictual in the United States. It is precisely this rationalization of 'whiteness' that sees 'race' rationalized as 'black' and 'white' and 'ethnicity' triumph as a marker of, not difference, but similarity. It is not without significance that some black Americans prefer to become hyphenated Afro-Americans, or that the black movement was, first, a civil rights movement and then split under the influence of a growing neo-*négritude* that served the same purpose within the United States as *négritude* served outside it. Indeed, the killings of Martin Luther King, Malcolm X and the Kennedys marked the end of a certain America internally as they did the vague possibility of certain alliances externally. Dashikis, black cosmetics, jerry curls, however, while certainly permitting the rise of a black petty bourgeoisie protected by an ethnic market itself served by black is beautiful, in no way guaranteed equality of either political or economic incorporation. The search for cultural equality delinked from political and economic power within American dominance permitted only this cultural equality to be granted. After all, that 'blacks as blacks invented everything under the sun' was only the continuation of that racialization of history that Aryanism had conceived. Not only did neo-*négritude* pose no threat to the category of race, it reinforced this category. For it is exactly the racialization of history and of cultures that is the most serious, because seemingly evident, underpinning of racism. Moreover, neo-*négritude* refused and eliminated the real questions of today and the passage to today's technological conquest by the very nature of its return to a mythical yesterday. This, served by a facile diffusionist cultural anthropology, evacuated culture by positing some primeval source increasingly geneticized and increasingly isolated by the very reification of blackness. Blacks know little of, say, the work initiated by Thapar on the possibility of the adoption of Aryan language on a Harappa base, of the refusal of Maoris to accept an Aryan heritage, of Needham's careful work on parallel and disconnected inventions in Europe and China, the whole body of modern historical research or the mixture of anthropology and archaeology that had begun to reconstruct the civilization of Southern Africa, the precolonial trade routes and the successive structures of greater Zimbabwe. These, in attacking the arguments for the Aryan racialization of history, also destroyed the basis for the black racialization of history.

Black Studies as a discipline encouraged this black racialization of history and became part of the social selection process through which blacks remained marginalized. For while black intellectuals were siphoned off into a multidisciplinary study of blacks that was only the name given to an encouragement to end a certain scientific rigour, blacks continued to be absent from the main stream of research, as witness the paucity of black professors at Harvard or Yale. Few were in the crucial area of archaeology, relatively few in the new push of the social anthropology of complex societies or historical sociology, to mention only the social sciences. Even where they are present, the weight of blackness has become a constraint against critical research and a method of attempting to ensure conservative conformity while maintaining the language of demagogy. Yet this critical research is needed if the analysis of black, as white, America is to proceed and the mechanisms by which social selection continues to structure racial discrimination, to ensure ethnic ranking and to affect the process of incorporation at all levels is to be understood in order to be effectively fought. Indeed, a reified blackness, itself a reaction to a reified whiteness, confused methods of political mobilization with methods of scientific research and was itself indicative of the real powerlessness of blacks after the end of the civil rights movement in the mid-1960s. Blacks, powerless as a group, sought individual social mobility through blackness. This, too, the Irish–Americans and the Jewish Americans had done. It was not a black affair. What was a black affair was that as a group blacks were too powerless to demand accountability either within the United States or outside it. Nor have they been able to combine a rectification of absence in American history with the sharing of control in the selection and accumulation of knowledge. It is their entry into the latter that will mark their entry into dominance.

The black petty bourgeoisie, following the example of the emerging bourgeoisie everywhere sought for their ancestral 'roots' in an aristocratic Africa. This, like the Irish–Americans' Ireland, was largely fabricated. Unlike Ireland, however, this fabrication interlocked with dominant groups in most of Africa and the Caribbean that were outside the Irish bourgeoisie–small farmer compromise of the First World War, and the bourgeoisie–working class–peasantry compromise of pre-1964. As such it served the interests of dominant African groups and as a linkage between these and American interests. Indeed, the very inter-class nature of race and the real fact of continuing racial discrimination served to create a bonding that preferred to suppress the historical reality of the slave trade and to focus attention only on a 'common' experience of racism. The nature of this could be seen in the debate on Columbus within the English-speaking Caribbean. What was at stake was not expansion. It was who first 'discovered' the Americas: white Columbus or black aristocratic Africans with gold-tipped spears. In Trinidad, with a 40 per cent population of Indian descent, to these two were added Aryans from India complete with reincarnation. All had found a savage, empty America on which they imposed their culture.

This cultural imagination in Trinidad was neither history nor simple borrowing from North America. It reflected the struggle for state power and the legitimation of 'first' Trinidadian claims. This struggle was accentuated by the decline of the economy and an ethnic struggle principally over subsidaries and state-financed casual employment. At the same time, integrist America organized, basing this integrism not on old-fashioned racism – in any case no longer needed – but on the rejection of the principles of Roosevelt's four freedoms and of the redistribution of income needed to eliminate black poverty. This new integrism fostered an ir-rationality in all religions while a new religious rationality occurred: the sale and consumption of religion as direct consumer–capitalist commodities in the form of multi-million tele-evangelist enterprises. It is within neo-nonrationalism that highly rational science and technology proceed, and indeed this neo-nonrationalism is functional to their new mode of operating.

Immigration to Europe

The mid-1960s also marked the beginning of 'immigrants' as a major issue in most European states. Not that the pre-1964 period was non-racist. Far from it. However, both the Nazi experience and the civil rights movement in the United States had made overt racism socially unaccept-able. The ending of full employment, the recovery of Europe, the seeming ease and good will with which most of the remaining colonies were 'given' their independence prepared the social base for a redefinition of 'others' in Europe. The new method of extracting surplus via the establishment of 'local' industries, the beginning of the debt syndrome and the new agricultural revolution provided its economic base. The immigrants were, even when citizens, 'immigrants' inherently unable to be absorbed as full Europeans except through some ambiguous 'integration' that no one defined or could define. Along the same lines as the USA fostered 'dia-sporas', Europe fostered 'others', granting a 'right to difference'. Indeed the widespread use of terms such as 'disaporu', 'multiculturalism', the 'right to difference' and 'ethno-development' occur at exactly the same time and serve the same purposes in the USA, Canada, Europe and Latin America, that is, the reshuffling of the dimensions of citizenship and limitations to participation in state power. There is no compromise with non-citizens (diasporas), on multiculturalism through birth, or with the inherently 'different' or ethnies, as opposed to real compromises sought before between, say, Protestants and Catholics. In each case primary loyalties are presumed to be elsewhere, as are the determinants of a conditonal incorporation into social institutions. The 'right to difference', which in any case cannot exist since 'right' is non-judiciable and 'difference' non-definable, seals differentiated citizenship. For citizenship implies non-differentiation in the public domain. Indeed, by the 1980s policies that were defended in the 1960s only by the far right had become respectable in the name of a new 'Europe' based on 'common' values and a 'common' culture. Exclusion was managed through a barrage of citizenship laws and by little-known administrative procedures. The 'new Europe' was already in the making. That it was fraught with ambiguities was one of the ways it proceeded. For some it was a return to the new respectability of Teutonic orders, for others the return to a refurbished Holy Roman Empire – Christian Europe. To others it was a move towards a Europe of liberties less and less defined in European historical terms and more and more in terms of the untramelled pursuit of happiness and profits of a neoliberalism fabricated not in Europe but in the United States. Human rights became not the hard-won achievement of modern man but a quasi-genetic legitimation of Greek descent, and the sealing of a new religious compromise under the curious terms of a Judaic-Christianism within which the Holocaust could take on a new ambiguity and in which the real lessons of the designation of racial category could be evaded. It was now citizenship that defined access to rights. Universality was being quietly scrapped at the same time that 'human rights' were being extolled. 'Citizenship' increasingly became a coded term in the same way as did 'immigrants'.

It is not by chance that 'human rights' becomes, not the moral code that gives a framework to real aspirations but increasingly a non-questioned format, that is, ideology. This emerges under Carter at the end of the Vietnam War and is at its most hysterical at a time when mega-publishing undercuts alternative sources of knowledge, the right to organize is increasingly constrained, the organization of education produces new pockets of illiteracy. In the greatest democracy in the world, the United States, fewer and fewer people worry about voting in the most important of elections: that for President of the United States.

In Latin America, where the demand for human rights is posited as the reply to the national security state, it would follow that political rights would in no way change economic structures, eliminate poverty or marginalization, or arrest the degradation of social relations. These, structurally achieved, structurally accentuated in the mid-1960s, symbolically signalled by the fall of Goulart in Brazil, could not be wished away because a truncated, ideologized version of human rights had been achieved. The riots in Venezuela, the continuing armed conflicts in Colombia and Peru are signals that a right to vote in the absence of the probability of change may call in question the democratic process itself.

New Europe was emerging at the same time that a common front of industrialized countries was forcing the structural adjustment policies on the Third World that Europe had refused for itself under the Marshall Plan, at the same time as Japan had become a major industrial competitor, that the USA attempted to redefine international politics, in spite of a severe internal economic crisis and a crisis in the financial 'honesty' that was the supposed hallmark of Protestant capitalism, and as the East European block collapsed. 'Structural adjustment' was the new word for structural change that was both external and internal. It crystallized around oil and was aimed at securing and maintaining control of the sources and of the price of oil. This, to be lasting, implied the effective fixing of petrol prices, control of petrol-producing countries, of tanker routes, and the reopening for foreign control of petroleum-producing countries. It was not only petrol prices that fell. So did the price of every primary product. The new 'export-oriented' economies, imposed by the World Bank and the International Monetary Fund and backed by all sources of external financing including the banking networks, tied financial liquidity to the terms set by the international lending agencies. The collapse of the Soviet Union and with it Eastern Europe raised hopes in Europe for a Europe stretching from the Atlantic to the Urals. It raised hopes in the more industrialized countries of Europe as well as in the United States of unlimited markets both for agricultural goods in the face of the Soviet Union's chronic agricultural inadequacies, for heavy industrial plant and for the finished products of consumerism.

At another level the immigrant 'others' could be replaced by what was thought would be a less politically divisive pool of immigrant labour. The collapse of Eastern Europe in the first instance tightened the policies of structural adjustment by both removing an albeit small and inefficient alternative market and, more crucially, destroying the fear of alternative military alliances.

States disintegrate

Structural adjustment expanded. It now included an ending of the era of industrial assembly plants in developing countries, of manufacturing substitution and of the protected markets that permitted some industrialization. A Third World labour reserve was assured by the 'conditionalities' of massive layoffs in the public service, while the rentability of denationalized industries was assured by 'rightsizing', that is, layoffs before denationalization. 'Conditionalities' enforced by the extreme ideologies of Thatcherism and Reaganism stretched from the virtual ending of free university education where this existed, to the dismantling of the beginnings of social welfare. State after state lost control of its budget, of internal policies, while 'advisers' ensured the direction of its civil service and police.

A state, if it is to function as such, must have some control within its borders; it was the state itself that disintegrated. Elected governments became intermediary administrators of 'structural adjustment' policies. If the extent of this collapse is only now beginning to worry the Europe of both sides of the Atlantic, it is because the consequences have proved that, whatever the so-called race, tribalism and the ensuing decomposition of the state occurs wherever the same structural conditions exist.

The 'others' were more and more impoverished – except for the richest of their elites. Indeed this impoverishment has begun to touch the middle class so carefully fostered and supposed to assure stability. There has been some concern with what had become the politics of poverty; however, the very definition of a Europe triumphant in the imagination and nowhere else, removed the 'others' from European consideration. Yet it is not at all certain that Europe does not share the same basic problems of its 'others', of which it remains a part. After all, debt repayment is the new form of tribute while free trade where the traders are not equal is the new way that external commerce deflects internal development. Nor did the dependency paradigm work: it supposed a real conflict of interest between dominant groups in the Third World forced to be dependent and dominant groups in the industrialized countries. While this was partly true it was a subsidiary cleavage. In fact, IMF (International Monetary Fund) adjustment policies are as internally functional to the maintenance of certain dominant groups within Third World countries as they are externally needed by the industrialized countries. Nor are these adjustment policies necessarily only directed to the Third World, as the 1991 OECD report on France has proved. They may also be directed to the achievements of the European working class already suffering from what has been considered an under-development disease: chronic unemployment. The Marxist paradigm turned out to be as misleading as the false hopes of neoliberals. The Marxist paradigm ignored Marx's own *Eighteenth Brumaire* and the importance of factions in all classes. In addition, the areas of conquests, race and sex were depressed, under class relations first and under neo-idealism afterwards.

The 'New' Europe

Extend this to the 'New' Europe. The pocketing of human rights provided a common lay religion that functioned through the 'imagination'. Indeed, at the same time that culture, multiculturalism, difference and the rest has come into vogue, Dallas or the Young and the Restless are on all screens, including those in Europe. The increased adoption of the *chador* has in no way influenced the extent of Arab purchases at chic Paris, London or New York boutiques. Moscow and Beijing rival each other more for the hamburger than for socialism, while Italy advertises that fast food is truly Italian. The TV news channel CNN's presentation of the Gulf War is the new exciting equivalent of MGM's Far Western epics. And this not only in the US, not only in the technologically backward Third World, but in Europe. It is 'imagination' that eliminates oil from the equation, that permits Saddam Hussein to be at one time the rampart against Islamic integrism and at the next the focal point of an Armageddon in which the allies are democratic Saudi Arabia and democratic Syria. It is imagination that refuses to see that the New Europe as Japan have been reminded of the limits of their 'independence' in the same way that the Third World has been unequivocally shown the ridiculous nature of a return to the past and the real nature of technological military might. Anyone who has believed in the separation of black America from general American policies has only to examine the composition of American forces in Panama or in the Gulf. That the high percentage of blacks is the result of poverty is partly true. That there is no real black attempt at even the refusal of war also is part of the heritage of the United States of William Penn and of the civil rights movement. That black Americans are American is what would be expected if the fiction of race does not intervene. It is precisely this fiction of some trans-Atlantic blackness that is the real spearhead of the Americanization of the Caribbean. Islands that have at great cost to themselves created and guarded cultures throughout colonial rule become increasingly not only Americanized, but subsidiary black ghettos of New York, Toronto and Miami removed from the complexity of an American heritage that can in no way simply be subsumed under 'imperialism', and increasingly alienated from the heritage of the Caribbean they have themselves created. 'The Cosby Show' may be attacked by black Americans. They share some part in the dominance that permits it. It is not as easily attacked within the Caribbean.

Haitians, in spite of the popularity of Toussaint L'Ouverture, are 'immigrants' in the Bahamas and suspected of evil all-powerful voodoo in Trinidad. Sympathy with the Haitian boat people does not necessarily follow from their blackness. Indeed, the Gulf War marks the victory of that 'other' America that lost the American Civil War, lost out to the upper bourgeois fraction and was threatened by what had been real American liberalism. To this extent the victory is within the US. It is the sealing of the structures set in place in the late sixties.

The Gulf War has also, perhaps at last, broken the fiction of some Pan-Arabism created in the nineteenth century, and already in fact broken in the Lebanon. For there is no reason to believe that inter-classism exists among Arabs more than it does elsewhere or that there is some bonding among Arabs that is greater than social reality. Nor is it certain that the shot in the arm given to Pan-Jewishness can last, except at the cost of the denial of the real – and now little-talked-about – historical reality of those of Jewish religion.

It is no wonder that decolonization has never been less popular, including among certain sectors of the formerly colonized. For the struggles of yesterday put into question the emerging dominant groups of today as rationality – on which the pre-1964 struggles were based – questions the reconstruction of quasi-racial historical pasts that foster the religious and racial integrisms of our time. These are in fact messianic movements created as a result of rapid economic decline of sectors of the economic segments of the population. In the absence of any political alternative, religion, good and evil are the only answers to a process that progressively eliminates many from the progress of today. This messianism is often financed by those who reap the most financial benefits out of the ethnic mobilization that ensues. It would be a mistake, however, to see ethnic mobilization as simple manipulation any more than racism is simply a question of attitudes. Both exist only where there are material reasons for their existence.

Yet, exactly as in black America, religious integrisms in turn reinforce the process through which marginalization is achieved, poverty is maintained and the continuum of external domination is perpetuated. Islamic science is no more real than white or black science. Islamic philosophy is only the non-emergence of a difference between theology and secular philosophy. Islamic law is as relevant to a modern state as medieval canon law to a European state today. That Islamic fundamentalists and Christian fundamentalists destroy the Lebanese state only removes that state from being a competitor in Middle East broker banking. Exactly the same is true with regard to rapidly growing Hindu fundamentalism. Indeed, the widespread nature of fundamentalism within all religions and at all levels of development in itself suggests that there are no 'others', for the same social processes can now be observed. In one place 'race' emerges, in another religion. While one is not the other, nevertheless either serves as the basis for perceived category and therefore for exclusion. That the collapse of state power implies the collapse of state cohesion is amply illustrated in Eastern Europe, and tragically in Yugoslavia. 'Ethnic cleasing' is the logical result of the end of national bonding and the inability of the new administrators to mediate in internal conflicts. 'Structural adjustment' in Eastern Europe has the added effect of containing Western Europe while, in the wake of the ending of a Europe from the Atlantic to the Urals, all that is left is a Europe increasingly susceptible to racial pogroms. Domination today is already having internal consequences within Europe and at a level that is likely to be more costly than the former colonial periods. The same irrationality that marks North America is at Europe's doorsteps. The 'others' outside are matched by a growing number of 'others' within, euphemistically called the 'new poor'. The untramelled search for markets gradually undercuts belief in and therefore the gains of the welfare state. The 'others' imply the reinforcement of category, which renders vulnerable in a crisis any group perceived as such. Free agricultural markets already render fragile many small European farmers – as the case of Ireland indicates. The 'freedom' of international finance can attack the pound, the lira, the punt, the franc as it can the Indian rupee or the Jamaican dollar. Unemployment is now taken for granted, and its increase predicted rather than its elimination. Much more serious, democracy itself is at stake as informed debate is replaced by selling, and as disillusionment in the political process follows the cynicism of political policies. Nor are there any longer the evils of communism with which to solder together a 'Free' Europe. Now there is only the conjuration of evil, disincarnated except in the 'others'.

The ideology of human rights has come near to emptying human rights of its real content; the use of international law has come near to ending belief in its objectivity. All that remains is a Europe whose competition is in the final analysis with Japan. For one of the losers of the Gulf War was a Europe proved incapable of an independent policy, of an independent military machine, incapable of independent negotiations, caught in the twin imaginations of crusades and the defeat of colonial policies. The socially perceived Europe was correct. Europe was part of American dominance and could not exist as Europe without it. But competition with Japan is seen as demanding what has already begun. Aggressive free trade abroad is part of the same coin as aggressive labour policies at home. The 'others' spread. They are now indeed Europeans.

The 'others' ceased to exist when European expansion created a world in which the 'others' were created. Struggles of the 'others' have triggered off social demands in Europe. European struggles have been part of the struggle of the 'others'. These struggles today remain the same. To suppose otherwise is part of the 'imagination' from which too many people suffer.

3

'Dying races': rationalizing genocide in the nineteenth century

Patrick Brantlinger

I see him sit, wild-eyed, alone,
Amidst gaunt, spectral, moonlit gums;
He waits for death …
(William Sharp, 'The Last Aboriginal', 1884)

In her free-trade fantasy *Dawn Island*, written for the Anti-Corn Law League in 1845, Harriet Martineau describes a society where, before the coming of the British, the 'savages' are so very savage that they threaten their own extinction (for more on *Dawn Island*, see Brantlinger 1988: 30–32). The wisest among them, old Miava, foresees the time when 'man shall cease'. In a reversal of the Malthusian nightmare, constant warfare, cannibalism, and infanticide will soon depopulate the island; fortunately the 'dawn' – the arrival of a British ship signalling the advent of commerce and civilization – saves the islanders from their collective suicide.

Martineau offers a paradigmatic version of one of the most frequent rationalizations for the 'vanishing' or 'passing' of non-Western peoples. The fantasy of what might be called auto-genocide, which Martineau makes virtually synonymous with savagery, is also the most extreme form of 'blaming the victim' through which the liquidation of 'primitive races' by European invaders was explained away. Such rationalizations share a number of characteristics, starting with the idea that a particular 'primitive race' either was already 'dying out' before the coming of the Europeans, or else is now dying out of its own accord, no matter whether Europeans treat it with benevolence or with fire and sword. Still another feature of these rationalizations is evident in Martineau's identification of 'savagery' as the prime or sole cause of the dying out of those who practise 'savage' customs. When 'savagery' is not identified as a direct cause of racial extinction, with 'civilization' its self-evident, supposedly humane cure, then it is frequently held that some groups of 'savages', at least, cannot be civilized, and are thus doomed to fall by the wayside no matter what customs they practise or fail to practise. And 'doomed' is the operative word: a third feature of such rationalizations (the ideological corollaries of imperialism) is that the extinction of at least certain primitive peoples – those incapable of becoming civilized – is viewed as inevitable.

I will examine a characteristic range of such rationalizations, from the 1830s to the end of the nineteenth century. I will then focus upon what appeared to many commentators, including Charles Darwin, to be the most dramatic – because the most total – case of the extinction of a primitive race, that of the aborigines of Tasmania. As anthropologist Lyndall Ryan has argued, the myth, for such it is, of the complete demise of the Tasmanians has served a number of insidious ideological purposes central to the imperialist imagination.

Why vanishing races vanish: arguments from Prichard to Darwin and beyond

As the British and other European empires expanded during the nineteenth century, 'savages' who stood in the path of 'civilization' were dealt with in ways that can only be called genocidal. According to the 1948 United Nations Convention on Genocide, 'acts committed with intent to destroy, in whole or in part, a national, ethnical, racial or religious group' include the following:

> ... killing members of the group; causing serious bodily or mental harm to members of the group; deliberately inflicting on the group conditions of life calculated to bring about its physical destruction in whole or in part; imposing measures intended to prevent births within the group; and forcibly transferring children of the group to another group.

In providing this summary of the UN convention, Lyman Legters points out that all of these practices were visited upon Native Americans in the nineteenth century and after. Moreover, 'when colonialism take[s] the form of settler colonies, the possibilities, even likelihood, of genocide come almost automatically to the fore' (Legters 1988: 771).

Imperialist expansion, including settler colonialism, of course gave rise to imperialism as an ideology, and central to that ideology was the myth that certain groups of 'savages' were uncivilizable. Sometimes all 'primitive races' were held to be doomed to extinction through mere 'contact' with civilization. The forms of 'contact' so often involved overt violence against the supposedly uncivilized, however, that civilization could hardly be whitewashed into the appearance of nonviolent benevolence, as in Martineau's fantasy. More often than not the violence that civilization was visiting upon the uncivilized was acknowledged, but treated as inevitable. Benjamin Kidd was echoing a widespread view when, in *Social Evolution* (1894), he wrote:

> The Anglo-Saxon has exterminated the less developed peoples with which he has come into competition ... through the operation of laws not less deadly [than war] and even more certain in their result. The weaker races disappear before the stronger through the effects of mere contact. (Kidd 1894: 49)

The word 'laws' not only lends legitimacy to violent extermination, it also makes such extermination appear 'inevitable', as Kidd goes on to say. Indeed, Kidd portrays the European colonizers as fundamentally pacific:

The Anglo-Saxon looks forward ... to the day when wars will cease; but *without war*, he is *involuntarily* exterminating the Maori, the Australian, and the Red Indian ... he may beat his swords into ploughshares, but in his hands the implements of industry prove even more effective and deadly weapons than the swords. (Kidd 1894: 62; my emphasis)

In similar terms, in 1869 Darwin's nephew Francis Galton could write that 'the number of the races of mankind that have been entirely destroyed under the pressure of the requirements of an incoming civilization, reads us a terrible lesson'. Galton then lists the numerous 'races' of 'savage men' that have been 'entirely swept away in the short space of three centuries' – why? '[L]ess by the pressure of a stronger race than through the influence of a civilization *they were incapable of supporting*' (Galton 1925: 332–3; my emphasis). So 'the human denizens of vast regions' of the world have perished because *they* could not 'support' the 'incoming civilization' from Europe!

Both Kidd and Galton voice the worst sort of racist/imperialist social Darwinism. It would be comforting to report that this quasi-scientific ideology is restricted to the late nineteenth century, the era of the so-called 'new imperialism' and 'the scramble for Africa'. But it is present earlier in Darwin himself (who has sometimes been falsely exonerated from being a social Darwinist), and elements of it can be found much earlier, in the first versions of nineteenth-century 'race science'. Thus in his 1839 paper 'On the Extinction of Primitive Races', James Prichard, pioneer of British anthropology, declares that 'wherever Europeans have settled, their arrival has been the harbinger of extermination of native tribes' (Prichard 1839: 169). Prichard does not assert that this result is inevitable; on the contrary, he expresses the hope that the newly founded Aborigines Protection Society will be successful in stemming the slaughter. But he nevertheless speaks of 'the progress of colonization', and the consequent 'progress' in the decimation of the 'aboriginal nations' of the world – strange language indeed for a humanitarian. Prichard, however, is interested in arguing that, if the 'progress' of civilization does indeed liquidate primitive peoples, it is urgent to establish an ethnographic science 'to record the history of the perishing tribes' (Prichard 1839: 170).

Writing for the Aborigines Protection Society, Saxe Bannister is attempting to counteract an already widespread opinion about the fate or destiny of 'primitive races' especially in South Africa when, in *Humane Policy* (1830), he declares that the 'destruction' of 'the natives' is 'contemplated by some persons with as much calmness as if a mere transition of inanimate elements, incapable of personal suffering, were in progress'. He adds that it is commonly held that 'the uncivilised man melts "as snow in sunshine" before "superior" capacities'. Or else, once again, it is held that the melting away of primitive peoples was going on before the advent of civilization, as when Dr A.K. Newman, writing in 1881, asserts that the Maoris of New Zealand 'were a disappearing race before we came here' – a view that allows him to look with equanimity on their complete demise: 'the disappearance of the race is scarcely subject for much regret. They are dying out in a quick, easy way, and are being supplanted by a superior race' (quoted in Pool 1977: 191–2). Similarly, in *Astoria* (1836), with Native Americans in mind, Washington Irving declares: 'There appears to be a tendency to extinction among all the savage nations, and this tendency would seem to have been in operation among the aboriginals of this country long before the advent of the white men' (Irving [1836] 1976: 158).

What may only have been a common opinion in New Zealand or the USA is presented as scientific fact by Dr Robert Knox, who in *The Races of Men* (1850) asserts that the 'dark races' of the world must fall before the onslaught of the 'energetic' 'Saxon and Celt'. As in Kidd, so in Knox: Europeans are identified with progress, and the historical march of progress dictates, as by inevitable 'laws' of nature, the complete extinction of many if not all the 'dark races'. 'Look all over the globe,' Knox writes; 'it is always the same; the dark races stand still, the fair progress' (Knox 1850: 149).

Knox claims, as Darwin does later, that 'the unity of man appears evident' (Knox 1850: 147). But if this is true, he asks, 'whence come the dark races? and why is it that destiny seems to have marked them for destruction?' (Knox 1850: 147) The failure of the 'dark races' to progress – indeed, the complete inability of 'the black races', at least, to 'become civilized' (Knox 1850: 162) – is identical with their failure to participate in history. Just as Hegel had declared the entire continent of Africa beyond the pale of history, so Knox: 'Of races which cultivate not the earth, which manufacture nothing, which progress not in art nor in science … their absence or their presence must in the history of man go for little. The inhabitants, for example, of Central Africa, have no history any more than if they had been so many bales of cotton' (Knox 1850: 107).

The alleged fact that 'the past history of the Negro … is simply a blank', however, does not begin to explain for Knox why, after having existed for perhaps as long or longer than the Saxon or Celt, the Negro should suddenly, in the progressive nineteenth century, be slated for extinction. It is not the supposed unprogressiveness of the dark races that has doomed them, since they have supposedly been unprogressive for ages; rather, the cause of their extinction lies in the alleged facts that the European races are both progressive and incapable of tolerating non-progressive peoples. So when the 'Saxon Hollanders' (or Boers) suddenly appeared in South Africa three centuries ago, Knox declares, the extermination of the Bushmen, Hottentots, and Caffres began – 'races which mysteriously had run their course, reaching the time appointed for their destruction' (Knox 1850: 66). But there is really nothing 'mysterious' in Knox's account: more clearly than most British writers about race and empire, Knox acknowledges that he is talking about genocide. Nor does he exactly approve of the violence 'Saxons' are visiting upon 'inferior races' around the world, though he treats that violence as a kind of unsavoury necessity or fact of life.

As Michael Banton remarks, 'Knox's racial theory taught that colonization was evil as well as useless. Though it stressed the powerful qualities of the Saxon race it also represented its members as cordially hating good government, outrageously boasting, arrogant, and self-sufficient beyond endurance' (Banton 1977: 48). The Saxons and Celts are also hypocrites according to Knox's account: professing Christianity, practising murder. Yet this seeming criticism of European behaviour is blunted by a racial essentialism that, as later in Kidd and also Darwin, makes genocide (or the 'extinction' of 'inferior races', to use Knox's language) the inevitable result of the 'progressive' nature of the white 'races':

> ... we must not advert ... to these drawbacks on the Saxon character; his onward principle diffused and spread him over the colony [South Africa]; the go-ahead principle was at work; this, *of course*, led to the seizure of land, the plunder and massacre ... of the simple aborigines. ... whilst I now write, the struggle is recommencing with a dark race (the Caffre), to terminate, *of course*, in their extinction. (Knox 1850: 156; my emphasis)

For Knox, history is nothing more nor less than the 'slaughter-bench' Hegel said it was (Hegel 1956: 21). Despite his apparent distaste for European hypocrisy and violence, Knox waxes enthusiastic in expressing his version of social Darwinism *avant la lettre*:

> What a field of extermination lies before the Saxon Celtic and Sarmatian races! The Saxon will not mingle with any dark race, nor will he allow him to hold an acre of land in the country occupied by him; this, at least, is the law of Anglo-Saxon America. The fate, then, of the Mexicans, Peruvians, and Chilians, is in no shape doubtful. Extinction of the race – sure extinction – it is not even denied. (Knox 1850: 153)

In addition to the certain doom of the Amerindians of both North and South America, Knox is just as sure about the fate of all other 'dark races', with the aborigines of Tasmania ('Van Diemen's Land') leading the way:

> Already, in a few years, we have cleared Van Diemen's Land of every *human* aboriginal; Australia, of course, follows, and New Zealand next; there is no denying the fact, that the Saxon, call him by what name you will, has a perfect horror for his darker brethren –

and therefore liquidates those 'brethren' wherever he finds them (Knox 1850: 153). These apparent facts of (human or inhuman) nature lead Knox to describe as 'folly' the humanitarian efforts of 'the philanthropists of Britain' – he seems especially to have in mind the Aborigines Protection Society – and also to invoke that thoroughly cynical *reductio ad absurdum* of political theory: 'might is the sole right' (Knox 1850: 312).

Knox was an influential figure in the development of British 'race science' – perhaps the most influential at mid-century – whom Darwin cites with respect if not absolute approval (Stepan 1982: 43). And in the section on the extinction of primitive races in *The Descent of Man* (1872), Darwin himself provides the most authoritative nineteenth-century examination of what might be called the 'inevitability of extinction' thesis: 'When civilised nations come into contact with barbarians the struggle is short, except where a deadly climate gives its aid to the native race' (Darwin n.d.: 543). Though humane in his anti-slavery views, Darwin clearly believes that the extinction of certain primitive peoples is inevitable and perhaps for the best. At times he seems almost to look forward to the complete triumph of civilized over primitive or 'lower races':

> Remember what risk the nations of Europe ran, not so many centuries ago, of being overwhelmed by the Turks, and how ridiculous such an idea now is! The more civilized Caucasian races have beaten the Turkish hollow in the struggle for existence. Looking to the world at no very distant date, what an endless number of the lower races will have been eliminated by the higher civilized races throughout the world. (Darwin 1959, I: 286)

Thus for Darwin as for Kidd, the progress of the world dictates not just the peaceful transformation of 'savagery' into its opposite, but its violent liquidation – the triumph of the 'civilized races' over the 'lower races' in 'the struggle for existence'. Darwin explicitly agrees with the co-discoverer of natural selection, Alfred Russel Wallace, who in 1864 wrote that the 'great law of "the preservation of favoured races in the struggle for life" … leads to the inevitable extinction of all those low and mentally undeveloped populations with which Europeans come in contact' (Wallace 1864: cxliv–clxv).

It seems unlikely, however, that by *all* 'low and mentally undeveloped populations' Wallace means *all* 'primitive' peoples, because by the 1860s it was evident to many observers that not all such peoples were withering away upon contact with civilization. Central Africans, for instance, might not avoid being sold into slavery, but many whom that catastrophe befell survived the horrors of the 'middle passage' and of slavery itself in the New World. The decimation of Native American societies contrasted to the successful establishment of African slavery in the New World seemed to prove both the unfitness of Native Americans and the at least physical fitness of the Africans.

It would be inaccurate to suggest that the idea of 'the inevitable extinction' of primitive races was consistently or uniformly applied throughout the British Empire and its history, or that it ever received any official sanction. Indeed, the great abolitionist crusade to end the slave trade and then to eliminate slavery in all British territories, coupled with missionary belief in the convertibility – if not necessarily civilizability – of all peoples, no matter how 'backward' or 'savage', diffused a humanitarianism that helped to counteract, at least partially, opinions like Knox's and Kidd's. 'This question of the fate of aboriginal populations is one closely concerning our national honour,' Florence Nightingale rightly declared in 1864 (Nightingale 1864: 557). But her view can hardly be said to have prevailed.

Moreover, humanitarianism (both religious and secular) and social Darwin -ist views were often combined in various ways. Darwin is as clear an example as any of an intelligent person who managed to be both human-itarian (as in the Governor Eyre controversy) and social Darwinist.

The case of the first and last Tasmanians

To Victorian commentators such as Knox and Darwin, whether scientists or not, one episode of genocide especially illustrated the inevitability thesis. As Knox suggests, the speed and thoroughness with which the British invaders killed off the original inhabitants of Tasmania provided a direct, apparently irrefutable lesson about racial extinction. Scientists, human-itarians, and government officials all struggled to understand and/or rationalize this seemingly minor episode in the history of genocides (not minor, of course, as far as the native Tasmanians were concerned).

From 1804 to 1830, the Tasmanian aborigines were harassed and killed with a haphazard but predictable ruthlessness that makes their extinction both unmysterious and unspecial in the history of genocides. What made the Tasmanian case special for the Victorians was partly that their final solution seemed really final, and partly that it first became apparent in the 1830s, heyday both of utilitarian belief in progress through secular industry and reform and of evangelical belief in extraworldly salvation. The 1830s were also the heyday of the antislavery crusade – time of the founding of the Aborigines Protection Society (see Bourne 1899). Furthermore, the Tasmanians were candidates, along with the Tierra del Fuegians, the Bushmen, and the Australians, for being the most primitive people on earth – lowest on the evolutionary totem pole and therefore closest to the apes (see Tylor 1893). From a Darwinian perspective this meant that they were potentially of great significance to science as perhaps one of the missing links between civilized humans and our simian ancestors. But from a social Darwinist perspective like Kidd's, this meant also that they were an unfit race, doomed to extinction.

The Tasmanians are Darwin's main exhibit in his consideration of racial extinction; they were apparently virtually extinct by the time of the publica-tion of *The Descent of Man* in 1872.

Although there are today several thousand racially mixed descendants with the legal status of Tasmanian aborigines, supposedly the last non-mixed Tasmanian man, William Lanney, died in 1869, while the last woman, Truganini, died in 1876. By then, the Tasmanians were the most notorious case of the liquidation of a primitive race through 'contact' with 'civiliza-tion'. And in many discussions the chief causes of their extinction – both genocide and disease – are forthrightly presented. But Darwin downplays genocide by focusing on the last remnants of the race, after they had been rounded up and relocated in a reservation or, as one recent historian of Tasmania puts it, 'concentration camp' on Flinders Island (Robson 1983: 220). 'When Tasmania was first colonised the natives were roughly estimated by some at 7,000 and by others at 20,000,' Darwin writes. One modern estimate puts the figure as low as 3,000 or 4,000 (Ryan 1981: 14), but in any case, as Darwin goes on to say, 'Their number was soon greatly reduced, chiefly by fighting with the English and with each other' (Darwin n.d.: 543). This is his only mention of bloodshed, and the fighting 'with each other' in his statement deserves comment: there was no evidence that the Tasmanians were warlike before the coming of the English, and very little to suggest that they were warlike 'with each other' afterwards. Meanwhile, Darwin emphasizes other factors, especially disease and infertility, though the latter mainly affected the few dozen final Tasmanians.

Maybe Darwin thought the violence that liquidated perhaps over half of the original population too self-evident to stress. Or maybe he naïvely reproduced the emphases of officials in Hobart Town and London, who after almost ignoring the slaughter of the vast majority of aborigines, paid lugubrious, microscopic attention to the demise of the final handful. Whatever the case, Darwin is much more interested in why this final handful failed to reproduce than in what happened to the vast majority. But quite obviously what happened to the majority was a main cause of the total demoralization of the last Tasmanians and of their consequent failure to reproduce. Darwin quotes various humanitarian observers (especially James Bonwick, whose *The Last of the Tasmanians* (1870) is a key text in the literature on race and extermination), all of whom stress the 'depression of spirits' suffered by the last, captive Tasmanians. Darwin neither agrees nor disagrees with what perhaps seemed to him mere psychological speculation, but after an additional consideration of the Maoris and some other supposedly dying races, he concludes that 'changed conditions or habits of life' seem to impair the reproductive capacity of primitive peoples, just as they impair the reproductive capacity of certain wild animals.

Two key points can be made about Darwin's discussion of how 'changed conditions' lessen the 'fertility' of 'the wilder races of man'. One is that Darwin reinforces the distinction counterposing on the one hand 'wild' or 'primitive' and on the other 'civilized', and he thereby implies that the distance between the two types of 'races' may be unbridgeable:

> It has often been said ... that man can resist with impunity the greatest diversities of climate and other changes; but this is true only of the civilized races. Man in his wild condition seems to be in this respect almost as susceptible as his nearest allies, the anthropoid apes, which have never yet survived long, when removed from their native country. (Darwin n.d.: 548)

Both 'civilized races' and 'domesticated animals' are immune, Darwin concludes, to the sterility that affects 'wild' varieties of men and animals under 'changed conditions' (Darwin n.d.: 550).

The second major point about Darwin's discussion is that, from his perspective, no matter whether primitive peoples are humanely or murderously treated, if their 'conditions or habits of life' change, their demise may be inevitable. Furthermore, it does not seem to matter whether the change is great or little; the final handful of Tasmanians were removed from the mainland to Flinders Island, but environmentally the difference was minor. Nevertheless, Darwin suggests, the Tasmanians failed to reproduce their race as if obedient to some invisible law of nature. If it were not for the apparent inevitability of this result, Darwin might almost be accusing the Tasmanians of wilfully failing to reproduce – blaming the victims with a vengeance! As it is, he has employed the Tasmanian example so as to suggest that the violence visited upon them by the colonists was just a minor aspect of the workings of 'changed conditions'.

But from any perspective, how could the extinction of even the most primitive, most 'unfit' savages, as opposed to their benevolent conversion to civilization, be called progress? The explicit answer in Darwin, echoed by later social Darwinists such as Benjamin Kidd and Karl Pearson, follows from the stress on the inevitability of the processes or 'laws' of nature: 'primitive' ways of life, if not clearly all 'primitive races', must and will disappear from the world as a consequence of the unilinear and progressive evolution of *homo sapiens*. At the start of *The Descent of Man*, Darwin asks: 'Do the races or species of men, whichever term may be applied, encroach on and replace one another, so that some finally become extinct? We shall see that all these questions ... must be answered in the affirmative' (Darwin n.d.: 395).[1] The elimination of one race by another is just the process of 'natural selection' at work – a process, however, leading to civilization and the ultimate perfection of humanity's moral and intellectual capacities. Darwin is sure, moreover, that England is in the vanguard of the forward march to perfection. He quotes approvingly the Reverend Mr Zincke, who asserts that the entire history of civilization up to the present has '"purpose and value [only] when viewed ... as subsidiary to ... the great stream of Anglo-Saxon emigration to the west"' (Darwin n.d.: 508). Darwin adds: 'Obscure as is the problem of the advance of civilisation, we can at least see that a nation which produced ... the greatest number of highly intellectual, energetic, brave, patriotic, *and benevolent* men, would generally prevail over less favoured nations' (Darwin n.d.: 508; my emphasis). 'Benevolent', of course, only suggests that the extermination of 'lower races' goes hand in hand with the highest of moral purposes.

About all that can be said in exoneration of Darwin is that he does not connect his prediction of the total extermination of all 'lower races' by 'higher', 'civilised' ones with advocacy of deliberate genocide. Darwin does not go so far as Charles Dickens, for example, who in 1853 declared that 'a savage [is] something highly desirable to be civilized off the face of the earth' (Dickens 1853: 337). Similarly, another great Victorian novelist, Anthony Trollope, could write in 1873, in social Darwinist fashion, that the 'doom' of the Australian aborigines 'is to be exterminated; and the sooner that their doom be accomplished – so that there be no cruelty – the better it will be for civilization' (Trollope 1967: 564).

Darwin was not psychologist enough to recognize that the 'changed conditions' which, he held, inevitably doomed primitive peoples might involve resistance to becoming 'civilized' – a resistance that, at least in the case of the Tasmanians, may have operated in their last days as a form of collective suicide. Nor did Darwin toy with any version of Rousseauistic admiration of primitive societies; 'civilization' appears in his writings as the inevitable goal of human history or evolution, and it is therefore – at least implicitly – a better state than what has come before, or a 'higher' condition than that of primitive society, which in turn is 'higher' (though not always by much) than that of any other species. Just exactly what Darwin means by his metaphors of lower and higher, and of progress, is often unclear. Yet he nowhere considers that the nomadic way of life of the Tasmanians (or other primitive peoples) may have been good or perfectly viable for the unchanged conditions in which Europeans discovered them, or that the invasion of 'civilization' was for them nothing better than an unmitigated disaster. He only suggests that the Tasmanians were uncivilizable; their dying out was largely a consequence, according to his argument, of their failure to reproduce under 'changed conditions', and one way to read that phrase is: under attempts to civilize them.

Along with disease, infertility and low morale, a less obvious cause of the final solution on Flinders Island – one mentioned by Bonwick and cited by Darwin, though he does not stress it – involved the misguided efforts of their white protectors to civilize the aborigines. According to this line of argument, not only did civilization kill by violence and by the spread of new diseases, it also killed by kindness, or anyway by conversion, through trying, in accord with its highest ideals, to transform Stone Age savages into progressive, enlightened humans. The point here is not that 'wild' people, like 'wild' animals, will die out under any changed conditions, as Darwin suggests; rather, they are somehow constitutionally unsuited to civilized life in particular. This point can in turn be construed in two antithetical ways: the first, more Darwinian, interpretation is that 'wild' people are 'unfit' for civilization; the second, Rousseauistic interpretation, offered by Bonwick, is that civilization represents a degradation of the way of life of primitive peoples, including a loss of freedoms enjoyed in a more natural state of existence.

Darwin quotes Bonwick quoting Dr J.F. Story, a Quaker humanitarian from Tasmania, who held that 'death followed the attempts to civilise the [aborigines on Flinders Island]. "If left to themselves to roam as they were wont and undisturbed, they would have reared more children, and there would have been less mortality"' (Darwin n.d.: 544; Bonwick 1870: 388). This argument had been offered as early as 1839, in reports to Parliament about the apparently well-intentioned but last-ditch efforts to save the last of the first Tasmanians. A Rousseauistic strain is evident throughout humanitarian commentary on the Tasmanian situation, and from the 1830s forward, though it is not part of Darwin's thinking. Officials in both Hobart and London, moreover, disapproved of the violence visited upon the Tasmanian aborigines and tried to stop it.[2] But of course, as Bonwick points out, the authorities had also turned Tasmania into a penal colony, and much of the most brutal violence against the aborigines came from escaped convicts or bushrangers.

Following the so-called 'Black Line' of 1830 (an unsuccessful attempt to kill or capture the few surviving aborigines), the aboriginal population of only about two hundred were rounded up and placed on Flinders Island by their would-be saviour and civilizer, George Augustus Robinson (see Plomley 1966 and also Rae-Ellis 1987). There, Robinson instituted an authoritarian Christian regime that involved frequent religious services and education by catechism, as well as '1. An aboriginal fund. 2. A circulating medium. 3. An aboriginal police. 4. A weekly market, and 5. A weekly periodical' (Robinson 1839: 399). The great arctic explorer John Hope Franklin, Governor of Tasmania after George Arthur, told Lord Glenelg that, in his opinion, Robinson's most effective civilizing tool was the 'aboriginal police' (Robinson 1839: 396), consisting of a grand total of four officers and two chiefs, but Robinson thought differently: 'of all the schemes put in force for the civilisation of the aborigines', he declared, 'the circulating medium is paramount' (Robinson 1839: 399). He could imagine no better means than the profit motive to get savages to practise the virtue of industry. 'With a circulation of coin not exceeding in amount fifteen pounds,' he wrote, 'labour in the value of upwards of one hundred pounds has been created' (Robinson 1839: 399). The aborigines were beginning to construct, purchase, and own property: the men were building roads and houses and tilling the soil for potatoes; the women were gathering grass for thatch, cooking, bird-snaring, and also learning the more 'refined' arts of needlework, knitting, and 'French net', under the tutelage of Mrs Clark, wife of the resident catechist. The aboriginal police, meanwhile, 'take a general surveillance over the entirety of the aborigines' (Robinson 1839: 401), though Robinson's own surveillance was far more thorough. Robinson even gave most of his charges new European names – no doubt part of their transmogrification into well-behaved Christian aborigines – though he declares that the aborigines themselves demanded new names. But it is hard not to think of these aliases as expressing a patronizing racism: 'Bonaparte', for instance, and 'Neptune', 'Romeo', 'Queen Cleopatra', and 'Lalla Rookh' (Bonwick 1870: 257–8).

Despite his claims to be civilizing the last Tasmanians, Robinson could not duck the fact that they continued to die out at an alarming rate. Critics began to accuse him of contributing to the bad health of his subjects by dressing them up and making them lead sedentary lives. Oblivious to these criticisms, Robinson declared that 'the only drawback on the establishment [at Flinders Island] was the great mortality among them' (quoted in Bonwick 1870: 255). The chief cause of the failure of his humane, godly conversion work was, he believed, the perverse, inexplicable deaths of his aboriginal subjects. 'Had the poor creatures survived to have become a numerous people, I am convinced they would have formed a contented and useful community' (quoted in Bonwick 1870: 258). Of course this is like saying had the poor creatures survived they would not have died out.

Bonwick for one is unwilling to let Robinson off the hook. 'Dr Story gives it as his opinion to me, that 'the deaths at Flinders Island and the attempt at civilizing the Natives were consequent on each other" (Bonwick 1870: 266). Both Bonwick and Story saw that what Robinson meant by civilizing the aborigines involved nothing less than the eradication of their former beliefs, customs and even identities. Although Bonwick did not know the word, 'brainwashing' would become the label for similar tactics in latter-day concentration camps. 'Even the Committee of the Aborigines' [Protection] Society were at last sensible of the folly of [Robinson's] over-legislation,' writes Bonwick; 'for, in their Report for 1839, they regretted that "from the first a system had not been applied more suitable to the habits of a roving people"' (Bonwick 1870: 255–6). In short, according to this logic, civilization in the guise of Robinson's conversion tactics killed the last Tasmanians, almost as surely as in more brutal forms it had killed the aboriginal majority.

At least Robinson was trying to preserve rather than to destroy the Tasmanians. But his efforts were too late and too little, a description that – despite the successes of abolitionism – fits nineteenth-century human-itarianism in general. The Aborigines Protection Society continued the work of the antislavery movement down to the end of the century, but was almost always reacting to genocidal violence that had already taken place. Humanitarianism may have prevented some violence, but it also gave the impression that every effort was being made to smooth the pillows beneath the heads of the inevitably dying races (see Bourne 1899). Nineteenth-century 'race science' was also too late and too little. Indeed, in partial contrast to James Prichard, Darwin nowhere indicates that his consideration of the extinction of primitive races is meant to produce remedies, as opposed to the mere 'scientific' understanding of the 'inevit-able' workings of natural 'laws'. And the new science of evolution lent powerful authority to the idea that what was happening to 'uncivilized' peoples around the world was not just natural and inevitable, but also an aspect of humanity's 'progress' upwards from the apes.

In the case of the Tasmanians, moreover, as Lyndall Ryan contends, the myth of their total extinction has meant that for decades the Australian government could ignore the claims of mixed-race Tasmanians: they simply did not exist. And that myth also, quite perversely, seemed to corroborate the view that other races would soon inevitably go the way of the Tas-manians. The Maoris of New Zealand were held to be 'passing away' as late as the First World War, and the Australian aborigines were 'vanishing' up until, perhaps, the Second World War, when demographic evidence began to point in the opposite direction. To this sorry legacy can be added at least two still operative ideological factors. One is a corollary of the inevitability thesis. According to this corollary, the past itself is the realm of the inevitable: what happened happened, and cannot be changed – there is therefore no point in criticizing the past. But there is every reason to criticize *the present* in light of the past, unless the present, too, is to fall victim to the paralysing myth of inevitability. And the second notion is that humanity has surely made great progress since the admittedly crude violence of the nineteenth century. But a glance at the twentieth-century record of genocides, down to the recent nightmare of 'ethnic cleansing' in the former Yugoslavia, should quickly dispel this dangerous illusion (see Bauman 1989). All of the illusions and rationalizations surveyed in this chapter have facilitated – and will continue to facilitate – genocides until they themselves have been eradicated from the colonized and colonizing imaginations that maintain them.

Notes

1. D.G. Ritchie is correct when, in *Darwinism and Politics* (1889: 7), he declares that Darwin 'looks forward to the elimination of the lower races by the higher civilized races throughout the world'. Ritchie adds that social Darwinism is a 'scheme of salvation for the elect by the damnation of the vast majority'.

2. Lord Glenelg, Secretary for the Colonies under Melbourne in the 1830s, was an evangelical infused with the humane spirit of the antislavery movement; partly through his influence, officials in both Tasmania and Britain tried (unsuccessfully) to curtail bloodshed. For a general account, see Turnbull 1948.

References

Banton, Michael 1977 *The Idea of Race* London, Tavistock.

Bauman, Zygmunt 1989 *Modernity and the Holocaust* Ithaca, Cornell University Press.

Bonwick, James 1870 *The Last of the Tasmanians: or, the Black War of Van Diemen's Land* London, Sampson, Low and Marston.

Bourne, H. R. Fox 1899 *The Aborigines Protection Society: Chapters in Its History* London, P.S. King.

Brantlinger, Patrick 1988 *Rule of Darkness: British Literature and Imperialism, 1830–1914* Ithaca, Cornell University Press.

Calder, J.E. 1874 'Some account of the wars of extirpation, and habits of the native tribes of Tasmania', *Journal of the Royal Anthropological Institute* 3: 7–29.

Darwin, Charles (n.d.) *The Origin of Species and The Descent of Man* New York, Modern Library.

Darwin, Francis (ed.) 1959 *The Life and Letters of Charles Darwin* New York, Basic Books.

Dickens, Charles 1853 'The Noble Savage', *Household Words* 337.

Galton, Francis 1925 *Hereditary Genius: an Inquiry into its Laws and Consequences* London, Macmillan.

Hegel, Georg Wilhelm Friedrich 1956 *The Philosophy of History* New York, Dover.

Irving, Washington [1836] 1976 *Astoria, or Anecdotes of an Enterprize beyond the Rocky Mountains* Boston, Twayne.

Kidd, Benjamin 1894 *Social Evolution* New York, Macmillan.

Knox, Robert 1850 *The Races of Men: A Fragment* Philadelphia, Lea and Blanchard.

Legters, Lyman H. 1988 'The American genocide', *Policy Studies Journal* 16(4): 768–77.

Martineau, Harriet 1845 *Dawn Island, a Tale* Manchester, J. Gadsby.

Nightingale, Florence 1864 'Note on the aboriginal races in Australia', *National Association for the Promotion of Social Science Transactions* 552–8.

Plomley, N.J.B. (ed.) 1966 *Friendly Mission: the Tasmanian Journals and Papers of George Augustus Robinson, 1829–1834* Hobart, Tasmanian Historical Research Association.

Pool, D. Ian 1977 *The Maori Population of New Zealand, 1769–1971* Auckland, Auckland University Press; New York, Oxford University Press.

Prichard, James Cowles 1839 'On the extinction of human races', *Edinburgh New Philosophical Journal* 28: 166–70.

Rae-Ellis, Vivienne 1987 *Black Robinson: Protector of Aborigines* Melbourne, Melbourne University Press.

Ritchie, D.G. 1889 *Darwinism and Politics* New York, Scribner and Welford.

Robinson, George Augustus 1839 'Report on the aboriginal establishment at Flinders Island', *Parliamentary Papers* 34: 397–403.

Robson, Lloyd 1983 *A History of Tasmania* Vol. 1, *Van Diemen's Land from the Earliest Times to 1855* Melbourne, Oxford University Press.

Ryan, Lyndall 1981 *The Aboriginal Tasmanians* Vancouver, University of British Columbia Press.

Stepan, Nancy 1982 *The Idea of Race in Science: Great Britain, 1800–1960* Hamden, CT, Archon Press.

Trollope, Anthony 1967 *Australia* (Edited by P.D. Edwards and R.B. Joyce) Brisbane, University of Queensland Press.

Turnbull, Clive 1948 *Black War: The Extermination of the Tasmanian Aborigines* Melbourne, Cheshire-Lansdowne.

Tylor, Edward B. 1893 'On the Tasmanians as representatives of Palaeolithic man', *Journal of the Anthropological Institute* 23: 141–52.

Wallace, Alfred Russel 1864 'The origin of human races and the antiquity of man deduced from the theory of "natural selection"', *Journal of the Anthropological Society* 2: clviii–clxxxvii.

4

Ethnographic showcases, 1870–1930

Raymond Corbey

Il n'y a ni bourg, ni hameau, ni maison séparée dans l'île; Zamé a voulu que toutes les possessions d'une province fussent réunies dans une même enceinte, afin que l'oeil vigilant du commandant de la ville pût s'étendre avec moins de peine sur tous les sujets de la contrée.

D.A.F. de Sade, *Aline et Valcour*

'To see is to know' – this motto was attached to the anthropological exhibits of the World's Columbian Exposition, 1893, one of the many world fairs during the era of imperialism and colonialism (Rydell 1984: 44). At these gigantic exhibitions, staged by the principal colonial powers, the world was collected and displayed. Natives from a wide range of colonized cultures quickly became a standard part of most manifestations of this kind. Together with their artifacts, houses, and even complete villages, so-called savages or primitives were made available for visual inspection by millions of strolling and staring Western citizens. Comparable places of spectacle such as zoos, botanical gardens, circuses, temporary or permanent exhibitions staged by missionary societies and museums of natural history, all exhibited other races and/or other species and testified to the imperialism of nineteenth-century nation-states.

In this chapter I will put these ethnographic exhibits into the wider context of the collecting, measuring, classifying, picturing, filing, and narrating of colonial others during the heyday of colonialism. All these modes of dealing with the exotic, with colonial otherness, functioned in a context of European hegemony, testifying to the successful imperialist expansion of nineteenth-century nation-states and to the intricate connections that developed between scientific and political practices. Of course, I cannot bypass the historical changes and national differences in exhibitionary practices in the period under study – the last decades of the nineteenth and the first decades of the twentieth century – but I will concentrate on the similarities, which in my view are predominant, arguing that it is possible to have a wide range of seemingly divergent modes of dealing with the Other within one single analytic field.

The world on show

World fairs or international expositions (the *exposition universelle, Weltausstellung*) were very large-scale happenings that combined features of trade and industrial fairs, carnival, music festivals, political manifestations, museums and art galleries. But primarily they were 'pilgrimage sites of commodity fetishism', as Walter Benjamin (1984: 441) pointedly put it. From 1851, when the first international exposition took place in London, onward, an enormous variety of industrial and technological products were exhibited, including steam-powered machines, lawn mowers, elevators, photographic cameras, mechanized weaving looms, and household appliances. In addition, colonial raw materials and products were displayed, along with archaeological artifacts. Various architectural styles were presented, and after 1885 the arts became a recurrent theme. The idea was to show progress in all fields – not only in industry, trade and transportation, but also in the arts, the sciences and culture. Meanwhile, there was no mention of poverty, sickness and oppression, or of social and international conflicts.

World fairs have been compared to gigantic potlatches, joyous ritual displays of richness and power, where possessions were given away and even destroyed in great numbers in order to gain prestige and to outdo others, as occurred among the Kwakiutl and other Indian cultures of the North American Northwest Coast (Benedict 1983: 7ff.). In both cases – world fairs and potlatches – ritualized competition, the gaining of prestige, and the reciprocal need to keep up with parties of comparable calibre played important roles. Both kinds of manifestations were large-scale, expensive festivals that – having social, economic, political, juridical, moral, and aesthetic aspects – displayed the character of a *fait social total* in the sense of Marcel Mauss, and both regulated relationships between rival groups (such as nations and large cities). Economic interests went hand in hand with cultural interests, and nationalistic ambitions were apparent notwithstanding the international character of the fairs, in which each country built its own monumental pavilion in its particular national style. The architecture was meant to impress; it could never be large, imposing, or unusual enough: the Crystal Palace (London), the Eiffel Tower (Paris), the Atomium (Brussels). The first world fair, the Great Exhibition of the Works of Industry of all Nations, held in the Crystal Palace in London in 1851, attracted 6 million visitors; the world fair in Paris in 1878, 16 million; the 1900 Paris fair, still before the era of cinema and television, 50 million.

So-called colonial exhibitions – such as the Colonial and Indian Exhibition in London in 1886, the British Empire Exhibition of 1924–25, or the Exposition Coloniale in Paris in 1931 – were even more closely associated with the idea and ideal of empire. But even for the 1851 Great Exhibition, the Society of Arts had fanatically developed scenarios for, as one of its spokesmen put it, 'promoting and spreading Christianity, civilization and commerce among peoples still steeped in barbarity and idolatry – in terms of quantity nearly half of humanity' (quoted by Haltern 1971: 314). World fairs quickly became inseparable from imperialism and nationalism. For the British Exhibition at Wembley in 1924, a historical pageant was staged with fifteen thousand participants, which took three days to pass (Benedict 1983: 47). With this gigantic spectacle, accompanied by music and texts written for the occasion, and structured like a heroic epos governed by a fundamental opposition between the civilized and the barbaric, the English people, self-consciously and full of pride, presented and represented their newly created world empire. Such manifestations are of interest in the present context, not only because colonial natives had a role to play too, but also because they express the civilizational idiom that formed the basis of contemporary views of 'primitives', tied up with imperialist ideology and social Darwinism.

In covering the Great Exhibition, the German newspaper *Allgemeine Zeitung* stressed the prevalent 'spirit of encyclopaedism' (Haltern 1971: 352). In the course of their development, the encyclopaedic character of world exhibits – an explicitly stated goal – became increasingly prominent. The history of subjects such as the home, labour, transportation was shown, while an equally panoramic variety of cultures was displayed. An inventory/census of the whole world and the whole history of humankind was constructed in a way reminiscent of medieval maps of the world – *mappae mundi*, offering an encyclopaedic survey of the world as creation – or of the cabinets of curiosity of the Renaissance. During the same period, journals like the French *Le Tour du Monde*, with their synoptic and panoptic illustrations, usually copied from photographs, had a comparable function, as did photography as such, not least as put to use at the world fairs (Favrod 1989; Lederbogen 1986; Theye 1989).

In all cultures, political and religious elites tend to accumulate and flaunt their rare and precious objects from faraway places in order to gain prestige and to display their knowledgeability. Everyone from Renaissance princes and cardinals to Chinese emperors owned collections of exotic animals, objects, and even people. Something similar happened at world fairs, where not individual collectors but states, metropoles and their elites were involved. Mary Helms offers the analogy of the tribal shaman's medicine pouch holding a collection of strange objects. The more rare and exotic these objects, the more effective they were and the more they contributed to the shaman's prestige and power.

> The emperor's zoo and botanical gardens, like the shaman's pouch, contained bits and pieces of the animate cosmos, power-filled natural wonders, examples of the rare, the curious, the strange, and the precious – all expressions of the unusual and the different attesting to the forces of the dynamic universe that by definition lies outside the (again by definition) controlled, socialized, civilized heartland. (Helms 1988: 166)

In each of these cases, a microcosm sampled and presented the macrocosm. The world fair can also be read as a microcosm, created by the Promethean Western middle classes, with their unlimited trust in Enlightenment ideas and the rational constructibility of the world – a world made after their own image, to European standards. Here, nature was only of secondary importance, appearing only in the shape of cultivated crops and painted backdrops; here, everything had been fabricated by man. Marx and Engels referred to the Great Exhibition as 'a pantheon in modern

Rome', where the bourgeoisie 'exhibits with self-congratulatory pride the gods it has created for itself' (quoted by Haltern 1971: 314). In high euphoria, the bourgeoisie celebrated progress, the attainment of world power, and the creation of Western middle-class culture by its own efforts – which, in its own eyes, was the purpose to which world history (and indeed cosmic evolution) had been directed from its earliest beginnings. Progress and civilization were the key concepts of these large-scale representations of middle-class 'selves' and savage 'others'. Another prominent theme was the Enlightenment ideal of universal brotherhood, connected with the Christian ideals of peace and love.

World fairs, as Carol Breckenridge (1989: 196) remarks, were part of a unitary, though not necessarily uniform, landscape of discourse and practice, providing a cultural technology for situating metropole and colony within a single analytic field, thus creating an imagined ecumene. The fairs told the story of mankind, the very same narrative that accompanied and legitimized colonial expansion. In this epic, staged by themselves, white, rational, civilized European citizens cast themselves in the role of hero.

Savages on show

Placed alongside all kinds of objects and products, colonial natives quickly became a standard part of world fairs, for the education and entertainment of Western citizens. Not only the citizens themselves, but also the natives figured as categories in Western representations of Self, as characters in the story of the ascent to civilization, depicted as the inevitable triumph of higher races over lower ones and as progress through science and imperial conquest. Often ethnologists were ahead of their times concerning interpretations of other cultures, but Charles Rau, for one, who created the ethnological exhibits at the Philadelphia Centennial Exhibition of 1876, on behalf of the Smithsonian Institution, stated that:

> ... the extreme lowness of our remote ancestors cannot be a source of humiliation; on the contrary, we should glory in our having advanced so far above them, and recognize the great truth that progress is the law that governs the development of mankind. (quoted in Rydell 1984: 24)

Two years later, the Paris world fair of 1878 was the first one in which people from non-Western cultures were exhibited, in especially constructed pavilions and 'native villages' (*Villages indigènes*). The display of 400 natives from the French colonies Indochina, Senegal, and Tahiti met with huge success, as did the exhibits of indigenous peoples from Java, Samoa, Dahomey, Egypt, and North America itself at the World's Columbian Exposition in 1893.

Native villages were a standard part of world fairs from 1878 onward. Equally popular were the 'foreign streets' such as the 'Rue de Caire'. Around the turn of the century, the International Anthropological Exhibit Company commercially exploited exhibitions of non-Western people in the United States in several settings, including world fairs. At the Dutch 'Internationale Koloniale en Uitvoerhandel Tentoonstelling' in Amsterdam in 1883, natives from the Dutch East Indies and West Indies were shown. The Greater Britain Exhibition of 1899 included a 'Kaffir Kraal – A Vivid Representation of Life in the Wilds of the Dark Continent', an exhibit featuring African animals and 174 natives from several South African peoples brought under control only shortly before. They were divided into four native villages, showing their crafts, performing 'war dances', and riding on ponies. Among them were San, who characteristically were exhibited as part of the natural history of Africa, together with baboons (MacKenzie 1984: 104). Often the European impresarios travelled from one world fair to another with the same group of people – the Senegalese who constituted the well-known 'Senegalese village', for example – and had them perform at other venues and on other occasions as well.

A brochure commenting upon the 'Village from Dahomey' at the Imperial International Exhibition of 1909 stressed the violent brutality of indigenous Africa, especially Dahomey with its 'bloodthirsty potentates' and woman warriors or 'Amazons' who were one of the main attractions of the village; it praised the French intervention of 1892 with the following words:

> Order and decency, trade and civilization have taken the place of rule by fear of the sword. France has placed its hand on the blackest spot in West Africa, and wiped out some of the red stain that made Dahomey a byword in the world. ... Today ... [the] days of savagery are passing away. (quoted in MacKenzie 1984: 116)

It was light against dark, order against violence, and a European nation as the bringer of civilization. The exhibited 'Amazons' – depicted as both barbarous and alluring, true personifications of the so-called Dark Continent – performed throughout Europe. When they appeared in the Moskauer Panoptikum in Frankfurt in 1899, they were introduced as 'wild females' – *wilde Weiber*. A group of women from Samoa, however, was described by the press and in brochures as a breathtakingly beautiful, always cheery, erotically permissive, and lazy people from the paradisiacal Pacific Ocean (*Plakate 1880–1914*: 257). North American Indians were similarly idealized and romanticized.

The 1909 world fair that featured the Amazons also included a native village of nomadic Kalmuks from Central Asia, brought under the control of the Russian empire shortly before. At the Berliner Gewerbe-Ausstellung of 1896, which led to the foundation of the Deutsches Kolonialmuseum, over a hundred natives from the German colonies were present, each group in its own carefully imitated cultural and natural setting. They had to call 'hurrah' at set times in praise of emperor and *Reich* (G. Schneider 1982: 167). Governments were keenly aware of the opportunity to publicize their colonial policies and to manipulate public attitudes toward the newly acquired territories. German, Dutch and Irish villages, among others, with native people in traditional clothing were also (re)presented at the world fairs as part of the national exhibits, staged however, by the exhibited peoples themselves, not by their colonizers.

It seems to have been quite usual for visitors to throw money to the performing natives and for the natives to beg for it. The exhibited peoples' behaviour and movement was strictly controlled. They were presented as 'different' and forced to behave that way. At most – though not all – manifestations it was unthinkable that they should mingle spontaneously with the visitors, and usually there were few possibilities for contact between parties. The living exhibits had to stay within a precisely circumscribed part of the exhibition space, which represented their world; the boundary between this world and that of the citizens visiting and inspecting them, between wildness and civility, nature and culture, had to be respected unconditionally. All signs of acculturation were avoided so long as the natives were on show. One of my colleagues who grew up in postwar Berlin has told me about his astonishment when, as a boy, he came across an African man, whom he had seen only hours before in native attire at Castan's Panoptikum, now in European clothes on a tramcar, smoking a cigarette. Primitivity was staged in minute detail.

The desirability of 'civilizing' North American Indian peoples was an important theme at the St Louis fair, as it was at other world fairs in the United States. Their 'dull-minded and self-centered tribal existence' had to be replaced by '[the] active and constructive and broadminded life of modern humanity' (Francis 1913: 529, quoted by Benedict 1983: 50). The imposition of cultural assimilation, as typical of internal colonialism in the United States as it was of French colonialism, was less important in the English colonial regime. English visitors to French world fairs and colonial exhibitions, therefore, often expressed astonishment when confronted with indigenous people in European clothing. In St Louis, the living exhibits were typically organized on a scale from civilized to barbaric. The lower a people or race was deemed to be, the further removed it was from the 'Indian School' that marked one pole of the scale, that of civilization. Filippine Igorots and African Pygmies were situated near the pole of barbarity at the other end of the scale.[1] At the World's Columbian Exposition of 1893 in Chicago, the opposition between 'wild' and 'civilized' and the desirability of civilizing peoples that were still wild was expressed by showing an old Indian in shabby traditional clothing next to his son in a neat new suit (Benedict 1983: 49ff.).

Hagenbeck's *Völkerschauen*

Persons from non-Western cultures appeared not only at world and colonial exhibitions, but also at special ethnographic shows called *Völkerschauen* in Germany, where this type of manifestation had proliferated since 1874. In that year Carl Hagenbeck, a dealer in wild animals in Hamburg and later director of a zoo and a circus, began exhibiting Samen – Lapps – as 'purely natural people' (*reine Naturmenschen*, Lehmann 1955) in several German cities, together with their tents, tools, weapons and other possessions, as well as reindeer. In 1876, he sent one of his collaborators to Egyptian Sudan in order to bring back Nubians and indigenous animals. This group of 'savages' with their 'wild' personalities, as Hagenbeck describes them in his autobiography (Hagenbeck 1909), was scrutinized by over thirty thousand German visitors on the first day of their appearance in Breslau. Subsequently the Nubians were exhibited in other European cities, including Paris and London.

When this venture became a success, Hagenbeck extended his profitable activities to include North American Indians, Inuit, people from India, and Zulus (*Zulukaffern*). He and other enterpreneurs also exhibited Sudanese, Bushmen, and *Somalinegerknaben* riding on ostriches; later, Dinka, Maasai, and Ashanti were recruited in Africa and brought to Europe (cf. Thode-Arora 1989: 168–78). The supply of natives closely followed the colonial conquests. Tuareg, for instance, were on exhibit in Paris within months of the French capture of Timbuktu in 1894, and natives from Madagascar appeared a year after the French occupation of that island (W. Schneider 1977: 101). The new genre quickly caught on, and ethnographic exhibits stayed very popular well into the twentieth century. Hagenbeck presented them to the middle classes with the stated intention of promoting the *Bildung* – the knowledge and culture a civilized person should possess – and stimulating the German people's nationalistic zest for colonial expansion. Often the members of *Naturvölker* ('natural peoples'), more closely associated with living nature than with civilization, were exhibited in local zoos behind bars or wire fences; fairgrounds and public parks served as settings, too. In France, the Paris Jardin d'Acclimatation, created in 1859 for the study and popularization of exotic animals and plants, became a popular setting for ethnological exhibits similar to the German ones.

For decades the German press wrote about the appearance, behaviour and nature of the foreign visitors in a very negative tone, expressing disgust and contempt for them. The general reaction of the public visiting the manifestations seems to have been the same; but near the turn of the century, press coverage began to change for the better, and more attention was given to ethnographic detail. Another reason for negative reactions to black Africans in particular, apart from deeply ingrained stereotypes of barbarity and primitivity, was the stubborn and often bloody resistance of several African peoples toward the European expansion in Africa, which was covered extensively by the European press. In the eyes of many Germans, a black African was some sort of savage monster. France consciously played on such fears in the French–German war of 1870–71 by pitting black *tirailleurs indigènes*, trained in Algeria, against German troops (Goldmann 1985: 258). In general, the more an indigenous people had resisted colonization, the more ferocity its representatives had to display when on stage.

Fear was but one of the mixed feelings German citizens experienced when visiting ethnological exhibitions. Another reaction was sexual fascination and curiosity, as is clear from contemporary press coverage and from preserved posters. Admiration of the supposedly large sexual potency of the scarcely clothed primitives competed with depreciation because of their alleged bestial lust (Goldmann 1985: 263–4; Thode-Arora 1989: 115–19). Disgust alternated with exalted attention, wonder and enchantment when Western citizens were confronted with picturesque scenes from savage life.

In the Netherlands, too, ethnological exhibitions took place. In the year 1900, for instance, the Groote Achantees Karavanen ('Large Ashanti Caravans') attracted much attention in Amsterdam, Rotterdam, The Hague, Utrecht and Nijmegen. The Ashanti, usually shown at the Jardin d'Acclimatation in Paris, now toured the rest of Western Europe.[2] In the Netherlands, they were described on a poster as 'old natives from the Gold Coasts of Africa ... Warriors, Fetish Priests, Snake-charmers, Women, Girls and Children. The most uncommon human race that has ever been seen in Europe. Most interesting for everyone' (Municipal Archives, Rotterdam). A few years earlier, *De Boschmannen of wilden van Afrika* ('the Bushmen or Savages of Africa'), as the title of the accompanying brochure reads, were on tour. Judging from their appearance, this brochure states, 'they show more similarity to Apes than to people. ... Notwithstanding their ferocity these Bushmen are nearly harmless, and even the most fearful person can approach and touch them all over with the greatest confidence' (Municipal Archives, Rotterdam). The suggestion that they could be touched indicates how close the attitudes towards these people was to the attitude towards animals. That the exhibited people were similar – metonymically, metaphorically, in appearance and behaviour – to animals, especially apes, was indeed a common perception, fed by contemporary scientific theory. In recent decades, in contrast, Bushmen once again came to play a positive role in Western imagination, similar to the one they played in the eighteenth century – that of noble savages, spontaneously and innocently enjoying a pure, natural, paradisiacal existence.

The natives performed in several roles. The American company William Foote & Co. African-American Characters exploited a show with African-Americans – as the letterhead of the firm stated – appearing as 'Savages, Slaves, Soldiers and Citizens' (Thode-Arora 1989: 41). Crafts, hunting techniques, rituals, dances, and songs were among the activities staged, as well as stereotypical 'authentic' performances such as warfare, cannibalistic acts, and headhunting. At the 1904 Louisiana Purchase Exposition in St Louis, Igorots from the Philippines could be seen eating dog meat, a food taboo in the West, while African Pygmies illustrated decapitation. The above-mentioned Dahomey 'Amazons', heavily armed, simulated fights. Aborigines from Queensland, Australia, presented as *Austral. Neger*, on exhibition at the Frankfurt Zoo and elsewhere in May 1885, were described on posters as cannibals and bloodthirsty monsters – 'wirklich blutdürstige Ungeheuer'. Another poster, printed for their appearance in England, continuing a European iconographical tradition reaching back to De Bry's late sixteenth-century *Grands Voyages* and earlier, depicts them engaged in a ferocious cannibal ritual, with the following text:

> Male and female Australian cannibals / R.A. Cunningham, Director / The first and only obtained colony of these strange, savage, disfigured and most brutal race ever lured from the remote interior wilds, where they indulge in ceaseless bloody feuds and forays, to feast upon each other's flesh / The very lowest order of mankind, and beyond conception most curious to look upon. (Plakate 1880–1914: 228)

How did the exhibited individuals themselves, often more or less coerced into participation, experience and cope with the exhibitions? Many had to battle with homesickness, emotional confusion, difficulties of adjustment to the European climate and food, and vicious infections. Often they actively resisted the roles forced on them, for instance by running away, and they could be put back in harness only by force. Now and then bad treatment led to court cases. In the *Zeitschrift für Ethnologie* of 1880, the prominent anthropologist and politician Rudolf Virchow described in detail how an Inuit woman whose measurements he wished to take literally ran into the walls of the room in total panic (quoted by Thode-Arora 1989: 129–30), an incident that was by no means exceptional. The percentage of those who died soon after their arrival in Europe was considerable. When the aforementioned group of Aborigines arrived in Germany in 1883, there were eight of them; in May 1885, when they appeared in the Frankfurt Zoo, five were still alive; in October 1896, when they were examined by members of the Berliner Gesellschaft für Anthropologie, Ethnologie und Urgeschichte, there were only three survivors. The members of two Inuit families from Labrador, on exhibition in several German cities during the year 1880 with their dogs and kayaks, all succumbed to an infection in January 1881 (Plakate 1880–1914: 236). At the cemetery of Tervuren, Belgium, close to the site of the 1897 colonial exhibition, a number of Africans lie buried who were part of the 'Congolese Village' and rowed canoes on the Tervuren ponds. In some cases, however, the exhibited natives were paid very well, treated with warmth and care, and offered sightseeing tours and dinners with local prominent people.

How the individuals on display – confronted with an alien world, unfamiliar food, strange customs, a different climate – experienced and handled their situation is an important question indeed. The relative scarcity of sources concerning their intentions and feelings should not lead us to underestimate their subjectivity or to leave it understudied. Who were they? How did they think and feel? How did they negotiate their identities? How did they creatively exploit the roles they were cast into to realize their intentions and express their reactions?[3] How did these roles influence their conceptions of themselves and of the Western people they met? How, for instance, did Penobscot Indian Frank Loring (alias Chief Big Thunder), Micmac Indian Jeremy Bartlett (alias Doctor Lone Cloud), and

Maliseet Indian Henry Perley (alias Red Eagle) feel about their roles as itinerant Native American performers (Prins 1991)?[4]

The diary of one of the males from the Inuit troupe touring Germany has been preserved (Taylor 1981). Much is known about Jefke, a black African boy on exhibition at the Antwerp Zoo, as well as about Ota Benga, a Pygmy boy displayed in a cage with a chimpanzee and later with an orang-utan at the Bronx Zoo (Bieder 1991; Bradford and Blume 1993). Less is known about Klikko, 'The Wild Dancing Bushman', a Khoi-San performing in London around 1913 (Parsons 1988). Mitchell (1988, 1989) quotes reactions of Egyptian scholars visiting the 'Rue de Caire' at the Paris Exposition universelle of 1889. How did Black Elk conceive of his appearances in Buffalo Bill's Wild West Show (see Neihardt 1988; Rice 1991), or Mary Alice Nelson, (alias Molly Spotted Elk), a Penobscot Indian, conceive of her dance performances in Paris, where she thrilled the public with her floor-length eagle feather headdress (McBride 1989)?[5] What was on the minds of the Indians from Surinam performing at the 1883 colonial exhibition in Amsterdam, who seem to have been wildly enthusiastic during the first days of exposure to their new world, but soon had to cope with boredom, sickness and the disappointment of not meeting their Dutch king as promised (Pieterse 1992: 34–5)?

Commerce and science

Hagenbeck was certainly not the first to exhibit non-Western people for profit. Although *Völkerschauen* became very popular during the period 1870–1930 and took place on a larger scale than ever before, the phenomenon was by no means new. During the 1820s, Captain Samual Hadlock of Maine toured Europe with a troupe of Inuit, which was exhibited in London, Hamburg, Berlin, Leipzig, Dresden, Prague and Vienna. Among his company was a 'Maori chieftain', whom he had come across in England. When this Maori suddenly died, his head was preserved chemically, and fixed to a model of his body. 'We do not even need the Captain's word for it to be convinced,' the Austrian *Allgemeine Theaterzeitung und Unter-haltungsblatt* wrote on the occasion of the exhibition of the reconstructed Maori at Vienna, 'that this man from New Zeeland, before he was taken aboard, really has eaten other people, because that's indeed the way he looks' (Goldmann 1985: 256).

In London, to give but a few more examples, 'Red Indians' could be seen in 1844; Bushmen in 1845, and again in 1847; south African 'Kaffirs' in 1850 and in 1853 – reflecting the renewed interest in that part of the world during those years. In London, as in Berlin or Paris, learned societies such as the Ethnological Society and the competing Anthropological Society showed great interest in the ethnological exhibitions. Here too, as in Germany, the general attitudes of the public were rather negative, not least under the influence of contemporary missionary propaganda. The *Times* wrote on the Bushmen in 1847:

In appearance they are little above the monkey tribe, and scarcely better than the mere brutes of the field. ... They are sullen, silent and savage – mere animals in propensity, and worse than animals in appearance. ... In short, a more miserable set of human beings – for human they are, nevertheless – was never seen. (quoted by Altick 1978: 281)

And Charles Dickens wondered: 'Is it idiosyncratic in me to abhor, detest, abominate, and abjure that noble savage?,' adding that he hoped something would happen to the stove these people slept around, so that they would suffocate. In his eyes, and in the eyes of most of his contemporaries, the savage was

> ... a prodigious nuisance and a gross superstition ... cruel, false, thievish, murderish; addicted more or less to grease, entrails, and beastly customs; a wild animal with the questionable gift of boasting; a conceited, tiresome, bloodthirsty, monotonous humbug ... if we have anything to learn from the Noble Savage, it is what to avoid. His virtues are a fable; his happiness is a delusion; his nobility, nonsense. (Quoted by Altick 1978)

We should add, however, that in later years Dickens traded his ideas on Anglo-Saxon superiority and progress for a form of cultural relativism implying much milder views on foraging and tribal peoples.

Columbus and Hernán Cortés had already brought back Indians and Aztecs from the New World. European princes, like the Medici in Florence, had scores of aliens at their courts, as curiosities and for purposes of prestige. During the age of European expansion, virtually every generation of Europeans could see Nubians, Inuit, Saami, North American Indians, and Pygmies at fairs, in inns – like the Amsterdam 'Blaauw Jan', precursor to the Artis Zoo – and theatres or, together with exotic animals, in zoos and princely menageries. An analogous practice was that of exhibiting the insane, usually presented in cages, for an admission fee. In eighteeenth-century France, insanity was seen as a decline to a state of wildness and unruly animality, associated traditionally with all that was wicked and unnatural (Foucault 1961), while at the same time there existed a whole body of publications theorizing on similarities of physical appearance between particular types of insanity and particular animal species. 'What was presented here,' as Dörner writes, as 'wild and indomitable nature, "beastliness", absolute and destructive unruliness, social danger, which, behind the bars installed by reason, could be staged the more dramatically for showing at the same time to the public reason as the necessity of controlling nature, as a constraint upon unlimited freedom and as securing the order of the state' (Dörner 1984: 22). Order was contrasted with chaos, reason with wildness.

Also comparable were the 'monsters' and 'freaks' shown at fairs, in circus sideshows, and in the amusement zones of world fairs: individuals with club feet, Siamese twins, bearded women, giants, dwarfs, and so on (cf. Bogdan 1988). A famous case is that of Merrick, the 'elephant-man', an intelligent and sensitive person terribly maimed by sickness, who was exhibited in a freak show in London at the end of the nineteenth century until a prominent surgeon took him into his custody (Montagu 1971). The so-called pan-opticums in large cities, such as Castan's Panoptikum and the Passagen-Panoptikum in Berlin, combined features of a museum of anatomy, a cabinet of curiosities and a horror cabinet. The way exotic animals were – and still are – shown and handled in circus performances elucidated practices of discipline and the concomitant idiom of wildness and taming that were present more implicitly in many exhibits involving people. P.T. Barnum's shows and, somewhat later, the German Circus Sarrasani for decades had ethnological acts on their programmes, often combined with acrobatics.

During the eighteenth and nineteenth centuries, exhibitions of live specimens were increasingly reframed in terms of science, especially phys-ical anthropology and natural history. Aside from their entertainment and curiosity value their educational value came to be stressed more and more. Hagenbeck for instance advertised his show as an 'anthropological–zoolo-gical exhibition' (*anthropologisch-zoologische Ausstellung*). In many ways exhibi-tions of human individuals were anyhow related to scientific practices and purposes. The lunatic asylums where the insane were put on show were in the process of being medicalized; what was monstrous or exotic was often as interesting from a scientific point of view as it was shocking or fascinating to the general public. At the beginning of the nineteenth century, the Khoi-Khoi ('Hottentot') woman Saartjie Baartmann was put on show when alive, and dissected by the famous Cuvier when dead. A mould of her body was then exhibited – in fact until a few years ago, at the Paris Musée de l'Homme – as was, half a century later, the skeleton of the Tasmanian woman Truganini, who was cremated and committed to the waves only in the 1970s. Anthropologists used to be represented on the committees heading the anthropological sections of world fairs, often quarrelling with those who wished to cater more to commercial than to scientific or educational interests.

In anthropometric and psychometric laboratories at the world fairs, visitors could witness and even take part in scientific research on racial characteristics. Phrenology, craniology, physiognomy and anthropometry shared the assumption that in the outward shape and physical appearance of the body the inner character – of different races, but also of criminals, prostitutes, deviants – was manifest. The outward shape, therefore, had to be measured and mapped meticulously (cf. Sekula 1986). Particularly manifest in this context are the interconnections between exhibiting colo-nial natives and scientifically collecting, measuring, classifying and filing them. At the same time, anthropological societies and museums of natural history accumulated tens of thousands of native skulls.[6] Saartjie Baartmann and Truganini are typical cases. According to contemporary views of the genetic variation of mankind, Khoi-Khoi, Tasmanians, Australian Abori-gines, and several native peoples from Tierra del Fuego stood closest to the apes and prehistoric apemen in the racial hierarchy, and therefore were outstanding examples of 'contemporary ancestors' and 'missing links'.

Exhibited colonial natives typically had to appear before anthropological societies such as those of Oxford and London or the Société d'Anthropologie in Paris. The Berliner Gesellschaft für Anthropologie, Ethnologie und Urgeschichte used to organize special sessions for this purpose, often at the same locations as the ethnological shows. On 28 March 1896, for instance, a number of members of the Berlin anthropological society studied an 'authentic Arabic harem' at the Passagen-Panoptikum (Theye 1989: 103). Usually anthropometric measurements and photographs were taken on such occasions, and it will come as no surprise that the objects of research, who were urged to undress, were often uneasy or even reluctant. The manufacture of plaster casts of different parts of the body was another research activity, as were linguistic and ethnomusicological observations. The learned societies gave certificates of authenticity of people exhibited, and suggested new target groups that would serve the financial needs of the impresarios as fully as their own scientific interests.

So science, commerce and imperialism went hand in hand. When Buffalo Bill's Wild West Show performed in Paris during the summer of 1889, Prince Roland Bonaparte, ethnologist and anthropologist, was present continuously in order to question and measure the Cheyenne and Sioux who took part in the show. J.A. Jacobsen, a Norwegian and one of the most important collaborators of the Hagenbeck family, also collected for the Berlin Museum of Ethnology, and supervised the manufacture of ethnographical dioramas featuring wax, plaster or papier-mâché mannequins. These were fabricated with the help of life casts and photographs, and showed dramatic scenes from ritual and daily life. The Hagenbecks maintained close relations with the Hamburg Museum für Völkerkunde, to the benefit of both parties. And museums of ethnography or so-called colonial museums often originated from world fairs that, despite their many aspects, were first and foremost commercial happenings: the Musée d'Ethnographie du Trocadéro – now called the Musée de l'Homme – in Paris, for instance, was created on the occasion of the 1878 world fair (Dias 1991), while the Koninklijk Museum voor Midden-Afrika at Tervuren, Belgium, resulted from the colonial exhibition of 1897.

William Schneider (1977: 98–9) signals a certain shift back to the traditional amusement-oriented character of – European – ethnological exhibits, which he situates at about 1890. In order to increase profits, the organizers began to stress the unusual and the bizarre, and to add spectacular performances, such as mock battles or cannibalistic rituals. What had begun to develop into a means of scientifically educating and edifying the public about faraway peoples and their customs turned into a form of amusement again, yet without impeding the persistence of a third function, that of political and imperialistic propaganda. Similar differences existed between the official ethnographic exhibitions and the less scholarly orchestrated midway amusement zones at North American world fairs, which also served as venues for ethnographic exhibitions and spectacles.[7]

Science and imperialism went hand in hand, and so, of course, did missionary activities and imperialism. I do not know of any human show-cases within the context of missionary propaganda, but other practices of categorizing, picturing, and exhibiting uncivilized, 'heathen' peoples had much in common with more profane happenings. During the first half of the twentieth century, many European missionary museums and countless missionary exhibitions, Roman Catholic as well as Protestant, tried to persuade their visitors to take certain views and certain actions concerning colonially dominated non-Western, non-Christian peoples. Such exhibitions, permanent or temporary, were staged by missionary societies with the help of objects, photographs, maps, and sometimes dressed mannequins or busts. On such occasions, the well-known narrative plots and metaphors, slightly modified, return: civilized or Christian whites bringing the light of civilization, or religion, to savages, or pagans, in the name of some higher instance, be it Progress or God. Missionary photography for propagandistic goals showed characters and scenes from such narratives.

On 24 December 1924, Pope Pius XI opened the World Missionary Exhibition at the Vatican, which attracted over 750,000 visitors during the following year. There was a Hall of Propaganda, a Hall of the Holy Land as the Cradle of Christianity, a Hall of the History of the Missions, and a hall dedicated to quantitative data concerning the missions. All these halls were crammed with ethnographical objects showing the customs and morals of the heathen cultures that were the target of the Roman Catholic civilizing and religious offensive, neatly arranged according to ethnologist Father Wilhelm Schmidt's theory of *Kulturkreise* and their historical develop-ment (Kilger 1925). Rome was represented as the centre of the world – a role that on medieval world maps was still reserved to Jerusalem, and in imperialist discourse was given to the metropoles of the leading imperial-ist nation-states. Roman Catholic missionary pageants in Belgium, the southern Netherlands, and elsewhere in Europe during the first decades of the twentieth century, with locals made up and dressed to represent black Africans, are reminiscent of Indian painter George Catlin's Indian Show in England during the 1840s, featuring native English people dressed up as North American Indians, or of the show in honour of King Henri II in the year 1550 near Rouen, France, where French sailors performed Brazilian Indians.

The 1930s witnessed the decline of the ethnological exhibition, at least in the specific form it had taken until then. Criticism of imperialism and racism increased, and ethnographic shows were found objectionable on moral grounds.[8] Ethnographic films and numerous scientific, semi-scientific, and pseudo-scientific anthropological treatises, abundantly illus-trated with photographs, took over much of the function of ethnological exhibits, as did colonial and missionary propaganda films. The increasing acculturation of colonial natives thwarted the creation of romantic or depreciating scenes of their natural lives. Recruiting exhibit groups in the German colonies became very difficult after 1901 because of new laws and regulations, and the First World War and its aftermath complicated things even more. During the 1930s, the *Völkerschauen* were prohibited by the National Socialists, who feared they would increase the sympathy of the German people for other races.

None the less, manifestations that are quite similar in several respects have persisted until today; for instance, the presence of Maori at the Te Maori exhibition at New York or of Sulawesi Toradja building a rice barn at the Toradja exhibition in the London Museum of Mankind during the 1980s. As a counterpart to exotic native villages at late nineteenth-century world fairs, a 'Dutch city' was opened in Nagasaki in spring 1992, featuring four miles of canals with full-scale replicas of well-known Dutch buildings such as the Utrecht Cathedral. The cinema, television, and tourism also share certain functions with the *Völkerschau*, which was often recommended as an opportunity to visit faraway cultures.

The story and the gaze

It is not difficult to show the pivotal role of narrative structures in nineteenth- and early twentieth-century world fairs, museums, or missionary exhibitions. Narrative plots are as pervasive in the civilizing, imperialist, missionary, and scientific discourses of the period as in the three-dimensional spectacles that, to a considerable degree, were governed by these discursive activities. As many contemporary book titles suggest, the history of mankind was narrated essentially as a heroic ascent toward the natural and ultimate goal of cosmic evolution: the industrial civilization of white, European, middle-class citizens of the nineteenth century. Other races followed the same path, it was postulated – especially in evolutionist ethnology, which was a scientific manifestation of the discourse on progress – but lagged behind culturally and physically. Imperialist expansion was represented in terms of a social Darwinist natural history, and European hegemony as a natural and therefore desirable development. There has been some controversy on the question of whether the master narrative of progress and civilization is essentially a secularized avatar of the Christian idea of world history as God's working, but in any case, it is not formulated in religious terms. The implied development is from a lack of civilization to a civilized state, from wildness to civility, achieved heroically by the white, Caucasian race under its own power, and by the other races with the help of the Caucasian race, insofar at least as their constitution allowed them to progress. The stagewise development from savagery through barbarism to civilization was suggested by organizing museum and world fair exhibits into evolutionary sequences.

Sekula's (1986: 58) stress on the spirit of optical empiricism and encyclopaedism of pictorial archives, with their purely iterative character, is heuristically useful and certainly justified to a certain degree; but in many contexts of collecting, filing and exhibiting, an order was imposed on the data that went beyond mere iteration and taxonomy. In many cases, all essential ingredients of the story, or at least of a certain type of story, are present: a beginning where some desirable good is lacking; an end that is somehow implied teleologically by that beginning; acting subjects; strife and struggle; and other plot elements. World fairs and museums not only categorized peoples, races, cultures, species and artifacts by creating taxonomies, but also ordered them syntagmatically, creating the well-known plots of civilized/Christian whites bringing light to the savage/heathen in the name of some higher instance. The same goes for many photographs from colonial contexts, showing moments from the story they presuppose and illustrate (Corbey 1988, 1989, 1990). Those well-known plots – flexible, capable of incorporating disparate elements, of outdoing alternative readings – are as pervasive in nineteenth-century civilizing, imperialist, missionary, and scientific discourses as in the spectacles and pictures that were governed by these discursive activities. The nineteenth century saw the proliferation of historicized, evolutionary frameworks of representation – of artifacts and natural history specimens, of human, racial and national origins.

One aspect of these spectacles, pictures and narratives was that they neutralized the cognitive dissonance and the threat to Western middle-class identity constituted by the baffling cultural difference of new peoples. Colonial others were incorporated narratively. In a *mise-en-intrigue*, they were assigned their roles in the stories told by museum exhibitions, world fairs, and colonial postcards. They were cast as contemporary ancestors, receivers of true civilization and true religion. The radical difference of the other was made sense of and thus warded off by a narrative discordant concordance between 'civilized' and 'savage'. Money, trade and exchange mediated between peoples (cf. Hinsley 1991: 362), but on another level stories were created in order to mediate the basic contradiction between the two perceived states of mankind. Here I concur with Lévi-Strauss's interpretation of myth as a struggle with contradictions or paradoxes, as a syntagmatic mediation of paradigmatic oppositions.[9] Carol Breckenridge (1989: 211) points out the analogy between the building of private collections by colonial officials (creating an illusion of cognitive control over a colonial experience that might otherwise have been disturbingly chaotic) and the world fair as a reminder of the orderliness of empire which consolidated the sense of imperial knowledge and control in the imagined Victorian ecumene.

But the resultant concordance will never be complete; the attempt to harmonize is ultimately bound to fail. For as the plot develops, the initial discordance between civilized and primitive, white and black, Christian and heathen, is slowly, but never totally overcome. Struggle develops into contracts, but some antagonism and difference is necessary all the way, to keep the story going. The story familiarizes and exoticizes at the same time.[10] Also, on a different level – that of the citizen's personal experience – the other seems to preserve an elusive quality; he or she never yields completely to incorporation within the framework of the familiar, stubbornly resisting a textualizing closure of spontaneous experience, of fascination, of wonder.[11]

To return now to the 1893 world fair motto we began with, 'To see is to know': of course we do not know how things are by simply looking. The eye is not innocent. The motto succinctly expresses an underlying ideology that is at work in a range of seemingly disparate practices in colonial times: photography, colonialist discourse, missionary discourse, anthropometry, collecting and exhibiting, and so on. What people saw, rather than reality as it is, was to a considerable extent reality as perceived, as actively constructed by images, conceptions, native taxonomies, stories and motivational attitudes in the spectator's mind (compare Mason 1990). The perceived order was an imposed one; the citizen's gaze on alien people was determined to a considerable degree by stories and stereotypes in their mind.

'Visualization and spatialization', Fabian writes in his study of the central role of the gaze and the visual in the history of anthropology,

> [became] a program for the new discipline of anthropology. There was a time when this meant, above all, the exhibition of the exotic in illustrated travelogues, museums, fairs, and expositions. These early ethnological practices established seldom articulated but firm convictions that presentations of knowledge through visual and spatial images, maps, diagrams, trees and tables are particularly well suited to the description of primitive cultures. (Fabian 1983: 121)

In this context, in line with our analysis of ethnological exhibitions, he stresses the ideological effects of *visualism* as a cognitive style. What is seen, the objectified Other, is looked at as coming not only from faraway places, but also, and more importantly, from a different, allochronic time. Fabian shows how a temporal gap is constructed between citizens and their 'contemporary ancestors', 'how anthropology has managed to maintain distance, mostly by manipulating temporal coexistence through the denial of coevalness' (Fabian 1983: 121)). This occurred in anthropology, just as it did in the political ideology of imperialism, in Christian discourse on heathens and the mission, at world fairs, and in certain photographic practices.

> When modern anthropology began to construct its Other in terms of topoi implying distance, difference, and opposition, its intent was above all, but at least also, to construct ordered Space and Time – a cosmos – for Western society to inhabit, rather than 'understanding other cultures', its ostensible vocation. (Fabian 1983: 111–12)

Besides plotting, there is a second aspect of the storied nature of the imperial imagination that has relevance to a proper understanding of ethnological exhibitions. It has to do with the encyclopaedic character of world fairs. 'As with other dimensions of the show,' Greenhalgh notes (1988: 87), 'the imperial dimension was underpinned by the belief that it was possible to present a complete knowledge, to create a physical encyclopedia capable of capturing and explaining a total world view.' What is interesting here is the cognitive position ascribed to the visitors: they are assumed to be situated high above the world they gaze upon. On a very basic level, activities such as narrating, taking pictures, or just plain looking create the illusion of the surveyability or transparency of reality, connected with the suggestion that those who narrate, take pictures, or look, find themselves in the privileged position of a panoptic spectator. In spontaneous visual perception, we already tend to experience ourselves as the natural centre of the world we see – a world that seems to be organized around the onlooker as its pivot. In other words, perspective is more than a neutral mathematical projection on external space. All three activities – looking, taking pictures, narrating – are perspectivistic, not only in a literal sense, as in the case of looking or photographing, but also cognitively, emotionally and ideologically. External reality is constructed from and around a central position, that of the onlooker, the photographer, the narrator – and also that of the citizen roaming the world fair. These spectators by their very activity seem to be panoptic, omniscient; their point of view is or seems to be panoramic, that of a bird's eye rather than that of a frog's eye. The narrator, hovering high above the plot, oversees time and space to a considerable degree, having relatively free access to what narrative characters are doing at different times and places. This panoptic gaze is very wide, and might indeed be coextensive with story or narrative as a highly general discourse structure, operating not only in fiction and literature, but also in the sciences and in philosophy, in religious practices and in everyday conversation.

The position of the narrator is usually external to the story, somewhere above the narrated events, permitting an overview of space and time, although it may be more limited, tied to one of the characters in the represented events and part of these.[12] External narrators find themselves in an excellent position to assign significance and value to the events and characters, including, in the case of a typical nineteenth-century master narrative, their own heroic role, natural superiority, and unshakable moral and cognitive orientation. 'The panoramic approach lays out the whole world conceptually in a Linnean classification or evolutionary scheme, or experientially in a scenic effect. ... The view is comprehensive, extensive, commanding, aggrandizing. As a prospect, it holds in it scenarios for future action' (Kirshenblatt-Gimblett 1991: 413). Panoramic landscape descriptions in novels or travel accounts, as well as landscape photographs and turn-of-the-century postcards, often embody a discourse of empire and domination, with the seer as a 'monarch-of-all-I-survey' (Pratt 1988; cf. Fabian 1983: 118–23), in firm control of the seen. The same gaze – self-confident, panoptic, voyeuristic – is to be found in many photos of colonial natives. 'There is an aggression implicit in every use of the camera,' Susan Sontag (1984: 7) has remarked, and indeed taking pictures was another means of taking possession of native peoples and their lands, as was narration.

A fine example of the encyclopaedic urge in an imperialist context was an ambitious project the Asiatic Society of Bengal tried to realize in Calcutta in 1865: a synoptic exhibition of living representatives of the races of the Old World (or at least of India), to be visited primarily by scientists (Falconer 1984–6). The idea was that of a kind of panopticon, as we know it from the writings of Jeremy Bentham and Michel Foucault. The spirit of the project once again was one of optical empiricism, as expressed by the Chicago motto 'To see is to know'.[13] The effort failed. A somewhat meagre but similar outcome realized instead of the exhibit of life specimens was constituted by E.T. Dalton's *Descriptive Ethnology of Bengal* (1872), illustrated with lithographs based on photographs, and the eight-volume *The People of India: a Series of Photographic Illustrations with Descriptive Letterpress of the Races and Tribes of Hindustan* (Watson and Kaye 1868–75), commissioned by the British government, both covering the native peoples from this part of the British empire. In a comparable way, richly illustrated publications like Karl Ernst von Baer's *Types principaux des différentes races humaines dans les cinq parties du monde* (1861) proffered the 'photographic museum of the human races' that had been postulated theoretically twenty years before by E.R.A. Serres (1845: 243; cf. Theye 1989) in France and had quickly become a quite common ideal, all the more so because it was felt that soon it would be too late to realize it. In the year 1872, the German ethnologist Adolf Bastian also formulated the project of 'a photographic museum of the human races', which was indeed created later by the Berliner Gesellschaft für Ethnologie, Anthropologie und Urgeschichte; tens of thousands of accumulated photographs were destroyed during the Second World War (Theye 1989).

In addition to illustrating the synoptic theme, the project of a photographic census of humanity also brings out nicely the role of photography in the complex of practices regarding colonial subjects: collecting, scrutinizing, measuring, categorizing, filing, controlling, narrating. The second half of the nineteenth century witnessed the quick rise of photography as another machinery of capturing and displaying the world. Here, too, we come across the illusion of authenticity, of unmediated encounter. Time and again the unbiased, true character of the photographic picture was stressed; photos were seen as windows on the world, as unmediated and therefore unbiased copies of nature itself. Photography was applied on a large scale in many scientific disciplines, in a spirit of optical empiricism. While the prospering middle classes of Western industrial societies presented themselves honorifically in self-congratulatory studio portraits, hundreds of thousands of photos of their others – other races, criminals, prostitutes, the insane, deviants – functioned in the context of repression. Publications like *The People of India*, Carl Damman's *Anthropologisches-Ethnologisches Album in Photographien* (*c.* 1872), or, somewhat later, the scenes-and-types postcard genre, were matched by photographic albums with 'types' of criminals. In this context, the needs of nation states went hand in hand with scientific purposes. Breckenridge (1989: 195–6) points out that agencies such as archives, libraries, surveys, revenue bureaucracies, folklore and ethnographic agencies, censuses and museums provided a context for the surveillance, recording, classifying, and evaluating called for by the new order of nineteenth-century nation-states with their imperializing and disciplinary bureaucracies – whether it concerned colonies abroad or criminals and slums at home.

Tony Bennett, in an argument that in many ways parallels and in other ways complements the argument developed here, has unravelled relations between power and knowledge in the development of what he appropriately calls an 'exhibitionary complex'. This encompasses museums of art, history and natural science; dioramas and panoramas; national and international exhibitions; arcades and department stores, serving as 'linked sites for the development and articulation of new disciplines (history, biology, art history, anthropology) and their discursive formations (the past, evolution, aesthetics, man) as well as for the development of new technologies of vision' (Bennett 1988: 73).

Conclusion

We have explored some of the complex interdependencies between the colonialist, scientific, and visual appropriation of cultural others in the context of world fairs and ethnographic exhibits. Persons from tribal cultures, on show in the West, were commodified, labelled (Bouquet and Branco 1988), scripted, objectified, essentialized, decontextualized, aestheticized, fetishized. They were cast in the role of backward, allochronic contemporary ancestors, receivers of true civilization and true religion in the stories told by museums, world fairs, and imperialist ideologies, thus becoming narrative characters in the citizen's articulation of identity – of Self and Other. Their own voices and views – ironically often as ethnocentric and omniscient as Western voices and views – were neutralized. Fitting cultural Others into narrative plots, we suggested, was a way the citizen's panoptic eye/I dealt with their wondrous, disturbing difference without annihilating this difference completely. These plots came with the illusion of the panoptic position of an omniscient spectator, functioning as another strategy of power – the illusion that 'To see is to know'.

Over the last centuries the 'we'-group, as an emic category of Western middle classes characterized by true humanity, has been expanding continuously to include many categories that were formerly excluded or considered ambiguous: women, slaves, peasants, the poor, and non-Western peoples.[14] In this chapter, occasional reference has been made to analogies between how other races and species were thought of and treated in the late nineteenth and early twentieth centuries. By now, the boundary of the human species has been reached and, in fact, is being questioned – not least as to its moral significance – and transgressed. The discussion is now shifting towards zoos, circuses, dolphin shows, bioindustry and animal experiments; towards 'simian Orientalism' (Haraway 1989) and other forms of anthropocentrism. It would seem that our observations on ethnocentric/ Eurocentric ethnographic exhibits during the heyday of colonialism are in many ways readily extendable to present-day forms, in theory and practice, of anthropocentrism and so-called speciesism.

Notes

This chapter is reprinted by permission from *Cultural Anthropology* 8 (1993). I wish to thank, among others, Ivan Karp, Peter Mason (who also suggested the motto from de Sade) and Bunny McBride and Harald Prins for their stimulating comments. Part of the archival and photohistorical research on which this chapter is based was carried out by Steven Wachlin, a photographic historian living in Utrecht, Netherlands.

1. In this context, Ivan Karp's analytical distinction between exoticizing and assimilating strategies of exhibition is relevant (in Karp and Lavine 1991: 375ff.); both strategies are examples of the cognitive strategy of assimilation – as opposed to accommodation – in the sense of Piagetian developmental psychology.

2. For a survey of ethnographic exhibits in the Jardin d'Acclimatation, see W. Schneider 1977.

3. A fruitful line of analysis not exploited here might pursue the infamous character of similar trades and professions; cf. Blok (in press).

4. Prins (1991) argues that these early showmen functioned as cultural mediators between dominant Euro-American society and their own respective native communities, and that their performances inspired the imagery currently used to express ethnic self-identity among tribespeople in the Northeast.

5. Bunny McBride (Manhattan, Kansas; cf. McBride 1989) is writing a biography of Molly Spotted Elk based on her diaries.

6. The Smithsonian Institution in Washington, DC, for instance, at this moment harbours the remains of about forty thousand non-Western individuals.

7. As remarked before, I am trying to bring out the general character of ethnographic exhibits in the period under consideration more than differences between nations, over time, or between types of manifestation. For an analysis of national differences, see Benedict 1991.

8. One would also expect conflicts between the scholarly and the popular imagination to have increased towards the end of the period 1870–1930 with the advent, in anthropology, of paradigms critical of evolutionistic anthropology.

9. At the same time, as may be clear to insiders, I take some inspiration from the structuralist narratology of A.J. Greimas and the Paris School – without necessarily subscribing to all its presuppositions, however. For an equally powerful but more radical, poststructuralist, analytical approach to exhibitionary practices, see Bal 1992.

10. Here again, Karp's distinction between exoticizing and assimilating strategies is relevant; see Note 1.

11. Stephen Greenblatt's (1991) stress on the the enduring fascination with 'the marvellous' complements the narratologically inspired perspective developed here.

12. In contemporary narratology, the narrator's perspective is analysed in terms of internal and external 'focalization'; compare Genette 1972, and Bal 1991, who stresses the ideological effects of focalization not only in texts but also in pictures and museums, developing the theory of focalization into a powerful tool of cultural criticism.

13. I am here, indeed, indirectly and loosely drawing upon certain ideas from the work of Michel Foucault, which has proved to be inspiring and heuristically useful in the field of cultural studies (cf. Mitchell 1988, 1989), despite its lack of historical precision, its too-sweeping generalizations, and its tendency towards sometimes rather obscure rhetoric.

14. Even early hominids may be included in this group. A poster announcing the 1989 exhibition 'Archéologie de la France: 30 ans de découvertes' at the Grand Palais in Paris shows a *Homo erectus* man with a modern baby on his knee, the caption reading 'Nous avons tous 400.000 ans', which only twenty years ago would still have been unthinkable.

References

Altick, Richard D. 1978 *The Shows of London: a Panoramic History of Exhibitions, 1600–1862* Cambridge, MA, Belknap.

Bal, Mieke 1991 *On Story-Telling: Essays in Narratology* Sonoma, Polebridge Press.

Bal, Mieke 1992 'Telling, showing, showing-off', *Critical Inquiry* 18: 556–94.

Benedict, Burton 1983 *The Anthropology of World's Fairs: San Francisco's Panama Pacific International Exposition of 1915* London, Scolar Press/Lowie Museum of Anthropology.

Benedict, Burton 1991 'International exhibitions and national identity', *Anthropology Today* 7(3): 5–9.

Benjamin, Walter 1984 'Paris, die Hauptstadt des XIX. Jahrhunderts', in *Allegorien kultureller Erfahrung: Ausgewählte Schriften 1920–1940* Leipzig, Reclam.

Bennett, Tony 1988 'The exhibitionary complex', *New Formations* 4 (Spring): 74–102.

Bieder, Robert E. '1991 Ethnographic zoo: race, sex and power', Bloomington, IN, unpublished MS.

Blok, Anton (in press) *Infamy* London, Routledge.

Bogdan, R. 1988 *Freaks Show: Presenting Human Oddities for Amusement and Profit* Chicago, University of Chicago Press.

Bouquet, Mary and Jorge Branco 1988 *Melanesian Artifacts – Postmodernist Reflections* Lisbon, Museu de Etnologia.

Bradford, Phillips and Harvey Blume 1993 *Ota Benga: the Pygmy at the Zoo* New York, St Martin's Press.

Breckenridge, Carol A. 1989 'The aesthetics and politics of colonial collecting: India at world fairs', *Comparative Studies in Society and History* 31: 195–216.

Chapman, Anne 1982 *Drama and Power in a Hunting Society: the Selk'nam of Tierra del Fuego* New York, Cambridge University Press.

Corbey, Raymond 1988 'Alterity: the colonial nude', *Critique of Anthropology* 8(3): 75–92.

Corbey, Raymond 1989 *Wildheid en beschaving. De Europese verbeelding van Afrika* Baarn, Ambo.

Corbey, Raymond 1990 'Der Missionar, die Heiden und das Photo', *Zeitschrift für Kulturaustausch* 40: 460–65.

Dalton, Edward T. 1872 *Descriptive Ethnology of Bengal* Calcutta, Office of the Superintendent of Government Printing.

Damman, Carl (n.d. – c.1872) *Anthropologisches-Ethnologisches Album in Photographien* Berlin, Wiegard, Hempel, and Parey.

de Sade, D.A.F. 1990 *Oeuvres* Paris, Bibliothèque de la Pleiade.

Dias, Nelia 1991 'Le Musée d'ethnographie du Trocadéro 1878–1908', *Anthropologie et Muséologie en France* Paris, CNRS.

Dörner, Klaus 1984 *Bürger und Irre. Zur Sozialgeschichte und Wissenschaftssoziologie der Psychiatrie* Frankfurt am Main, Europäische Verlagsanstalt.

Fabian, Johannes 1983 *Time and the Other: How Anthropology Makes its Object* New York, Columbia University Press.

Falconer, John 1984–86 'Ethnographical photography in India', *Photographic Collector* 5: 16–46.

Favrod, Charles-Henri 1989 'Voir les autres autrement', in *Étranges étrangères: Photographie et exotisme, 1850–1910* Paris, Centre National de la Photographie.

Foucault, Michel 1961 *Folie et déraison. Histoire de la folie à l'âge classique* Paris, Plon.

Francis, D.R. 1913 *The Universal Exposition of 1904* St Louis, Louisiana Purchase Exposition Company.

Genette, Gerard 1972 *Figures III* Paris, Seuil.

Goldmann, Stefan 1985 'Wilde in Europa', in Thomas Theye (ed.) *Wir und die Wilden. Einblicke in eine kannibalische Beziehung* Reinbek, Rowohlt, pp. 243–69.

Greenblatt, Stephen 1991 'Resonance and wonder', in Ivan Karp and Steven D. Lavine (eds.) *Exhibiting Cultures: the Politics and Poetics of Museum Display* Washington, DC, Smithsonian Institution Press, pp. 42–56.

Greenhalgh, Paul 1988 *Ephemeral Vistas: the Expositions Universelles, Great Exhibitions and Worlds Fairs, 1851–1939* Manchester, Manchester University Press.

Hagenbeck, Karl 1909 *Von Tieren und Menschen. Erlebnisse und Erfahrungen* Berlin, Charlottenburg.

Haltern, Ulrich 1971 *Die Londoner Weltausstellung von 1851. Ein Beitrag zur Geschichte der bürgerlich-industriellen Gesellschaft im 19. Jahrhundert* Münster, Aschendorf.

Haraway, Donna 1989 *Primate Visions: Gender, Race and Nature in the World of Modern Science* New York, Routledge.

Helms, Mary W. 1988 *Ulysses Sail: An Ethnographic Odessey of Power, Knowledge and Geographical Distance* Princeton, Princeton University Press.

Hinsley, Curtis M. 1991 'The world as marketplace: commodification of the exotic at the World's Columbian Exposition', in Ivan Karp and Steven D. Lavine (eds.) *Exhibiting Cultures: the Politics and Poetics of Museum Display* Washington, DC and London, Smithsonian Institution Press, pp. 344–65.

Karp, Ivan and Steven D. Lavine (eds.) 1991 *Exhibiting Cultures: the Politics and Poetics of Museum Display* Washington, DC and London, Smithsonian Institution Press.

Kilger, Laurenz 1925 'Die vatikanische Missions-Ausstellung 1925', *Die Katholischen Missionen* 53(6): 167–79.

Kirshenblatt-Gimblett, Barbara 1991 'Objects of Ethnography', in Ivan Karp and Steven D. Lavine (eds.) *Exhibiting Cultures: the Politics and Poetics of Museum Display* Washington, DC and London, Smithsonian Institution Press, pp. 386–443.

Lederbogen, Jan 1986 'Fotografie als Völkerschau', *Fotogeschichte: Beiträge zur Geschichte und Ästhetik der Photographie* 6: 47–64.

Lehmann, Alfred 1955 'Zeitgenössische Bilder der ersten Völkerschauen', in W. Lang, W. Nippold and G. Spannaus (eds.) *Von fremden Völker und Kulturen: Beiträge zur Völkerkunde. Hand Plischke zum 65. Geburtstag* Düsseldorf, Droste, pp. 31–8.

McBride, Bunny 1989 'A Penobscot in Paris', *Down East* August: 63–5, 80–81.

MacKenzie, John M. 1984 *Propaganda and Empire: the Manipulation of British Public Opinion 1860–1960* Manchester, Manchester University Press.

Mason, Peter (ed.) 1992 *Indianen en Nederlanders, 1492–1992. Wampum* 11, special issue.

Mitchell, Timothy 1988 *Colonizing Egypt* Cambridge, Cambridge University Press.

Mitchell, Timothy 1989 'The world as exhibition', *Comparative Studies in Society and History* 31: 217–36.

Montagu, Ashley 1971 *The Elephant Man: a Study in Human Dignity* New York, Outerbridge and Dienstfrey.

Neihardt, John 1988 *Black Elk Speaks* Lincoln, University of Nebraska Press.

Parsons, Q.N. 1988 'Frantz or Klikko, the Wild Dancing Bushman: a case study in Khoisan Stereotyping', *Botswana Notes and Records* 20: 71–6.

Pieterse, Evelien 1992 'Amerika binnen handbereik', in Peter Mason (ed.) *Indianen en Nederlanders, 1492–1992 Wampum* 11: 16–39.

Plakate 1880–1914 (n.d.) exhibition catalogue, Historisches Museum, Frankfurt.

Pratt, Mary Louise 1988 'Conventions of representation: when discourse and ideology meet', in Willie van Peer (ed.) *The Taming of the Text: Explorations in Language, Literature, and Culture* London, Routledge and Kegan Paul, pp. 15–34.

Prins, Harald E.L. 1991 'Public performance and ethnic identity: Chief Big Thunder and the peddling of 'Indian' culture'. Paper presented at the American Society for Ethnohistory Annual Meeting, 7–10 November.

Rice, Julian 1991 *Black Elk's Story: Distinguishing its Lakota Purpose* Albuquerque, University of New Mexico Press.

Rydell, Robert W. 1984 *All the World's a Fair: Visions of Empire at American International Expositions, 1876–1916* Chicago, University of Chicago Press.

Schneider, G. 1982 'Das deutsche Kolonialmuseum in Berlin und seine Bedeutung im Rahmen der preussischen Schulreform um die Jarhhundertwende', in *Die Zukunft beginnt in der Vergangenheit. Schriften des Historischen Museums* XVI, Frankfurt, Historisches Museum, pp. 155ff.

Schneider, W. 1977 'Race and empire: the rise of popular ethnography in the late nineteenth century', *Journal of Popular Culture* 11: 98–109.

Sekula, Alan 1986 'The body and the archive', *October* 39: 3–64.

Serres, Etienne-Renaud-Augustin 1845 'Observations sur l'application de la photographie à l'étude des races humaines', *Comptes Rendues de l'Académie des Sciences* 21: 243ff.

Sontag, Susan 1984 *On Photography* Harmondsworth, Penguin.

Taylor, J. Garth 1981 'An Eskimo abroad, 1880: his diary and death', *Canadian Geographic* October/November.

Theye, Thomas 1989 '"Wir wollen nicht glauben, sondern schauen": Zur Geschichte der ethnographischen Fotografie im 19. Jahrhundert', in Thomas Theye (ed.), *Der geraubte Schatten: Die Photographie als ethnographisches Dokument* Munich, Münchner Stadtmuseum, pp. 60–119.

Thode-Arora, Hilke 1989 *Für fünfzig Pfenning um die Welt: Die Hagenbeckschen Völkerschauen* New York, Campus.

von Baer, Karl Ernst 1869 *Types principaux des différentes races humaines dans les cinq parties du monde* (2nd edn) St Petersburg.

Watson, J.F., and J.W. Kaye 1868–75 *The People of India: a Series of Photographic Illustrations with Descriptive Letterpress of the Races and Tribes of Hindustan* (8 vols.) London, India Museum.

5

Liberalism and colonialism: a critique of Locke and Mill

Bhikhu Parekh

Liberalism is full of strange paradoxes and reveals different faces depending on one's angle of vision. It offers one of the most inspiring statements of human equality, yet some of the greatest liberal philosophers justified colonialism with a clear conscience. Liberals condemned racist prejudices and misuse of political power in the colonies, but endorsed both the economic exploitation of the colonies and arrogant assertions of cultural superiority. They insisted on protection of the material interests of the colonial subjects, but thought little of destroying their ways of life. John Stuart Mill led a most creditable campaign against the brutality of Governor Eyre of Jamaica, but saw nothing wrong with the colonial context that made such things possible.

Nearer home, liberals stressed the virtues of individuality, autonomy and moral self-development, but they vigorously supported the nineteenth-century capitalism that made these virtues unrealizable for masses of men and women, and they often resisted attempts by the state to regulate the evils capitalism produced. They advocated freedom of choice, civil liberties and an inviolable area of privacy, yet many of the liberal architects of the New Poor Law of 1834 wanted the workhouses to become 'objects of terror' and to enforce strict segregation of the sexes. Liberalism claims to be sceptical of all claims to absolute truth, yet for decades liberal economists and politicians entertained no doubts about their *laissez-faire* economic theories, even when the havoc they caused at home and in the colonies, including Ireland, was too stark and horrendous to be missed.

More recent liberal thought and practice have revealed similar paradoxes and contradictions. American liberals opposed the McCarthyite witchhunts, but many of them, including such distinguished liberals as Sidney Hook, Irving Kristol and Daniel Bell, insisted that their communist fellow citizens could be legitimately barred from teaching on the grounds that communism was not an 'opinion' but a 'fanatical conspiracy' and that its academic supporter had 'engaged his intellect to servility'. The Vietnam War was in some of its crucial phases a liberal's war, started and supported by liberals and powered by a missionary liberal ideology. Even as late as 1989, British intellectuals of impeccable liberal credentials were unhinged when a small group of British Muslims burned a copy of Salman Rushdie's *The Satanic Verses* and supported Khomeini's death threat against the author. Liberals who had a good record of fighting racism and promoting black, including Muslim, interests became fiercely anti-Muslim. Even Roy Jenkins, father of the Race Relations Act 1976, lamented that 'we might have been more cautious about allowing the creation in the 1950s of a substantial Muslim community here'.[1] He went further and reached the most bizarre conclusion that the Muslim book-burners' behaviour had strengthened 'my reluctance to have Turkey in the European community'. Apparently all Muslims, like the proverbial Chinese, looked the same to him, and a threatened misdeed by a section of them was enough to damn the lot. It was depressing to note how the legitimate liberal rage against the Ayatollah Khomeini's murderous impertinence and the outrageous Muslim support for it escalated step by even sillier step to a wholly mindless anger at first against all Bradford Muslims, then against all British Muslims, then against all Muslims, and ultimately against Islam itself. Some liberal commentators, a few of them with a leftist past, became instant experts on the Koran, attacked its 'bloodthirsty' conception of Allah, and compared it unfavourably to the Bible and its 'loving God', in the process offering most valuable insights into the tensions and contradictions of the structure of liberal self-consciousness.

Even this brief and sketchy account is enough to indicate that liberalism contains contradictory impulses. The contradiction is not just between liberal thought and liberal practice, but within liberal thought itself. Liberalism is both egalitarian and inegalitarian, it stresses both the unity of mankind and the hierarchy of cultures, it is both tolerant and intolerant, peaceful and violent, pragmatic and dogmatic, sceptical and self-righteous. The origins of its contradictory impulses, the way it accommodates and reconciles them in different contexts, the tensions they create in liberal thought and practice, and so on, raise fascinating questions. Since I cannot pursue all of them in this short chapter, I shall concentrate on one of them, namely the liberal attitude to colonialism. For analytical convenience I shall examine this question through the writings of John Locke and John Stuart Mill, two of the greatest liberal philosophers, who lived during the two distinct phases of colonial expansion and reflected, articulated and deepened the prevailing liberal discourse on the subject.

Locke's savages

When England began to colonize the so-called New World in the seventeenth century, its actions provoked a muted but fascinating debate. As William Strachey, First Secretary to the Colony of Virginia, put it:

> [Of the] clayme which we make to this part of America ... I have observed more in clamour (me thought) than at any tyme in force, to cry out still upon yt, calling yt, an unnationall and unlawfull undertaking ... Why? Because

injurious to the naturalls; and ... yt must then necessarily followe (saye they) that yt can be no other than a travaile of flat impiety, and displeasing before God.[2]

Critics of English colonization argued that it violated the rights of the American Indians to their property and territorial integrity. The Indians had cultivated and lived on their land for centuries and it was their 'rightful inheritance'. They had also established stable societies which, like their counterparts elsewhere, were entitled to non-interference by outsiders. England had no 'right or warrant' to 'enter into', let alone 'go and live in the heathen's country', and was acting in an immoral and un-Christian manner. The Revd. Roger Williams, the minister of Salem, criticized the British king because he had 'no right to grant the lands on which the colony was founded since they belonged to the Indian tribes'. He was arrested, put on trial, and eventually banished.[3]

Locke, who had both a philosophical and a financial interest in the Americas, was greatly interested in the controversy. He asked the English settlers for information about the Indian way of life, and built up an impressive collection of books dealing with the European exploration of the Americas. His philosophical interest sprang from the fact that unlike Hobbes's largely imaginary state of nature, the Indian way of life offered a realistic contrast to, and provided most valuable insights into, the nature and structure of political society. Locke's interest was not entirely intellectual. His patron the Earl of Shaftesbury had strong financial interests in the New World and, in the words of Locke's distinguished biographer Maurice Cranston, shared Locke's 'zeal for commercial imperialism ... and the possibilities it offered for personal and national enrichment'. Locke was also secretary to the Lords Proprietors of Carolina (1668–75) and to the Council of Trade and Plantations (1673–76). In both these capacities Locke played an important part in formulating colonial policies. He was in no doubt that English colonization of North America was fully justified, and provided its most articulate and influential philosophical defence.

For Locke, reason was man's natural, highest and unique faculty. It was a natural capacity because man was born with it. Society did, of course, develop and cultivate it, but it did not create it. Reason was also the highest human faculty because it alone enabled man to know and control the natural and the social worlds. And it was unique to man in the sense that no other species in the world possessed it. Although Locke's analysis of the nature of reason was complex and inconsistent, by and large he thought that it analysed and reflected on the sense impressions, perceived similarities and dissimilarities between different events and entities, traced their causes, and formed universally valid generalizations. Though it was susceptible to the influences of the passions, prejudices and superstitions of the wider society, it was in principle capable of transcending them all and delivering a universally valid body of knowledge about the nature of man and the world, morality, politics, the truly good life, and so on. Being trained to reason correctly and rigorously and to rise above the distorting influences of personal passions and popular prejudices, philosophers were particularly equipped to exercise reason and guide mankind. They not only discovered the true principles of moral and political life but also demonstrated their validity, and played a vital cultural role.

Locke advanced a set of what he regarded as universally valid propositions about man and society. God created men and gave them the world in common. By this Locke meant not positive but negative communism, that is, the world was not a collective human property to be used for collective well-being, but rather it belonged to no one and was available to all for their individual use. God's gift entailed both rights and duties. Every man had a right to mix his labour with nature, and to use its fruits to satisfy his needs consistently with a due regard for others. Since God wanted men 'to be fruitful and multiply', every man also had a duty to develop the earthly resources to the full and maximize the conveniences of life. As Locke put it, 'God gave the world to man in common, but … it cannot be supposed he meant it should always remain common and uncultivated. He gave it to the use of the Industrious and Rational.'[4] Locke's juxtaposition of 'Industrious' and 'Rational' is striking.

Since all men had identical faculties including and especially reason, and since they were all ontologically dependent on their creator and hence independent of one another, they were all equal. For Locke, equality was one of the most basic features of human relationship, and had several important implications. It implied that all human beings had equal dignity and rights, that they were entitled to the equal protection of their basic interests, that no authority was legitimate unless it was based on their uncoerced consent, that no one had a right to injure another in the pursuit of his interests, that each should exercise his rights with a due regard for others, and so on. As rational beings, humans were expected to govern their affairs rationally. Since the use of force signified rejection of reason, whoever used it without due authorization opted out of the human community and could be punished and treated like an animal.

Locke had no doubts as to how a truly rational man should live and how a truly rational society should be organized. The former exhibited such qualities of character as industry, energy, enterprise, self-discipline, acknowledgement of others as his equals and all that followed from it: control of passions, obedience to the law, and reasonableness. A truly rational society established the institution of private property and provided incentives for industry and the accumulation of wealth, without both of which men could not discharge their duty to develop the earth's resources and create a prosperous society. Locke was deeply haunted by the idea of waste and wanted all the material potentialities of the earth to be fully realized. The duty to be fruitful and multiply 'contains in it the improvement too of arts and sciences', and hence a truly rational society encouraged these as well. As for its political structure, it had a clearly defined territorial boundary, a cohesive, centralized and unified structure of authority entitled in peace and in war to speak and act in the name of the community in all matters of collective importance (which Locke called sovereignty, 'decisive power' or 'one supreme government'), and a will to persist as an independent polity that made it 'too hard' for its neighbours to attack and overrun it. A truly rational society was governed not by customs and traditional practices, but by general and 'positive laws' enacted by the supreme legislature and clearly specifying who owned what and how transgressions were to be punished. Political power in it was institutionalized, subject to clearly stated procedures and checks, and separated into legislature, executive and judiciary.

Locke analysed English colonialism in America in terms of his theory of man and society. He argued that since the American Indians roamed freely over the land and did not enclose it, it was not 'their' land; they used it as one would use a common land, but they had no property in it. The land was therefore free, empty, vacant, wild, and could be taken over without their consent. This was odd for, although the Indians did not build fences or barriers to demarcate their land, they knew what land was theirs and what belonged to their neighbours, and had thus enclosed it in a manner intelligible to them. That was not acceptable to Locke, who only recognized the European sense of enclosure. Even then, Locke faced a difficulty. Whilst some Indians did not enclose their land in Locke's sense, the coastal Indians who lived in villages and engaged in nonsedentary agriculture did. English settlers were covetous of these lands, and sought to take them over to avoid the hard labour of clearing land themselves. They had argued that although the Indians enclosed and owned the land, their practice of letting it rot and compost every three years for soil enrichment demonstrated that they did not make rational use of it. Locke agreed that enclosure was not enough. He observed:

> ... if either the Grass or his Inclosure rotted on the ground, or the Fruit of his planting perished without gathering, and laying up, this part of Earth, notwithstanding his Inclosure, was still to be looked on as Waste, and might be the Possession of any other.[5]

Even when Indians enclosed and cultivated land, they were not industrious and advanced enough to make the *best possible* use of it and produce as much as the English could. Indeed, since they produced not even one-hundredth of what the latter could, they were for all practical purposes guilty of wasting the land. In Locke's view, the trouble with the Indians was that they had very few desires and were easily contented. Since they lacked the desire to accumulate wealth, engage in commerce, produce for an international market, and so on, they had no interest in exploiting the earth's potential to the fullest. In this regard the English settlers were vastly superior and had a much better claim to the land. After all, since God Himself had imposed on man the duty to maximize the conveniences of life, the English had both a right and a duty to replace the Indians. Locke acknowledged that the principle of equality required that the Indians should not starve or be denied their share of the earth's proceeds. Since the English colonization increased the conveniences of life, lowered prices, created employment and so on, and thus benefited the Indians as well, Locke though that it did not violate the principle of equality.

But even this was not the end of the problem. Locke had hitherto discussed America as if it were no more than a mass of land, and the Indian tribes as if they were no more than a collection of individuals. Vacant lands in Locke's sense existed in several parts of Europe as well, but he would not allow their colonization because they fell within the boundaries of specific political societies, whose independence and territorial integrity had to be respected under international law. As Locke put it, vacant lands in a political society were under the jurisdiction of the law of the land and not available to 'all mankind'. Could this not be true of the Indians as well? And could not their vacant lands be seen as part of their territory, and hence unavailable for colonization? Locke did not think so. He acknowledged that the Indians called themselves nations and were ruled by elected kings, but argued that that was a misleading way of describing their society, which was not really a political society at all.

First, they lacked sovereignty, that is, a single, unified and centralized system of authority.[6] Their structure of authority was fragmented and chaotic because the right to make peace and war resided 'either in the people or in a council', whereas the responsibility to conduct the war rested on the kings. In a properly constituted political society, such a vital right as the right to make peace and war ought to be vested in a king or a 'federative' authority. To locate it in the people implied that they had not yet developed a structure of authority entitled to speak in their collective name, and were thus in a state of nature. And to locate it in a council, which had no other functions, implied that the society in question was divided up into different centres of authority, lacked centralization, and thus again was not a political society. As for the Indian kings, Locke contended that they were 'little more than generals of their armies' who, although active and absolute during war, normally exercised 'very little dominion' and possessed 'but a very moderate sovereignty'.[7]

Second, as we saw, Locke maintained that political authority in a political society should be institutionalized, exercised through general positive laws, and be divided into legislature, executive and judiciary. In his view all these were missing among the Indians. He admitted that since they had 'no temptation to enlarge their possessions of land, or contest for wider extent of ground', and since there were therefore 'few trespasses and few offenders' among them, they had 'no need' for these institutions. Such few and relatively trivial disputes as occurred among them were settled on an informal basis by turning to their neighbours or to arbitrators chosen by the parties concerned. In Locke's view that only showed that the Indians did not need and therefore did not possess a political society.

Third, Locke argued that the Indians were not 'one people' and lacked a sense of collective identity. They did not speak 'one language', had not

developed arts, sciences and a distinct culture, neither asserted their
independence against outsiders nor insisted on a clearly demarcated territorial identity, lacked internal solidity and were therefore a soft target for
their neighbours, and so on. Locke could not see how a people devoid of
all this could be said to constitute 'one society'. Since he had a specific
notion of its oneness or singularity, he insisted that a political society
must be unified in terms of a single and unified system of authority
culminating in a 'decisive power' located in a single and clearly identifiable
centre.

Locke summed up his view as follows:

> Let me ask you, Whether it be not possible that men, to whom the rivers and
> woods afforded the spontaneous provisions of life, and so with no private
> possessions of land, had no inlarged desires after riches or power, should live
> in one society, make one people of one language under one Chieftain, who shall
> have not other power to command them in time of common war against their
> common enemies, without any municipal laws, judges, or any person with
> superiority established amongst them, but ended all their private differences, if
> any arose, by the extemporary determination of their neighbours, or of arbit-
> rators chosen by the parties.[8]

Having shown to his satisfaction that Indians lacked a political society,
Locke argued that they were not entitled to have their territorial integrity
respected by others. Theirs was a porous and unstructured society devoid
of a clearly established political boundary and without settled ideas on
who were insiders and who were outsiders.[9] He admitted that they were
not just a collection of isolated individuals and had developed a society
with at least an elementary structure of authority, but insisted that this
only placed them at an advanced stage of the state of nature. The insistence
that they were in some kind of state of nature was vitally important for
his defence of English colonialism. It enabled him to draw a qualitative
distinction between Indian and English societies, to argue that the relations
between the two could only be governed by the individualistically oriented
law of nature, and to maintain that the English conflict with Indians, not
being a case of war, was not subject to the laws regulating wars between
nations.

For Locke, Indians were 'wild', 'like savages', and devoid of the capacity
to raise themselves unaided to the level of the 'civilised part of mankind'.
Since they lacked the basic drive to accumulate wealth and engage in
international commerce, without which property, the arts and sciences
and political society were impossible, they would, if left to themselves, for
ever remain in the state of nature. The English guardianship was in-
dispensable for their historical transition to civility and civilization.

Since Indians were in a state of nature, their relations with the civilized
Europeans were to be governed by the law of nature and not by the law
of nations which presupposed equality between those subject to it. The
law of nature enjoined that, as human beings, Indians had rights to life,

liberty and property, which the English settlers had a natural duty to respect. They were not therefore at liberty to hunt and kill Indians as if they were animals, or to enslave them, or to deprive them of the fruits of their labour. Beyond that, the English settlers had no obligations to them. Since Indians had no property in land, the English were fully entitled to compel them to live closer together and to acquire the 'surplus' land. Locke also hoped that once the economy was monetized, English settlers would be able to buy up Indian lands and turn the erstwhile owners into their employees. He was in no doubt that these arrangements were in the interests of all concerned. He was prepared to admit that Indians might not see things this way, but was convinced that in the long run they would 'think themselves beholden' to the English. In Locke's view, English colonization not only did them no harm, but also respected their natural rights and conferred on them great economic, moral, cultural, scientific and political benefits. If the obstinate Indians resisted the settlers, they would have behaved irrationally, and '[might] be destroyed as a lion or tiger, one of those wild savage beasts'.

Locke distinguished two modes of colonization, one based on 'conquest by sword' and represented by the Spanish, the other based on commerce and represented by the English.[10] He unreservedly condemned the former and welcomed the latter. Spanish colonialism violated the natural rights of the natives, and additionally failed to establish a civilized way of life in the colonies. In Locke's view it was also self-contradictory, for the colonial expansion was motivated by a desire for economic gain, whereas the right of conquest on which it rested 'extends only to the lives of the conquered' and did not give the conqueror a right over the latter's property. English colonialism was not open to these objections. It respected the natural equality of Indians, it was relatively peaceful, it used force only when they did not voluntarily part with their vacant and wasted lands, it civilized or morally uplifted them and drew them into an economically interdependent world, and it furthered the interests of mankind. Locke had no doubt at all that in colonizing America, the English performed the remarkable moral miracle of serving God, mankind, Indians and themselves.

Why Locke went wrong

Locke stressed human equality yet justified the English subjugation of Indians, including annexation of their land. How could an egalitarian premiss yield such patently inegalitarian conclusions? Only two explanations are possible. Either his reasoning was faulty and involved illicit steps, or it rested on assumptions with inegalitarian implications. As we saw, by and large his reasoning was impeccable. The fault lay with his assumptions which, despite his confidence, were anything but self-evident and morally innocent.

First, Locke's thought rested on a narrow view of human nature. For him, man was essentially rational; reason had a natural and uniform

structure and mode of operation; reason was detachable from, and functioned best when insulated from, feelings and passions; man had a natural
desire to accumulate wealth and enjoy a life of plentiful material comforts;
and so on. Judged by such a view of man, Indians appeared defective and
not fully human. Locke was not wrong to assume that human beings
shared several basic capacities, needs and desires in common. His mistake
was twofold. First, his list of universal human capacities and desires was
narrow, and uncritically universalized those characteristic of the Englishmen
of his time. The desires to accumulate wealth, enjoy maximum comforts
and master nature are historically contingent, and there is no obvious
reason why all human beings should develop them or why these desires
should be given the importance that Locke gave them. Again, Locke was
right to stress human rationality, but wrong to think that reason is inherently calculating, utilitarian, result-oriented or concerned to obtain the
maximum possible advantages from a given unit of human effort. Second,
Locke did not appreciate that even the universally shared human capacities
and desires are shaped, structured, related and valued differently in different
societies. All men reason, but they do not do so in an identical manner,
nor do they all dissociate reason from feelings and sentiments, nor do
they all give reason the same importance. Locke was wrong to think that
just because Indians did not give reason as much importance as he did or
exercise it the way he thought proper, they were subrational. Like many
other liberal philosophers after him, he had great difficulty coping with
difference and equated it with deficiency.

Locke's second assumption related to his monistic vision of the good
life. He derived this vision from his view of human nature and, since the
latter was taken to be universally common and used to ground his moral
theory, he assumed that only one form of individual and collective life
was worthy of human beings. He judged the Indian way of life by these
standards and found them wanting. Locke's moral imagination was characterized by a simple-minded dualism. All ways of life were either civilized
or primitive, and those falling within each category were in turn homogeneous and differed at best only in degrees. He never asked if the Indian
way of life might not be good in its own way, represent a different view
of human flourishing, and contain elements missing in his own way of life
and from which he might learn something. Even when Locke noticed that
Indians led peaceful and contented lives, were 'free of hurry and worry'
as a contemporary missionary put it, did not quarrel over property, settled
disputes peacefully, avoided litigation and generally did not commit of-
fences, the qualities he himself admired in other contexts, he did not ask
how these qualities were developed and nurtured by the Indian way of life
and whether it might have useful lessons for him. Instead he dismissed
them as deficiencies born out of lack of ambition and drive. Since he
considered Indians savage, he was convinced that they could not have
anything good about them, and since their way of life was treated as an
undifferentiated and homogenous whole, Locke did not think it necessary

to approach it with sensitivity and discrimination and distinguish its good and bad features. Convinced of the absolute superiority of the civilized way of life, he was unable to view the Indian society with critical sympathy and use it to interrogate his own. In Locke's naïvely dualist framework, the Indian way of life was the 'absolute other' and had no moral claims to his respect.

Third, Locke not only saw nothing valuable in the Indian way of life but uncritically analysed it in terms of culturally specific English categories, and totally misunderstood it. As a result, his analysis of it was unable to protect him against the understandable European bias. For him land must be owned, or else it was not property. It never occurred to him that land might be used but not owned, that it might be owned but not to the exclusion of others, or that the very idea of owning land may appear odd and sacrilegious to communities who define their identity in terms of, and therefore see themselves as an inseparable part of, their land. For Locke, owning must involve enclosure. It did not occur to him that one might own land but leave it open to the use of those whose needs are greater or who require occasional or regular access to it for their survival. Even so far as enclosure was concerned, Locke insisted that it must be of only one kind. It had to involve unambiguous and physical demarcation, fencing, the drawing of a boundary; an informal, notional and relatively permeable boundary would not do. For Locke, labour too had to be of a specific kind to qualify as such. It had to involve physical appropriation such as plucking a fruit or picking up the animal one has killed. He dismissed planting, hunting, trapping, fishing and nonsedentary agriculture as 'spontaneous provisions' or products of 'unassisted nature' and, except for the very last step of picking or killing, not forms of labour. Locke said that land must be used and not wasted, but again he defined 'waste' and 'use' in extremely narrow and utilitarian terms. Land that was used for hunting, roaming for fun, or chasing animals was said to be wasted. Cultivation too was narrowly defined to mean 'improvement', and the latter in turn was taken to mean a maximum yield of the conveniences of life. As a result, the Indian practice of not exploiting land to the fullest, letting it 'rest and breathe for a while', and allowing animals their share of access to it was dismissed as irrational and wasteful. Locke insisted too that claims to property must be based on labour, be it one's own or one's servants'. This culturally loaded argument undermined Indians' claim to their land, based as it was on the ground that they had lived on it for decades, that their Gods and dead spirits inhabited it, that their customs were interwoven with it, and so on. They did, of course, labour on it but that was incidental. It was not their land because they laboured on it; rather, they laboured on it because it was their land, which they owed it to their ancestors to keep in good condition.

Locke's conception of political society displayed a similar European bias. He uncritically universalized the emerging European, especially English, state, and he condemned other societies for failing to be like it. For him, a political society properly so called must have a single seat of sovereignty, it must clearly distinguish between and institutionalize the legislative, executive and judicial powers, it must be governed by positive or deliberately enacted laws, it must feel possessive about its territory, it must be powerful and cohesive enough to stand up to its neighbours, and so on. He could not imagine that other societies might organize their collective life differently. Since he looked for Indian analogues of European institutions, he totally misunderstood the Indian way of life. He did not notice that even though the exercise of power was not formally institution-alized among Indians, it was governed by an intricate system of procedures and contained its own checks and balances; he did not appreciate that although disputes appeared to be settled on an individual and *ad hoc* basis, the settlement was embedded in and sanctioned by the authority of the wider way of life; and he did not notice either that although the Indian 'laws' were not formally enacted and written down, there was a clear consensus on what counted as 'laws', how they derived their authority and who was entitled to interpret and enforce them. Some European travellers, and even English settlers, had written reports about the Indian political system that corrected these and other misunderstandings. Locke chose to believe only those that confirmed his preconceptions.

Fourth, for Locke humanity was a status, a rank, with its own dignity and corresponding rights and obligations.[11] Man occupied a middling rank within the universe. Infinitely inferior to God, he was the equal of his fellow humans and vastly superior to the animals. It was because he was human, that is, a being endowed with reason, that he was entitled not to be treated like an animal and to enjoy equality with other men. But precisely because he was human, he had a duty to lead a certain kind of life. For Locke, humanity was not a state of being to be accepted with gratitude, and human capacities were not faculties to be exercised and enjoyed as one preferred. Human life had a purpose, an overarching goal, namely to understand and master the world, and human capacities were a means to that goal's realization. Life therefore was a task to be diligently executed, a responsibility to be conscientiously discharged. The misguided Indians treated life as fun and as a festival, and lacked the kind of moral seriousness Locke expected of human beings. Since they failed to live up to the full demands of their human dignity, status or rank, they were not yet fully equal to the English and could be legitimately subjected to the process of civilization.

Given these and related assumptions, it is easy to see how Locke deduced his defence of English colonialism from an egalitarian premiss. Indians were human beings, and, like the rest, entitled to protection of their basic rights and interests. This is why Locke condemned in the strongest possible terms the outrageous Spanish treatment of the Indians, and took great pains to show that English colonization was in their ultimate interest. Precisely because Indians were human beings, they were expected to live up to the rational and moral imperatives of their human status. Since they had not fully yet developed their rational capacity and lacked an adequate understanding of what it was to be human, they were not equipped to define their interests themselves and could not be allowed to lead their self-chosen way of life. Locke's principle of equality accepted them and other 'savage' people as equal *objects* of concern, but not as self-defining *subjects* entitled to full and equal self-determination. The manner in which Locke defined and defended equality thus had both egalitarian and inegalitarian implications, and *both* justified colonialism and regulated its excesses. It had an egalitarian form but its inegalitarian assumptions gave it an inegalitarian content, and it legitimized violence against the poor at home and the 'savages' abroad provided, of course, that that violence did not exceed certain limits and served their long-term interests as defined by their masters.

Whilst Locke's principle of equality offered at least some moral protection to Indians, it offered them no *political* protection. Indians were entitled to equality as individuals, but not as an organized society. As individuals their basic rights and interests were to be fully protected. However since, in Locke's view, they had failed to establish political societies and were not nations, their ways of life and territorial integrity had no moral claims on outsiders and could be dismantled. As Locke defined equality, it obtained only between the civilized nations and placed the non-civilized societies outside the pale of international law and morality. Interpersonal relations between all men were subject to the laws of nature, but not international relations. The distinction between an egalitarian interpersonal morality and an inegalitarian political and international morality is central to Locke's thought, and indeed to most of the liberal tradition.

Mill and the Indians

During the late eighteenth and the early nineteenth centuries, European colonialism entered a second phase. Hitherto the 'empty spaces' of such areas as North America, Australia and New Zealand had been subject to colonization. Now it was the turn of the heavily populated countries of Asia and later of Africa. Europeans were interested primarily not so much in unburdening their surplus population and settling in these countries as in trade, commerce and political control. This new phase of colonialism, usually called imperialism, needed a philosophical defence. Although Lockean arguments were not without value, they needed to be revised to suit the new circumstances. Among the many liberal writers who provided such a defence, John Stuart Mill was the most influential. Just as Locke was closely associated with English colonization in North America, J.S. Mill was closely associated with the East India Company. He entered its service in 1823, was eventually promoted to the highly influential post of examiner, and remained one until 1858, the year the British government abolished the company and took direct control of India.

For Mill, man was a progressive being whose ultimate destiny was to secure the fullest development of his intellectual, moral, aesthetic and other faculties. 'Among the works of man, which human life is rightly employed in perfecting and beautifying, the first in importance surely is man himself.'[12] As a self-creating being, his 'comparative worth as a human being' consisted in becoming 'the best thing' it was possible for him to become. He was constantly to improve himself, develop new powers, cultivate a 'striving and go-ahead character', and evolve a life best suited to his 'natural constitution'.[13] For Mill only such an autonomous and self-determining being had 'character' or 'individuality'. 'One whose desires and impulses are not his own has no character, no more than a steam-engine has a character.'[14]

For Mill, as for other nineteenth-century liberals, individuality was an extremely difficult and precarious achievement. It required the courage to be different, the willingness to make choices and to accept responsibility for their consequences, thinking for oneself, and so on, which most human beings found painful. In Mill's view, human beings had both a natural and a historically acquired tendency towards conformity, which only a few were able to fight successfully on their own. The tendency to conformity was for obvious reasons reinforced by vested interests, including not only rulers and religious establishments but also corporate and self-reproducing institutional structures. For Mill as for most other liberals, individuality represented human *destiny*, but it was not underwritten by and even went against some of the deepest tendencies of human *nature*. There was a profound tension between human nature and human destiny, between what human beings tended to do and what they ought to do. The liberal way of life required them to rebel against themselves, and only a few, the 'salt of the earth' as Mill called them, were capable of it. The rest had to be educated into it and, until such time as they were ready, held in check.

Like Locke, Mill divided human societies into two, but his principle of classification was different. In some societies, which he called civilized, human beings were in the 'maturity of their faculties' and had 'attained the capacity of being guided to their own improvement by conviction or persuasion'.[15] In his view most European societies had 'long since reached' that stage. By contrast all non-European societies were 'backward', and human beings there were in a state of 'nonage' or 'infancy'. Mill did not think much of Africa, a 'continent without a history'. And although he thought that India, China and 'the whole East' had begun well, he was convinced that they had been 'stationary for thousands of years'.

Such backward societies were incapable of being improved by 'free and equal discussion' and lacked the resources for self-regeneration. Like Locke, he argued that 'if they are ever to be farther improved, it must be by foreigners'. He did not think much of the likely objection that all societies, including the backward, had a right to territorial integrity. Like Locke, he argued that the right to nonintervention, like the right to individual liberty, only belonged to those capable of making good use of it, that is, to those 'mature' enough to think and judge for themselves and to develop unaided. Since backward societies lacked that capacity and were basically like children, the right to nonintervention was 'either a certain evil or at best a questionable good for them' and only perpetuated their peoples' primitive and subhuman existences. For Mill, as for Locke, the right to non-intervention only applied to the relations between civilized societies.

Mill's defence of colonialism was based on his theory of man sketched above. Since, according to this theory, non-Europeans were moral and political infants, and thus below the age of consent, a 'parental despotism' by a 'superior people' was perfectly 'legitimate' and in their own long-term interest. It facilitated their transition to a 'higher stage of development' and trained them in 'what is specifically wanting to render them capable of a higher civilisation'. As human beings, such backward individuals had equal *moral* claims to the pursuit and protection of their interests with the members of civilized societies, but as collectivities they had no *political* claims to independence and self-determination. This is precisely the argument Locke had made in relation to American Indians.

Unlike the Canadians, Australians and other British dominions who were of 'European race' and of 'her own blood', non-Europeans were only fit for a 'government of leading-strings'.[16] Their affairs were best run by a body of carefully selected, well-meaning and professionally trained bureaucrats free from the control of elected politicians who were all bound to be subject to the influence of shifting public opinion. Mill was convinced beyond a shadow of doubt that the colonial bureaucracy should not be accountable to the 'second and third class' of elected representatives either in Britain or in the colonies. That was why when the British parliament abolished the East India Company and brought India under direct British rule, Mill chose to take early retirement rather than cooperate with the new arrangement even on an experimental basis.[17] That was also why he kept resisting right until his last working days every parliamentary attempt to give the Indians a measure of self-rule. Even when Ceylon, which was directly under the Colonial Office, was granted considerable local autonomy with no apparent adverse results, Mill continued to argue against its extension to India.

Mill maintained that just as a civilized society had a right to rule over a primitive or semi-civilized society, a more civilized group or nationality within a civilized society had a right to 'absorb' and dominate inferior groups. He had no doubt that the Breton and the Basque stood to benefit greatly if absorbed into the French 'nation' and given the opportunity to share in the latter's dignity, power and civilization. The Scottish Highlanders and the Welsh too would gain if absorbed into the British, by which Mill meant the English, way of life. This view lay at the basis of Mill's approval of Lord Durham's Report on Canada. Lord Durham was hostile to the 'backward' French Canadians' 'vain endeavour' to preserve their cultural identity, and insisted that their true interests lay in being subjected to the 'vigorous rule of an English majority', that 'great race which must ... be predominant over the whole' of North America.[18] Although Lord Durham advocated responsible government for Canada and was genuinely liberal in several respects, he had very little understanding of the strength of ethnic loyalties and even less sympathy for the desire to preserve ethnic identities. Nor surprisingly, many Canadian commentators have criticized his cultural 'chauvinism', and some have even accused him of racism. Mill enthusiastically welcomed the Durham Report, calling it an 'imperishable memorial of that nobleman's courage, patriotism and enlightened liberty'.[19] Just as Lord Durham wanted the French Canadians to become English, Macaulay wanted to make the Indians English in all respects save the colour of their skin. Liberals in other parts of the British Empire felt the same way about the indigenous ways of life and thought. Drawing inspiration from Mill they wondered why people should remain attached to their traditions and customs, and why the colonial rulers should not use a subtle mixture of education and coercion to get them to adopt the liberal ways of life and thought.

Although Mill stressed the value of diversity, he defined its nature and permissible range in narrow terms. As we saw, he linked diversity to individuality and choice, and valued the former only in so far as it was grounded in the individualist conception of man. This ruled out several forms of diversity. It ruled out traditional and customary ways of life, as well as those centred on the community. It also ruled out ethnically grounded ways of life as well as those limited to a 'narrow mental orbit' or 'not in tune' with the dominant trend of the age. Although he did not dismiss them, Mill took a low view of ways of life that stressed contentment and weak ambition rather than a go-getting character, or placed little value on worldly success and material abundance. As one would expect, Mill cherished not diversity *per se* but liberal diversity, that is, diversity confined within the narrow limits of the individualist model of human excellence. In his relation to nonliberal ways of life, Mill displayed considerable intolerance. His intellectual tools were too blunt to allow him to make sense of them, and he thought them inhuman and stifling. He dismissed them as illiberal and sought to dismantle them. If that required a vigorous policy of assimilation, he saw nothing wrong in it. And if some measure of coercion and violence was necessary, he accepted it as morally legitimate. More so than Locke, Mill condemned the racist arrogance of and the misuse of political power by the colonial bureaucrats, so much so that many of his countrymen called him a lover of the blacks and some of his obituarists could not restrain their relief at his death. And yet he had no difficulty sharing the colonial contempt for native cultures and approving of the violence used to dismantle them.

Although Mill is separated from Locke by a century and a half and sometimes speaks in different idioms, there are remarkable similarities between their vocabularies, approaches and assumptions. Both talk of reason, progress (Mill more so than Locke), liberty, autonomy, civilization. Both divide human societies into 'civilized' and 'primitive', and treat each category as homogeneous and undifferentiated. Both treat non-European ways of life with contempt, think that they have nothing to learn from a critical dialogue with them, and make no effort to understand them from within. Both use educational metaphors to conceptualize colonial rule, and see it as a pedagogical process. This allows them to assimilate colonial violence: to legitimate chastisement, to conceal its true nature, to blame the victims for provoking it, and to justify it in terms of the latter's long-term interests as well as those of the human civilization itself.

Both Locke and Mill shared a firm belief in the equality of men and used it to justify and regulate colonial rule. Unlike the conservative defenders of colonialism, they were concerned (Mill more than Locke) about the well-being of the natives, and condemned the racism, misuse of political power, and violation of basic human rights that accompanied colonial rule. While respecting the demands of equality up to this point, neither writer recognized the natives as self-determining subjects entitled to define their true interests themselves and to lead their preferred ways of life. The transition from the equality of all men to the unequal treatment of some was effected by both writers by means of such steps as belief in the uniformity of human nature, a monistic vision of the good life, contempt for those who differed from the latter and the consequent failure to allow them to speak for themselves, a recurrent tendency to see difference as deviation, and a pervasive mood of cultural narcissism.

Both Locke and Mill also failed to understand the extremely complex relationship between human beings and their cultures. They rightly insisted that being reflective and self-critical, human beings were able to take a critical view of their cultures and possessed capacities that were not always realized in their cultures. This meant that while cultures could be graded, human beings could not. The separation between human beings and their cultures protected the two writers against racism and gave them the conceptual tools to criticize it. But it also created problems. While rightly stressing that human beings were not prisoners of their cultures, Locke and Mill took the simple-minded view that cultures were like clothes, external to those involved and to be discarded when more fashionable ones became available. This prevented them from noticing that cultures could not be dissociated from their human bearers and judged (let alone graded) in the abstract, and that even if European culture could be shown to be superior to non-European cultures, it was not necessarily *better* for non-European societies to whose tastes, traditions, temperaments and habits of thought it was ill-suited. This does not mean that cultures could not or should not be criticized and changed, but rather that demands for changes must come from within them, and that changes do not take roots unless they are grafted onto the critically teased-out resources of the cultures concerned. The task of civilizing other societies is deeply problem-atic, and rests on dubious assumptions.

Why liberalism becomes illiberal

I have so far concentrated on showing how and why Locke and Mill, starting with egalitarian premisses, reached inegalitarian conclusions, of which justification of colonialism was one but not the only expression. Since both writers drew upon and developed the liberal tradition of thought, it is hardly surprising that their assumptions continue to inform that tradition and explain some of the actions and utterances listed at the beginning of this chapter. Liberals believe in equal respect for persons, tolerance, fairness, and so on. They are also convinced, however, that the individualist way of life is the best and even the only rationally defensible one, that those that differ from it are mistaken and in need of education and even perhaps coercion, that liberals can only feel safe in a world that has become thoroughly liberal, that human beings are only contingently related to their cultures, and so on. Although liberalism has mellowed over the years and become self-critical, these and related assumptions still continue to dominate it and emasculate the force of its liberal and egalitarian impulses. Liberals do believe in equal respect for all human beings, but they find it difficult to accord equal respect to those who do not value autonomy, individuality, self-determination, choice, secularism, ambition, competition and the pursuit of wealth. In the liberal view, such men and women are 'failing' to use their 'truly' human capacities, to live up to the 'norms' of their human 'dignity' or 'status', and are thus not 'earning' their right to liberal respect. For reasons of prudence and out of respect for the liberal principle of tolerance, liberals do not generally persecute nonliberals, but they feel uneasy and even threatened in their presence and do all in their power to undermine them, even exerting enormous social and political pressures and using schools as tools of cultural engineering. This explains the liberal attitude to communists in the 1950s and to the ethnic minorities, Muslims and other religious groups, today.

Liberals grant equality to all men on condition that they share and live by the narrowly defined liberal values of choice, autonomy, self-determination, and so forth. Equality as defined by the liberal therefore is a dubious gift and often serves as the ideological means to mould its recipients in the liberal image. The liberal views on tolerance, fairness, justice and personal responsibility have a similar thrust. When critically examined, the central assumptions informing liberal thought turn out to be problematic. As pointed out by critics of liberalism from Hegel onwards, the socially transcendental individual as imagined by the liberals is a fiction; human beings and the cultures they both inherit and re-create are infinitely varied, and their visions of good life are sometimes incommensurable. Unless a theory of man recognizes the legitimacy of deep differences and gives them an ontological status, it cannot avoid setting up narrow norms and throwing up inegalitarian and even imperialist impulses. Obviously, we cannot tolerate all differences, but the determining principle should be dialogically derived and consensually grounded, not arbitrarily imposed by a narrowly defined liberalism. Liberals cannot consistently be dogmatic about their own beliefs and sceptical about all others, or talk about an open-minded dialogue yet both exclude some and conduct the dialogue on their own terms. They need to take a sustained critical look at their basic assumptions that both generate, and prevent them from noticing and restraining, their illiberal and inegalitarian impulses.

Notes

I am grateful to my friend Jan Nederveen Pieterse for his valuable comments. The section on J.S. Mill draws on my 'Decolonising liberalism' in Alexsandras Shtromas, *The End of 'Isms'?* (Oxford, Blackwell, 1994). I am grateful to Will Kymlicka for his many helpful comments on that essay.

1. *The Independent*, 4 March 1989. For a detailed discussion, see my 'The Rushdie affair and the British Press', in Parekh (ed.), *Free Speech* (London, Commission for Racial Equality, 1990).

2. William Strachey, *The Historie of Travaile into Virginia* (London, 1612), pp. 1f.

3. For an excellent discussion of these critics and of Locke, see James Tully, *An Approach to Political Philosophy: Locke in Contexts* (Cambridge, Cambridge University Press, 1993), Chapter 5. For a discussion of Roger Williams's case, see *The Cambridge History of the British Empire*, Vol. I (Cambridge, Cambridge University Press, 1929), pp. 163–4.

4. *Second Treatise*, §. 34.

5. Ibid., §. 38.

6. Ibid., §. 107f.

7. Ibid., §. 108.

8. *The Third Letter Concerning Toleration*, cited in Tully, p. 152.

9. That a political society should be 'too hard' for its neighbours is discussed in *Second Treatise*, §. 42. I have so far concentrated on showing that contrary to Locke's assertions, the Indians had established the two vital institutions of property and political society. This challenges his conceptualization of and conclusions about them, but not his premises. To challenge the latter, one would need to criticize his views on man's relation to the shared earth, the nature of equality, the way he justified private property and limited others' claims on it, and so on. I do not mount such a critique here.

10. Ibid., §. 180, and chapter XVI in general. See also Patrick Kelly (ed.), *Locke on Money* (Oxford, Oxford University Press, 1991), pp. 222f.

11. The ideas of status and rank occur in almost all of Locke's moral and political writings and are packed with normative implications. Mill's conception of human dignity, with its quasi-aristocratic connotation, bears a close resemblance to it and plays a similar role in his thought. A good deal of the liberal tradition presupposes an unarticulated cosmology and a view of man's status in the universe.

12. J.S. Mill, *Utilitarianism, Liberty and Representative Government* (London, Dent, 1912), p. 117.

13. Ibid., pp. 117, 118 and 125.

14. Ibid., p. 118.

15. Ibid., p. 73.

16. Ibid., pp. 377, 378 and 199.

17. Ibid., pp. 386f and 391f.

18. Sir C.P. Lucas, *Lord Durham's Report on the Affairs of British North America* (Oxford, Clarendon Press, 1912), Vol.11, pp. 285ff.

19. *Utilitarianism, Liberty and Representative Government*, p. 377.

6

Samurai and self-colonization in Japan

Hiroshi Yoshioka

Japan, colonized?

Decolonization of imagination – what does it mean in a Japanese context? Before answering this question I should define what I understand by the expression 'decolonization of imagination'. If we can talk about decolonization of imagination, there should be something like 'colonization of imagination'. What does it mean to 'colonize' imagination? What happens to someone or a culture when his or her imagination is 'colonized'? The first thing we can say is that the phenomenon of colonization at this level involves our ways of seeing, thinking and talking about other people and cultures. In other words, this issue of colonization can be discussed in the realm of cultural representation and discourse. This does not mean we are always forced by some noticeable power to represent or talk of others in a certain way. On the contrary, forces that distort our images of others function most effectively when we are not aware of them, that is, when we feel ourselves free to see or think about the world. The domain of these distorting forces is in the unconscious, and they reach very deep into our everyday life through the process of communication in families, school and social education as well as daily exposure to mass media.

If we talk of colonization of imagination as colonization of culture in this sense, we can deal with it more or less separately from actual, political colonization which operates under visible forces such as military power, law or economic control. Compared to the painful history of this actual colonization, colonization of imagination might seem a more obscure, abstract matter, because theoretical study of the problem deals with representations and discourse instead of bare facts. It is true that, in cultural criticism, we cannot do without terms such as 'politics', 'power', 'institution' and so on, but in many cases their use is metaphorical, not literal. Because of this, cultural criticism (especially in its postmodern or poststructuralist styles) is often regarded as being only of indirect importance in relation to the problem of colonization, or sometimes as merely playing with jargons. I believe it is quite wrong to see contemporary theories in this way. Cultural criticism is one of the most urgent tasks for these theories, and the most important point of cultural criticism is to change our ways of seeing and talking, not to characterize or describe them within an established frame. Many contemporary theories transgress any fixed realm of research, making use of the vocabularies of philosophy, linguistics, anthropology, psychoanalysis and so on, to invent new styles or textual strategies. They do so because the objects of contemporary cultural analysis are, in principle, too complex to be dealt with by any single methodology. Every cultural image is complex because it is generated by an interplay of fundamentally different languages, different systems of representation. And that is the field in which the argument about the decolonization of imagination occurs.

I hope this prefatory argument will help introduce the current problem – decolonization of imagination – in a Japanese context. How does Japan stand in relation to the question of colonization? As far as actual colonization is concerned, Japan's position is clear enough. Except for the American occupation after the Second World War, Japan has never been colonized. Japan was so quick to Westernize itself that it avoided political colonization. In fact, it stood on the colonist side as one of the modern imperialist states. In this respect, we can regard Japan as a part of the West in modern history. One might find a colonizing mentality even today in, say, Japan's economic 'invasion' into markets in other countries. And it is true that there still exist in Japan many institutional and psychological restrictions that separate its own people from foreigners. But I do not think it useful to regard these cases as essentially the same as racial discrimination in the Western world. The basic relation to the other and to the West, in contemporary Japanese society, is deeply involved with an inward process of cultural domination, and when we turn our eyes to the inner process of colonization, the situation turns out to be not so simple. We will miss the point if we formulate the problem of cultural colonization in Japan as a simple problem of following the Western or American value system. By this I mean neither to say that it is wrong to see Japan's modernization as something realized by following or reproducing the West, nor to claim some original quality in Japanese culture. Rather, what I want to attack is the very opposition of *reproduction* and *originality* in cultural formation. Or, more precisely, even if modernization is undertaken merely as reproduction, reproduction itself is no simple question. Reproduction, copy and repetition (together with their doubtful opposition to originality) constitute a complex theoretical subject, and this becomes pertinent when we talk of colonization of culture.

No one could deny Japan's surprisingly fast development as a modern state since the Meiji period. And after defeat in the Second World War, Japan has surprised the world again by its remarkable economic recovery. One tends to think there is a certain kind of secret in such national toughness. Many books are published every year identifying such a secret in Japan's miraculous success in the business world. Instead of talking of a secret, however, I see the whole situation under the hypothesis that Japan's strength was attained at the cost of a certain distortion in its cultural and psychological structure. In the course of rapid Westernization,

Japan experienced radical change in its cultural system. What is important is that this change was not felt to be something forced from outside. If Westernization were only an imposed factor in modern Japan, we could get to the 'true' Japan merely by eliminating such foreign factors. But Westernization in Japan is not a process of intrusion of the other, but a kind of simulation done by Japanese people themselves. In the process of simulation, information can be taken in without confronting any counterpart in another culture.

In short, colonization, at least in the normal sense of the word, has no place in the self-understanding of Japanese culture. But that is the very reason I am going to use this term to analyse the deep structure of the Japanese cultural self. To make the point clearer, I present an exemplary response which will suggest how Japanese people feel about their relation to the West. If one asks a Japanese if there is some colonized aspect to Japanese culture, a possible answer would be: 'Japan, colonized? Well, as we are very good at copying Western cultures, you know, there must be a lot of features which look like those of a colonized culture. But that is the result of imitation, not colonization. And however Western our culture may look, the core of our mind remains Japanese.'[1] What is missing in this kind of remark is the consciousness of cultural contradiction. In most Asian countries people feel some form of contradiction between the West and themselves. In most areas of Asia, the Western element was once imposed by actual colonization, but now in many cases it is so deeply established that one cannot easily get rid of it, while, on the other hand, one can never be free from the idea that there is a totally different stratum in one's self, which is rooted in one's own, traditional culture. Most countries that experienced colonization are suffering more or less from such a double identity, or inconsistency of two cultures. But Japan seems to be an exception. Japanese people have only a faint consciousness of such doubleness. There is very little awareness of contradiction between different elements in this culture. Japanese people appear not to suffer any cultural colonization. Coexistence of the Western and Japanese elements in one single culture is felt to be natural and harmonious. According to such a naturalized view, there is no need to decolonize culture because there is no element of colonization in it.

What I wish to do in this chapter is to reconsider Japanese modernization in the context of this kind of naturalization. In order to see the current cultural situation in a different way, I will use the term 'colonization' in an abnormal way, so that the cultural subject of modern Japan can be seen as the result of a hidden process of colonization. According to my image of Japanese culture, its calm outlook (often represented as oriental calmness, impersonality, unity with nature and so on) is created as the effect of incessant identification between the subject and an object, an outside 'other'. To put it in another way, I argue that a certain complex and dynamic process mediates the immediate character of Japanese cultural ideals. The harmonious coexistence of different cultural elements is, of course, not a lamentable thing in itself. In the case of modern Japan, however, it seems to me that there is a mechanism concealed underneath this outlook of harmonious coexistence. To bring this hidden mechanism to light, I will make use of the most popular cultural image for Japan: samurai.

Functions of cultural stereotypes

It may not seem very serious to mention a cultural stereotype such as samurai when talking of a hidden process of colonization in the Japanese mind. But seriousness may not be of much help in the area I am approaching, because the function of stereotypes comes from their arbitrary and floating character. Instead of taking samurai seriously, maybe I should ask whether the samurai himself is serious or not. At first sight, the samurai may look totally serious with his silence, bravery, loyalty, suppression of personal emotions, and of course that famous, ceremonious way of suicide. But for all that, the samurai is not serious in the same sense as the modern Western subject is said to be serious. If the modern subject can be characterized by rationality of action, samurai belong to a value system utterly different from that of goal-seeking rational ethics. If modernity is defined by its separation of science, morality and art (Habermas 1983), the samurai lives somewhere outside such a separation. He does have an ethic, but not in the modern sense. It is something that works as aesthetics, religion and practical knowledge at the same time.[2] So, if he is put within the world of modern capitalism the samurai looks strange and funny. The more serious he is in his own way, the more comical the role he plays. But I think this unserious character of the sign *samurai* helps to stabilize Japanese cultural identity, as well as to encourage this critical attempt of mine.

Here I do not use the samurai in a serious sense either. In using this term I do not mean the warrior in the Japanese feudal age, either as an individual or a social class. Instead, I choose the term samurai to give some form to a complex representational mechanism that is at work in the relation of Japan to the West. It bears only a limited relationship to the historical fact of what a samurai really was. I do not know whether there ever was a 'real' or 'true' samurai, but I am sure that people like to imagine that there was (and still is?). In my view, the samurai stands for the desire for cultural essentialism. In the West the term has been used to identify something or someone as typically Japanese, and sometimes it even seems to be synonymous with what Japan is like. In the West it is a privileged sign that points to the very core or essence of the Japanese mind. But what do people imagine by it? Like many other cultural stereo-types, it derives its totalizing effect from its vagueness, its lack of distinct content. The samurai slips out of the hands of criticism because it is too ambiguous to be criticized as a false image. In other words, it functions almost as a pure signifier which, by its very senselessness, provokes people's imagination strongly. In the world of advertising or tourism, for example, samurai can be associated with almost every aspect of Japan.

Strangely, this ambiguity has been rarely pointed out by Japanese people themselves. On the contrary, Japanese people seem to feel at home in finding themselves represented in this stereotyped way. Or rather, they enjoy representing themselves as samurai just as much as the West enjoys representing them in that way. The samurai is an exotic image even for the Japanese, but this exoticism is in some curious way entangled in people's self-image. The sense of historical discontinuity is anaesthetized. I am thinking of the endless samurai dramas broadcast daily on Japanese television. They are very popular, but few watch them out of historical interest. The samurai in these dramas are by no means different from their modernized descendants except for their clothing and hairstyles. Their popularity comes from their contemporary character. Their way of thinking, feeling and acting in society is very much like that of the contemporary Japanese, and the society they live in is exactly what we think present Japanese society is, only situated in the Edo period. Office workers see their own struggle in business, their problems of maintaining good relations with their boss, their desires to move upwards in an organization and so on, in dramas situated some hundred years ago. It is as if the business world of late capitalism were transplanted to the feudal age.

What one finds in these dramas is not so much historical continuity as an immediate fusion of different ages. What samurai drama is showing every day is not the past but something like an eternal present. Samurai images function to negate historical incompatibility and to identify the past with the present. But if the samurai is a sign of blind historical consciousness, why do modern Japanese need it? Why should our imaginations identify the modernized present with the premodern past? It may be that in such dramas the samurai image functions as something to negate the radical transformation of culture caused by Westernization. Samurai provide people with a fantasy that the world has not been changed by the impact of modernization. The samurai in these television dramas serve as an image of the deep self of a Japanese office worker, who is often in everyday conversation compared to a warrior. The world of business is often described as a battlefield, in which a strong and loyal male subject of production is celebrated as a samurai. Every month many business magazines feature success stories of business champions, comparing them to a shogun in the Age of Strife, or even stories of a shogun comparing him to an executive of Sony or Toyota. By imagining himself as a warrior, an office worker can avoid facing the difficult reality. In this sense, the samurai serves as a sign to imply continuity with a premodern golden age. The sign can represent the strength of the nation, but that strength is gained by forgetting cultural discontinuity, forgetting the peculiarly complex character of the Japanese self. I suppose the samurai was generated as a kind of psychological defence against the strong modern subject of the West. It has played a certain role in the struggle to develop a strong ego (collective as well as individual) which could confront the West. It has been an unconscious self-image for the nation. In the course of integrating people in the islands, who were really of various different cultures and traditions, into a single nation it played a role similar to the modern Western self. In the process of modernization, however, this samurai image had a far more ambivalent character. For Japanese modernizers in the late nineteenth century, the values of the historical samurai were something to be abandoned because they belonged to the past. They felt it necessary to distance themselves from the past and they looked at it in the same way colonists looked at native cultures. But, at the same time, people found it hard to develop Japan into an industrialized imperialist state without assuming a strong, independent, male subject in their mind, through which they could have a national identity. Thus the samurai was interpreted as something similar to the Western modern ego, in its individual, stoic and masculine character. This is not a simple act of recovering or maintaining the past. There was an identification with an other in the process of constituting that self-identity, because it is through the eye of the other that Japan could make up its own self. The very core of the national identity was constituted through the internalized eye of the West.

The samurai, then, is nothing but a modern invention. The samurai provided a homogeneous space of representation when Japan recognized and located itself in relation to the other. Once such a homogeneous space was established it became very hard to imagine anything outside it. The samurai belong to a perspective restricting the imagination of modern Japan. In this sense, I resist the accepted idea that the samurai is something like a core of the Japanese mind. The samurai as the archetype of the Japanese spirit is but an invention constructed as the result of the relationship between Japan and the West during the last 120 years. And it was invented not only by Westerners but also by Japanese themselves. In contrast to their behaviour in the field of current international trade, Japan and the West have been and remain deeply cooperative in establishing this stereotypical view of Japan. Westerners use 'samurai' as a key word to interpret the behaviour of the Japanese, some of which appears too irrational to understand, for example the eccentric suicide of the writer Yukio Mishima.[3] On the other hand, it was Mishima himself who played the role of samurai. Mishima, together with nationalist and romantic thinkers in modern Japan, wrote and behaved as if we Japanese could restore Japan's native spirit by eliminating the 'imposed' Western or American cultural standard. This trend of thought was effective as a means of resistance to postwar Americanization and superficial democratization, in which the trauma of defeat fatally weakened the culture. But there is one question this nationalist movement has always failed to ask: what if the innermost tradition is nothing but an image represented by the other? What if our desire to return to the original spirit is itself mediated by an alien element? What if we were born with mixed blood from the very outset?

Mind as a colony

If the samurai were simply a distorted image imposed from outside, the strategy of criticism would be relatively simple. All we would have to do is to show how the colonized culture has been misrepresented and distorted by the colonizer, and what false images and stories have been made up in the process of colonization. But, in fact, criticism of the samurai is faced with a certain ambiguity and instability, caused by the tricky character of the sign itself. The samurai is neither inside nor outside Japan, it is on the surface – on the interface connecting Japan to the other. It is like a semi-transparent mirror put between Japan and the West. As one gazes into it, one's reflection looks strangely doubled with that of the other beyond the mirror. For modern Japanese this may have been the main function of the sign. In other words, the samurai has made it possible to imagine oneself as Japanese and Western at the same time. If we use 'samurai' as a name for such a representational system rather than a representation, we could say that the samurai exempts one from, or makes one blind to, asking who one really is. It allows the subject to be ambiguous about his position to the other, or it enables one to speak as if there were no others. Protected by the samurai guard, Japanese culture can behave within its own language, within its closed community, without facing the fact that true contact remains closed.

This ambiguous doubleness of the Japanese subject is reflected in many aspects of culture. It also applies to academic discourse. In Japanese academic discourse, especially in studies based on Western ideas, the speaker's position is always very unstable. As the speaker's position in relation to the West is seldom stated, we never know whether he or she speaks as a Western subject or as someone who feels uneasy with the Western way of thought. Sometimes it even seems that it is this ambiguity that activates academic discourse. And this situation can be generalized. Modern Japanese people are basically living in an imaginary identification with the West. Visitors to Japan might wonder why many mannequins in display windows and heroes and heroines in comic books have Caucasian faces, blue eyes and blond hair. A more interesting example of this doubled cultural identity is a famous theatre in which young girls play in an opera about the French Revolution, with blond wigs and special make-up to make them look like Western males. Am I going too far if I say that the theoretical subject in Japanese academic discourse is like those girls? The subject is almost perversely disguised, but totally innocent.[4] What makes this possible is the representational space we called 'samurai' above, and the innocence is also the Samurai's innocence. There is no contradiction between appearance and truth, because they are merged into the same thing in the samurai. The samurai appears here as a political guiltlessness.

In another aspect, the paradoxical effect of the samurai simultaneously opens and closes the space of information in modern Japan. Today, most Japanese are badly informed about colonization, and not because there is powerful censorship or explicit control violating freedom of speech. Of course there is some control upon information, exerted mainly through the influence of the mass media. This control is anonymous and collective. It affects people's imagination not so much by selecting or distorting the contents, as by manipulating the form of information. Japan lacks the distribution of heterogeneous and multiple types of information. Information is excessively uniform and politically neutralized so that people are hardly aware of other angles from which to look at a situation. The amount of information itself is great, but every alien element is eliminated from it. An average high-school student can learn many facts about history from a textbook, but facts are only one kind of information, information on the first level. They are not given any information on the second level, knowledge of how to interpret facts, because authors are afraid of being regarded as ideological and dangerous. Neutralized description in authorized textbooks completely lacks this secondary information. No matter how many books are published we cannot say that information is plentiful, if what is written is the same in all the books. This does not apply only to textbooks. To some extent, it applies to general publishing, as well as to the general structure of information in Japan.

As a result of my experience as a teacher, I have wanted to give a name to such a closed, uniform cultural system. The invitation to speak at the conference on 'Decolonization of Imagination' in 1991 gave me the chance to consider such a name together with the theme of colonization. In opposition to the general impression that Japan today has nothing to do with colonization, I tried to present an idea of internalized colonization, and its comical agent: the samurai. The point of this idea is that Japan has colonized itself and that in the course of modernization and the drastic transformation of its culture, the Japanese have played the role of the colonizer and the colonized at the same time. What has been basic in this process has been the fusion of the subject and the object of domination. That has made the structure of this culture unbelievably complex, and this is why Japanese people cannot simply adopt a critical position against represented images of themselves and why they even appear to act as accomplices to such representation. A certain implicit mechanism is at work here. By creating a completely superficial sign, by sharing a pure signifier, the difference between subject and object is eliminated. If you ask what is the dominant ideology in Japan, I would answer that it is an ideology of non-difference.

I know that internalized colonization is an abnormal expression. A colony often means a distant area, so it may sound strange to relate it to something within one's own culture. As mentioned before, the cultural image of samurai was formed by Japanese people creating an imaginary distance from their own culture, treating it as if it were a colony. But if this expansion of meaning is allowed, there is still something misleading in the formulation 'internalized colonization'. It sounds as if the process of colonization is repeated within a culture, in which we are divided into either the colonizer or the colonized. It is partly true that the whole culture can be divided into these opposing camps. But what I refer to by this term is a deeper structural element in which the colonizer and the colonized are mutually implicated, in which normal social criticism has no power. I do not mean to insist there are (or are not) colonizers in Japan. What I am suggesting is that every Japanese is a colonizer of his own mind. This has greatly speeded up modernization in Japan, by avoiding discrepancies in the course of radical cultural change. But this process of colonization is not exercised by any conscious personal subject. Rather, it is through the absence of such a subject that such self-colonization became possible.

Why did this absence of the subject accelerate modernization, internalize colonization, and help prevent actual colonization? Let me explain this as a story. When Japan was faced with a totally different cultural system, the modern Western world, in the middle of the nineteenth century, it knew it was useless to resist and keep itself closed. So Japan opened itself to the world and set about the task of building itself into a modernized state as soon as possible. The problem was that the Japanese mental structure and cultural system were completely different from those of the West. In particular, in Japan there is no such thing as the integrated modern ego of the West. It would take many decades or even centuries to build up such a thing by itself. In order to grow into a modern state in a short period, it was more effective to give up striving to become the strong subject, and cultivate instead an amorphous subject and ambiguous identity. The strong self-image of the samurai was invented, but it was invented as a dummy to confront the Western subject. It is a mask to cover the absence of the subject. From the standpoint of consciousness, such an operation might be repudiated as a form of self-deception. If we see a whole cultural system as an organism, however, this operation can be thought of as a strategy for survival in a difficult environment. Thus, the absence of the self turned out to be a solution to the task of achieving the modernization of society, to some extent even more effective than the original modernization in the West, because it was unnecessary to face difficulties caused by the opposition of the individual and the society.

Samurai discourse

With the expansion of its economic activities, Japan is now having more and more opportunities to face real others in the world, and other criteria of other cultures, instead of represented pictures of them. This is happening both outside the country (by expanding business abroad) and inside (as a result of increasing numbers of foreign residents). But the Japanese way of communication so far has not turned out to be very effective in this new situation. The tendency of Japanese people to stick to the rules of their own community, trust in tacit agreement, and avoid expression of personal feelings – all the characteristics of the samurai – makes it difficult to communicate with others in the current internationalized situation. Samurai characteristics are often praised for their refinement from an aesthetic point of view, but aesthetic refinement alone does not work in the effort to develop relations with people who have completely different cultural standards. The present time may be the first historical opportunity for modern Japan to open its fundamentally inward-oriented community. In other words, the Japanese are coming to the end of the homogeneous space of representation, the dead end of simulated modernization apparent since the Meiji period. This means a true crisis for the samurai, and now is the time for him to say something about his own plight.

The samurai speaks out most clearly in political discourse, though eloquence is inconsistent with his ethic of keeping silence and enduring without words. To speak cynically, by speaking out the samurai is no longer a samurai. At any rate, in 1989, a small book was published that seemed to challenge the Japanese to abandon shyness and to escape from the thirty-five years of trauma caused by the country's unconditional surrender in the Second World War. I think this book tells us how Japanese people, after achieving industrial success, felt about the world in the late 1980s. The book encourages people to overcome their collective inferiority complex by saying no to the superior, the United States. It provoked political disputes both in Japan and the United States. In Japan it had sold more than 1 million copies by the beginning of 1991, largely thanks to its controversial title, *The Japan That Can Say No* (Morita and Ishihara 1989). What does this title mean exactly? It says that Japan otherwise cannot resist the stronger partner, even when it really wants to. This title takes for granted that Japan has its own distinct subjectivity, and that free utterance is suppressed only by an exterior power. It simplifies the problem and reduces it to a question of having the manly courage to express one's will. This way of encouragement seems to belong rather to the American mind than to the samurai ethic. The samurai functions to simplify the situation and to present Japan as a single personality.

Though the book was primarily intended for Japanese readers, it provoked a sensation also in the United States, because it criticizes the United States as unfair. It is not my intention here to decide whether the authors are right in this matter, or to what extent they are right. I agree with them on many points, but we are dealing now with the paradoxical dimension of basic cultural structure, something that can be seen only by bracketing straightforward judgement. Instead I would like to call attention to another reason the book appeals to the West: it implies a certain way of representing Japan to the West, the perspective basically rooted in the West, that is, to assume some 'real' or 'true' tradition in the Japanese mentality which survives all the cultural and social transformation caused by modernization. In this sense this book was implicitly written for the Westerner, including the Western self in the Japanese mind. This type of utterance I call samurai discourse. I define samurai discourse as the discourse generated by Japanese when they desire to be agents of the West, while at the same time they seek to appeal to a 'genuine' Japanese tradition. As an agent of the other, the samurai often projects and repeats his relation to his superior in his followers' relation to him. 'Genuineness' of a cultural tradition is, as I have already argued, a fiction created through the eyes of the other. The samurai is a modernist promoting westernization and a nationalist conserving tradition, and he speaks English, the ability praised in this country as a symbol of intelligence and power. Thus, to the Japanese he appears as a representative of the West, while to Westerners he embodies native Japanese tradition. This double motion is the very core of Japanese modernization so far. The dominant tone of this book is embodied in suggestions such as 'Don't hesitate any more. Trust yourself and speak your mind clearly!' This sounds in some strange way similar to suggestions that English teachers often give to shy Japanese students. The enlightening voice of this book comes from the common fact that the authors play the role of the Westerner in the position of educating the Japanese, while, on the other hand, they claim that the Japanese no longer need to follow the West. The book confronts the West (the United States), representing the nation as one the authors hope is not going to be subordinate any longer, trusting in talents that it has by nature.

The book as a whole can be read as a statement that it is necessary now to recover the original tradition of a Japanese spirit strong and harmonious at the same time. It implies that such a 'true' tradition exists, but has been distorted by some 'wrong' process of history. This type of political discourse is not at all new. In the 1930s, when Japan was developing increasingly antagonistic relations with the West, many arguments suggested that the nation must overcome modernity by returning to its original self. In that movement, the Westernization of mind of the Meiji Restoration was attacked from the standpoint of a 'genuine' Japanese tradition, and this culminated in the worship of the Emperor as a living god. Some might think it symptomatic to see, sixty years later, political discourse that claims to be overcoming dependency upon the United States appealing to some 'original' tradition of the Japanese spirit. However, the prewar project of overcoming modernity, like its contemporary counterpart, has its own truth. It is wrong to associate every nationalistic movement with war and aggression. The truth of nationalism consists in its opening of the possibility of reconsidering modernization from an angle different to the one imported from outside. But in samurai discourse, the paradigm in which Japan is opposed to the West is itself a borrowed one, because it assumes an identical Japanese subject, which is fundamentally commensurate with the Western subject. This basic function of the samurai remains the same, even when, instead of the imperial system, technological achievement is celebrated as a symbol to enhance national identity.

In the opening sentences of *The Japan That Can Say No*, the author expresses his worry that the Japanese today have brains too large for their weak bodies to support, and he compares the 'monstrous' Japanese figure to that of ET in the Steven Spielberg film. (This was not criticized as another case of racial discrimination since ET is not a representative of a race.) It is interesting that he chooses an extra-terrestrial as an image of a holder of a highly advanced technology. For by calling it 'monstrous', he perhaps unconsciously admits that contemporary Japan may appear to the West as alien and monstrous. Am I going too far if I say this reveals that he (as well as many Japanese in leading positions) looks at recent techno-logical developments with fear, just as do many in the West? In any case, strength, as he contrasts it with intelligence here, seems at first sight to be physical strength. He wishes the Japanese had won more in the most recent Olympic Games. But on the next page, the reader is told that the main strength of the nation consists not in its physical strength but in its highly developed technology. But technology is achieved only by 'large brains', and this remarkable contradiction suggests that technology serves as a substitute for some more clearly masculine symbol of power, such as military power. Another equally interesting point is that the author espe-cially admires technological progress in the fields of integrated circuits or superconductivity, where precision, purity and refinement are required more than in any other field of industry. This high technology is praised as something more than just complicated know-how. It is, he argues, an embodiment of the nation's spirit and, as such, something valuable in itself. Strength appears here in an almost artistic form, just as the sword of the samurai is praised as a work of art, though it is actually a weapon intended to kill. This aestheticization of strength is another side of samurai discourse, and the artistic, fetishistic character of technology/strength also appears in later passages, when we find the excellence of Japanese techno-logy compared to the artistic achievements found in traditional arts that show the taste of high culture. Since the samurai is an ideal self for the modern Japanese, there is always a longing for the refined culture of the aristocracy.

Technology is not the only ground on which this book intends to restore Japan's self-confidence. The co-author, Akio Morita, the president of Sony, emphasizes the universality of the idea of the company as a family. He attributes the success of his company to the sense of community shared by employees even in a factory in a foreign country, and he emphasizes the merit of this idea by comparing it with the American way of treating employees, in which little effort is made to develop loyalty to the company itself. In the Japanese way of organizing people as a harmoni-ous community, both employers and employees are said to share a common fate. This idea, he says, should be universally acceptable. This includes, certainly, a kind of idealization and sentimentalism, but it is not groundless. The idea of the company as a family might be called an illusion, but as a matter of fact this illusion works quite effectively in the Japanese social context. It is also derived from what can be called the ideal of harmonious coexistence, a crucial part of the samurai ethic. In principle, harmony in human relationships can never be called a bad thing. Nevertheless, in Japan what is called 'harmony' often has the effect of suppressing

individual initiative and thinking, and as a result inhibits open communication. The central function of the idea is to assimilate the reality to
the ideal: by sharing a common illusion individuals can endure hardship.

Why do I call this book an example of samurai discourse, though I
basically agree with the suggestion that Japan should become more open-
minded? It is not simply because of any expressed ideas or opinions, but
because of its basic standpoint. The book addresses readers from the
position of the double identity I mentioned before. The authors are
speaking as the Japanese and the Western subject at the same time, without
any sense of contradiction. This arises not from the authors' particular
fault, but from a certain basic structure of the Japanese subject of speech.
As mentioned before, this basic structure is not limited to this recent
bestseller, but is shared by academic discourse as well as dancing girls
with Western makeup on the stage. And I do not want to say that
something is fundamentally wrong with it. It has worked for Japan, at
least so far. This doubleness may be possible simply because Japan is
situated far from the West. Japan has acted as a member of the West,
though it is not in the West. The geographical distance might have helped
create the internal colonization discussed here, and samurai discourse may
be seen as the end product of the situation. But when Japan faces the real
other, and when it comes to theorize critically about this situation, samurai
discourse is distinctly weak, because it looks at Japan with the eyes of the
West, and in so doing fails to grasp the central issue in the relation of
Japan to the West. A book such as *The Japan That Can Say No* can encourage
people to speak their minds clearly to the West and assert that Japan's
exclusiveness is the main weakness it has to overcome. In reality, however,
it is this very peculiar exclusiveness that enabled and accelerated Japan's
modernization. Japan's real power has been derived from its distorted
acceptance of Western cultures, the translated, secondary character of its
own culture and the only halfway-enlightened structure of its self. In
short, Japan has been effectively modernized because its modernization
has always been a strongly modified one, which may sometimes look
superficial, fake and kitsch. This has brought about an unprecedented
complexity in the cultural and sociopolitical life of the country. What we
need now is not a single-step political decision or change of attitude, but
an attempt to create a new discourse to cope with this complexity.

Notes

1. This is based on a discussion I had with my university students.
2. A classic example of the introduction of the samurai ethic to the West is
Nitobe 1969.
3. On Mishima's own representation of the samurai ethic see Mishima 1977.
4. About such an innocent character found in many aspects of Japanese culture
see Buruma 1984.

References

Buruma, Ian 1984 *A Japanese Mirror: Heroes and Villains of Japanese Culture* Harmondsworth, Penguin.

Habermas, Jürgen 1983 'Modernity: an incomplete project', in Hal Foster (ed.) *The Anti-Aesthetic* San Francisco, Bay Press.

Mishima, Yukio 1977 *Hagakure: the Samurai Ethic and Modern Japan*, translated by Kathryn Sparling, Harmondsworth, Penguin.

Morita, Akio and Shintaro Ishihara 1989 *'No' to ieru Nihon* Tokyo, Kobunsha.

Nitobe, Inazo 1969 *Bushido: the Soul of Japan* New York, Charles E. Tuttle.

7

Metaphors and the Middle East: crisis discourse on Gaza

Toine van Teeffelen

Crisis discourse

A major methodological problem in the study of Western images of the non-Western other is how precisely such images surface in discourse. Much post-structuralist theorizing, pre-eminently concerned with texts and self–other contrasts, pays scant attention to the concrete manifestations of images as they are evoked, negotiated, and adapted in talk and in writing. In the modern media, self–other divides cannot be taken for granted. Powerful as they are, such divides are not immune to interrogation and challenge; in fact, their viability partially depends on their adaptive capacity in the face of new arguments and new developments. Critical discourse analysis is an approach intended to reveal the subtle linguistic re-creation and negotiation of self–other oppositions against a background of commonsense reasonings. In following one strand of this tradition, I will inquire here into the workings of a set of metaphors commonly brought into association with the Arab–Islamic world. Since the 1970s regular media hypes about the dangers of terrorism, Islamic fundamentalism and (nuclear) war have suggested the Middle East to be a 'powder keg' where problems are 'explosive', or a 'volcano' where crises reach a 'boiling point'. In associating the domains of physics and nature with a political situation, these crisis metaphors give expression to a fear of a Middle East out of control.

A political issue in the Middle East that has long been regarded as defying control is the Palestine question, and of all the various events and places related to this conflict those pertaining to the West Bank and especially to the Gaza Strip have obtained special metaphoric treatment. During the Intifada, soldiers petitioned for withdrawal from the Gaza Strip, feeling they were 'sinking' in an 'ocean' of hostility, 'engulfed' by crowds. In a reversal of the image, Israeli prime minister Rabin wished the Gaza Strip, in an offstage remark made in 1993, 'to sink into the sea'. An article headline such as 'West Bank explodes' or 'Gaza explodes' has for a long time been routine in the Israeli media in the same way as similar metaphors dominated the coverage of violence in Soweto during apartheid. In the case of the West Bank and the Gaza Strip some Israeli journalists have in fact become aware of the cliché:

> Expressions like 'pressure cooker', 'powder keg', 'playing with fire', and a 'match liable at any moment to ignite a terrible conflagration here' sounded especially true this time. (Gid'on Levi, 'The Gaza Strip: "A dog in Tel Aviv lives a more normal life than we do"', *Haaretz* weekly supplement, 12 June 1992.)

In its turn the Western press took over crisis discourse on the Occupied Palestinian Territories. It is quite likely that this discourse has contributed to the political viewpoint, gradually endorsed by a dominant current of Israeli society, that Israel should abandon Gaza; not as a matter of principle, out of concern for Palestinian political rights, but rather to protect Israeli lives and interests, and to realize control by other means. This viewpoint became reality after the Gaza–Jericho agreement between Israel and the PLO made in 1993–94.

Here I consider a number of articles on the Occupied Palestinian Territories, and especially Gaza, written in the 1980s by Israeli and Western (Dutch) journalists, in order to show the ideological implications of the above-mentioned metaphors; how they shaped attitudes and definitions of reality within an argumentative context not without ambiguity.

The explosion metaphor

Recently communication studies, psychology and social anthropology have paid a great deal of attention to metaphors. As has been argued by Lakoff and Johnson (1980), metaphors should not be treated as simply rhetorical decorations or conventions of figurative language but rather as keys to people's imagining and reasoning about the world. Some cognitive studies regard metaphors as economic devices – frames or schemas – suitable to grasp quickly divergent or new situations where a non-metaphoric, literal approach would render understanding and reasoning laborious. More socially or culturally inclined authors (for instance, Quinn 1987, and contributions in Fernandez 1991) regard metaphors as linguistic cues to widely shared cultural models. Whereas metaphors can be applied in a deliberate way, as handy devices to think through dilemmas or to shed light on new realities, most of the time they are employed routinely and unconsciously to express commonsense notions.

Although such approaches have helped to give metaphor a more prominent status in cognitive and cultural studies they run the risk of losing sight of the constructive as well as ideological potential of metaphor. Metaphors are not mere windows on or tools to understand a pre-existing reality, but rather they take part in a situated practice of defining reality (see Haste 1993 and Lupton 1994 for recent case studies on the political use of metaphors). In conveying authority to a particular reasoning about reality they discredit or de-emphasize rival interpretations. They thus have a bearing upon social and political reality, including relations of domination and control.

In much crisis discourse about the Gaza Strip we see the elaborate use of a metaphoric construction of politics in which increasing tension or pressure is said to culminate in an explosion. Consider an example from David Grossman's preface to the Dutch translation of his *Yellow Wind* (1988). In this book Grossman, a widely known Israeli journalist and an acclaimed writer, relays his experiences during his journeys in the Occupied Palestinian Territories just before the Intifada began.

> [T]he first stone was thrown in Gaza. ... Emotions and forces which were repressed for twenty years erupted in an explosion of violence. (p. 8, translation TvT)

> In December 1987 the Palestinian uprising started. It was not planned: it was the fruit of prolonged dissatisfaction. The violence suddenly erupted, nourished by years of bitterness and hatred. Not only were the Israelis surprised. For the Arab countries and the PLO the uprising was a surprise as well. Indeed, the Palestinians themselves were surprised. Until that moment they had never dared to make use of the energy which they had bottled up for twenty years without action. (p. 10, translation TvT)

The main metaphors suggest the situation at hand, the beginning of the Intifada, is to be understood through the consecutive stages of built-up 'energy'/'tension' followed by 'eruption'/'explosion'. In the commonsense schema presented here, three conditions seem to influence the explosion's intensity: the repression of tension, the 'prolonged' duration of this repression as emphasized by the repeated mentioning of the occupation's length, and the lack of an opportunity to release the 'bottled-up' tension. The level of tension apparently determines the size of the explosion. Concepts of energy and tension refer to the emotions and unspecified 'forces' of the refugees; concepts of eruption and explosion refer to the resulting violent behaviour.

This reasoning seems primarily based upon ordinary metaphoric thinking about the psychology of anger. Lakoff and Kovecses (1987) have demonstrated how Western discourse tends to understand anger in terms of a central metaphoric construction: 'the heat of a fluid in a container'. Examples are when somebody 'boils over', 'seethes with rage' or 'makes your blood boil'.

Their analysis indirectly suggests why anger metaphors can be effective devices for constructing self–other relations. The metaphor tension–explosion suggests a breakdown of self-control and a loss of rationality that violate a broadly shared set of Western values. Ideally speaking, the expression of anger should be guided by reason, which means that it must be based on a legitimate grief; that other ways should be tried to redress the grief; that when anger is allowed to come out, it should happen in a controlled way, and that it should be directed towards the wrongdoer, and retributive in proportion to the grief (Lakoff and Kovecses 1987).

Apparently, all this does not apply here: the Palestinians simply release their tension; they are even 'surprised' by their own anger. The Intifada appears to lack planning or a meaningful target.

Both literary criticism and the social sciences provide authoritative sources for the reasoning associated with the deviant anger model that is imposed upon the Palestinians. The literary prototype of *ressentiment*, extensively theorized by Nietzsche, has been a common device in Western novels to discredit forms of resistance of the working class or the non-Western Other as being reactive and based on griefs and feelings of envy and hate that can be easily manipulated to suit exterior ends (Jameson 1980). In the social sciences the 'volcanic' model of rebellion or revolution equates collective violence with the 'periodic eruption of social–psychological tensions that boil up in human groups like lava under the earth's crust' (Aya 1979: 14, quoted in Farsoun and Landis 1991: 17). In this model, society is epitomized by the 'mass', the fearful phenomenon which, according to popular psychologies, is not only a threat to the social order but in fact its very negation. In mass society there is 'lurking ... the undefined mass, the anonymous crowd, a formless aggregation of little entities, each isolated from the others' (Moscovici 1990: 70). The individual is nothing but 'a molecule in an expanding gas'. Such a society is prone to explosion.

Social reasoning here easily ties in with the above-mentioned conception of the individual being overpowered by emotions. When society is nothing more than a sum of individuals, it can only reflect the laws of individual behaviour. According to this line of thinking, discontent, if not put into constructive action, transforms itself into madness and hysteria which in their turn are prime sources of criminal individual behaviour or destabilizing mass action when people mindlessly imitate each other's behaviour (a process that Gustave Le Bon, a writer who was particularly instrumental in popularizing mass psychology, called 'contagion'). Isolated from their political context, oppositional violence or resistance can thus be easily dismissed as destructive, senseless and dangerous from a functional point of view.

More generally, these reasonings are informed by the reason-versus-emotion dichotomy that permeates Western discourse. Emotion points to a fearful threat to order: to wildness, chaos, nature, femininity; alternatively, rationality points to control, order, predictability, culture, masculinity. Both person and society are viewed as being physically divided into spheres of rationality and spheres of emotion. This division, and the wish to keep it intact, also seem to inform the metaphors under discussion here. By evoking two domains separated by a physical border vulnerable to penetration – when the tension explodes, the lava erupts, or the hot water flows over – the metaphors graphically construct a fragile boundary in need of protection (van Teeffelen 1994).

By naturalizing 'Others' and making them the object of uncontrollable forces, the energy–tension and eruption–explosion metaphors also downplay human agency. Although it is impossible to discuss linguistic elements other than metaphor in detail here, it should be noted that the example above contains syntactic devices that serve to reinforce the draining of discourse from human agency (Kress and Hodge 1979), especially intransitives ('the violence ... erupted'; 'emotions and forces which were repressed ...') and nominalizations (when processes or actions are represented by nouns, as in the clause 'bitterness and hatred'). They make it easier to suggest that human properties are part of a quasi-physical rather than a moral realm.

Let us move from the linguistic construction of a self–other divide to the ideological implications for the situation described, the Israeli control over the Gaza Strip. In describing a border situation that defies control, the discourse of fear is said to accomplish a double purpose: the justification of suppression and the mobilization of support for the colonizing power (Abu-Lughod and Lutz 1990: 14). It is pertinent here to reflect upon the question of to what extent Grossman, in creating a self–other boundary by emphasizing the Other's deviant expression of anger, in fact exploits such a discourse of fear for ideological ends.

To begin with, those familiar with the journalistic and literary work of Grossman will remark that the example above should be considered in relation to the remainder of the book, and also in the context of the public climate in Israel. Grossman is a journalist who was courageous enough to present the Israeli public with the harsh reality of Palestinian daily life in the Occupied Palestinian Territories before the Intifada started. In the Introduction to the book he asserts that his account of the Occupied Palestinian Territories delivered all the facts needed to understand the emergence of the Intifada. The crisis metaphors served to urge Israel to realize that long-term control over Gaza is untenable.

It may seem paradoxical that Grossman constructs a self–other contrast while at the same time opting for a liberal politics of changing the political *status quo*. Here we arrive at a point of supreme importance for understanding the politics of metaphor, namely, its employment to lend authority to a particular definition of reality as opposed to rival definitions. In other words, political metaphors attain their rhetorical effect within what Billig (1987) calls 'a context of controversy'.

Like many other Israeli liberal writers, Grossman pursues two polemics. He objects to the normalizing discourse practised by the Israeli right, which pretended that the army was in control of the West Bank and Gaza Strip and that the occupation was benevolent in nature. Yet he also warns against a definition of Palestinian reality in terms of curtailed political rights, a definition supported in many liberal Western circles. In addressing a Dutch public Grossman explicitly states that his descriptions of the occupation must not be misunderstood as evidence of support for the Palestinian cause.

The use of the tension and explosion metaphors in crisis discourse serves to effectuate this dual demarcation vis-à-vis normalizing discourse and political rights discourse. On the one hand, the metaphors negate the idea of a normal situation; they ring the bell warning that something may happen. On the other hand, they maintain and even reinforce a self–other divide by casting the reasoning in a mechanistic form. This device creates distance and prevents identification with the victims of the occupation. It does not matter what emotions they have: grief, anger, hatred, or whatever. All emotions are lumped together as potential sources of violence. It is difficult to sympathize with undifferentiated emotions or with people who function in a mechanistic way and are controlled by outside forces; the more so when they internally 'build up tension' and 'explode' at an unpredictable time. You had better get out of their way.

In the Grossman example, the interaction with the other discourses remains implicit. I now turn to other examples to show how the metaphors function when conflict between the rival discourses surfaces in the text, and how the metaphors are used to reframe a definition of the problem from one based on a denial of political rights to one created by a loss of control. At the same time, the new examples render it possible to illustrate some other theoretical issues that inform the politics of metaphor.

'The impulses strike you like waves'

The following passage is from an article in the centre–liberal Hebrew-language paper *Haaretz* by the Israeli writer and journalist Amos Elon, written at a time (1981) that the Gaza Strip did not receive much media attention. He describes the refugee camps:

> [The camps] are the great reservoir of dreams and frustrated hopes, of 'next year in Ashdod' and 'next year in Beer Sheva'. Here the refugees have been hanging, for 33 years, like marionettes in an eternal present. From hand to mouth. And it will go on if alternatives are not set up for them. But none are being prepared. The dense mass accumulates tension, here are the assaults and large explosions, the demonstrations and the executions, the hand grenades and the collective punishments, one sparking off the other. (*Haaretz*, 24 April 1981, translation Israel Shahak)

The main metaphors here – 'marionette', 'reservoir' and the 'dense mass' that accumulates tension and generates explosions – portray the refugees as being completely deprived of human independence and agency. As in the previous example, the Gazans' political actions seem to lack reason, context and direction. After their emotions surface as violence, this violence subsequently becomes self-generative and escalating; one kind of violence 'sparks off' other kinds. How the violence-generating process precisely occurs is not altogether transparent. For instance, it is unclear to which entity the 'dense mass' that stands at the base of the violence exactly refers; it can refer to the 'dreams' and 'frustrated hopes' of the people but also to the high population density of the Gaza Strip.

Two themes in this description are stripped of their potential political significance. The first is the reference to the refugees' wish to return to their birthplaces. While the use of quotes ('next year in …') suggests the presence of an authentic voice, this well-known Palestinian political aim is cast in an adaptation of the Jewish saying 'next year in Jerusalem'. The irony here prevents this longing from being understood as equally legitimate to the Jews' wish to return to Jerusalem; rather, it is rendered inauthentic as a mere imitation. Even more significantly, the will to return is framed not as the fulfilment of a natural right but as an emotional state of frustration that enhances tension and generates explosions.

Another political theme is present in the last sentence, which describes the escalating spiral of violence. In this case all political actions, whether they derive from Palestinians or the Israeli military, and whether they represent legitimate protest ('demonstrations'), illegitimate violence ('executions', 'hand grenades') or oppression ('collective punishment'), are brought under the common denominator of violence 'sparking off' other violence. Thus, opposing political actions are lumped together as quasi-physical elements contributing to the amplification of tension and violence in the way previous examples showed the amalgamation of different emotions.

Other, even more conspicuous, instances of depoliticization concern the refugees' voice.

> You sit with them [Gaza refugees] in their rooms, or in their small coffee houses, listening to their stories. … A house. The fatherland, the family. Independence. Oppression. Israel. Palestine. The impulses strike you like waves and you feel yourself drowning in a bottomless sea, with no shoreline in view. (ibid.)

Again, two physical metaphors appear: the discharge of electricity and the 'drowning' in a deep sea, connected through the double meaning of 'wave'. The first one describes the source of the tension; the second the loss of control due to physical shock. In the drowning metaphor, the water is without bottom and shore: in other words, without container. Elon's domain of rational observation here seems to collapse under the pressure of the inhabitants' emotional voices, which are represented as 'impulses' by way of one-word sentences. No information is provided about the source or the details of the utterances, or the particularity of the experience. Even the words are interchangeable. Brought forward in this way, they seem to be imitations of slogans or propaganda. Being thus stripped of credibility and authenticity, the utterances are appropriated in the metaphoric model to constitute the base material for striking waves. Obviously, utterances which 'strike you like waves' are not particularly conducive to reflection or dialogue.

'The fundamental causes of the unrest'

One of the particularities of Elon's metaphors is that the Gazans are primarily described as victims of outside forces. (Incidentally, their victimization contains an ironic note through the implicit use of the Christ metaphor when Gazans are said to be 'hanging' for thirty-three years). The Gazans are not a prime target of blame. It is indeed illogical to attribute blame to people who are presumably governed by mechanical forces. In fact, the explanations evoked by such crisis discourse usually pass beyond the refugees' apparently ephemeral intentions to reflect upon the 'real' causes of the unrest. Many explanations for the appearance of the Intifada in the Gaza Strip concentrate upon circumstantial or background factors which are said to determine the Gazans' response to the occupation. The next passage, which delineates one set of such background factors, is taken from an article by the prominent military correspondent of *Haaretz*, Zeev Schiff. He is writing at the beginning of the Intifada, when crisis discourse about the West Bank and the Gaza Strip permeated the Israeli media. Schiff provides alarming predictions about the population increase in the Gaza Strip. Like Elon and Grossman, he warns that in the long term the situation in the Gaza Strip will get out of hand. The article carries the headline 'A human time bomb'.

> The worst prediction concerns the population. ... Within some 12 years up to the year 2000 the population of the Strip will increase by about 50%. [Details about the numbers follow]
>
> In this human sea and in the area which is contained in a narrow strip, whose length is 45 km and whose breadth is between 5.5 and 12.5 km, there also exists a group of Jewish settlers. Their number is 2,500 only, and this includes 150 Yeshiva [religious] students, all together 0.4% of all the inhabitants. [Details about their numbers]. ... those settlers have already received 28% of the state lands of the Gaza Strip, although it is clear that the human density in the Strip and the lack of land reserves will cause a future population explosion. (*Haaretz*, 13 December 1987, translation Israel Shahak)

Instead of the semi-literary discourse of the Elon example, here we meet a discourse that derives its authority from a rhetoric of science. Among other things, an effect of objectivity is created by the many figures which suggest the facts and reasoning to be part of a perspective that takes distance from the immediate situation at hand. The metaphoric schema triggered by the expressions 'human time bomb' and 'population explosion' suggest the projected future size of the population of the Gaza Strip to be a threat to social order and control. Note that the attention paid to the population size coincides with a flat homogenization of the Palestinians, who are described in terms of 'human density' and a 'human sea ... contained in a narrow strip'.

The references to the size of the population, to the small area of the Gaza Strip that must sustain such a large population, and to the 'human time bomb' or 'population explosion' jointly provide a clue to the reasoning elicited here. A growing population size combined with a small 'container', namely, the small area of the Gaza Strip, enhances tension. It thus creates a human time bomb, and carries the risk of future explosion. The schema resembles the use of the metaphor of explosion in previous examples except that the demographic element replaces the emotional state of the people. The commonsense theory applied here seems to contain an economic component: the smaller the area, the more doubtful the economic possibility of sustaining a rapid population increase.

As in other examples, this definition of the problem is depoliticized to the extent that other conditions than the occupation constitute the central matter of concern. Schiff's criticism of Israeli policies does not pertain to the dispossession of land, or the right to settle in occupied territory, but to the fact that the settlers occupy sparse land in the Gaza Strip and thus increase population pressure.

The population density in the Gaza Strip plays a prominent part in other, more general observations. The following passage is from an article that relays the experiences of Salomon Bouman, the correspondent in Israel for the Dutch mainstream 'quality' newspaper *NRC-Handelsblad*, on a visit to the Gaza Strip at the beginning of the Intifada. In the article he describes the opinions of Palestinians by way of short quotes. Naturally, his sources strongly object to Israeli repressive measures, to the privileged position of Jewish settlers and to the occupation in general.

> 'It is quite possible that the situation in the Gaza Strip will calm down after two or three days. Until the next explosion, which will be greater than the one now,' says a young Palestinian in Jabalya. 'We want peace. Honourable peace with Israel,' he continues. 'But if 2,500 Jewish colonists in the Gaza Strip grab 40 per cent of the best land there is no possibility for such a peace.'

After the Palestinians' accounts, the journalist goes on to provide his own explanation of the origin of the Intifada in the Gaza Strip.

> The fundamental causes of the unrest in the Gaza Strip, whose intensity yesterday diminished, are pushed to the background by the rising emotions.
>
> Overpopulation, bad hygiene in the large refugee camps, exploitation by the Israeli labour market and the lack of perspective for a political solution, and thus the occupation's continuation and the resulting infringement on rights, have made the Gaza Strip into a Palestinian powder keg in the Middle East.
>
> At the end of this century a million Palestinians will live in the Gaza Strip, 80% of whom will have been born under Israeli occupation.
>
> Whatever the political or sociological definition of the current explosion may be, it is a signal to Israel that a political solution cannot wait much longer.
> (*NRC-Handelsblad*, 17 December 1987, translation TvT)

Bouman couches his account in objective and scientific rhetoric by speaking about the 'political or sociological definition' of the unrest and about its 'more fundamental causes'. The situation is framed in terms of a causal schema of circumstances or background factors which apparently determine the refugees' attitudes and behaviour. The factors are listed without indication of their relative importance, or of how they mutually relate or precisely impinge upon the uprising. A general category of what can be called 'adverse circumstances' is constructed, similar to the way that previous examples constructed undifferentiated categories of people's emotions, behaviour and voices. Taken in a broader context, his account is reminiscent of traditional descriptions of the city-slum in (historical) Europe or in Third World countries as being completely conditioned by environmental factors such as overcrowding, poverty and bad hygiene.

Overpopulation is put at the head of the order and is the only factor to be elaborated. Conversely, the political situation seems to be less important and is set at the end of the summary. The overall reasoning, characteristic of many Israeli and Western articles on Gaza, points to the adverse circumstances as the fundamental determining influence, to the 'rising' emotions as the intervening factor, and to the explosion as the outcome.

The Bouman example is perhaps especially interesting because it shows the limits of a static and decontextualized interpretation of metaphor (see Lee 1992: 3, for a note of caution on this point in his analysis of similar metaphors in press reports of oppositional actions in South Africa during apartheid). It may look surprising that the Palestinian source quoted him/herself speaks about the danger of new explosions to come. Assuming the quote is a verbatim account of the speaker's words, the speaker seems to legitimize a dehumanizing discourse to interpret the situation of Gaza.

In itself it is not a particularly strange phenomenon that people employ a political discourse that embodies a viewpoint different from their own. The classic model to explain this is the attribution of a false or alienated consciousness which reflects the influence of ideology as disseminated through the mass media. However, in this case it makes more sense to assume that the Palestinian appropriates the metaphors for well-considered reasons. In the first place, contrary to the Israeli accounts, crisis discourse is here paired to a political discourse based on human rights, despite the fact that both discourses are historically at odds with each other. Rather than taking for granted that people can only mould their opinions in an ideologically coherent manner, it is a reasonable assumption that speakers also make use of divergent and even conflicting ideological resources. In this context Wetherell and Potter (1992) speak about the 'patchwork' of interpretive repertoires which stand at people's disposition when they argue about a social issue. Moreover, it is also quite common to turn particular metaphors against their original users. Especially since the start of the Israeli–Palestinian negotiations, Palestinian diplomatic discourse has been marked by the repeated use of crisis metaphors in relation to the Israeli presence in the Occupied Palestinian Territories, as when settlements are called 'time bombs' to underline the urgency of Israeli withdrawal.

In addition, by adopting the metaphor of explosion, the Gazan spokesperson rhetorically creates a distanced viewpoint towards the Gazan people potentially involved in the violence. This bolsters his or her credibility as a privileged observer of the crisis. The speaker conveys a warning on behalf of the Gazans which the Western journalist is supposed to transmit to the West. Yet of course this speaker does not have the final say. While quoting a Palestinian spokesperson and momentarily granting the Palestinian the role of knowledgable interpreter, Bouman subsequently disempowers the voice by considering it too 'emotional' for an objective analysis of the situation. By liberally granting speaker rights to the 'other', even though only in order to be superseded by the journalist's opinion, crisis discourse is imputed here with a credibility-enhancing maturity (McKenzie and van Teeffelen 1993).

Conclusion

This discourse analysis suggests a couple of interrelated conclusions which may have a broader significance for understanding Western images of the Other. In the first place, crisis metaphors such as tension–explosion impose homogeneous and decontextualized images of person and society on a population that is presented as being without agency. The images are informed by a wide array of commonsense reasonings which have an authoritative base in social psychology, sociology and literature, and can therefore be adapted to fit both an objective or a scientific rhetoric as well as a more literary style of presentation. A basic schema is the understanding of political action in the form of stages: a preparatory stage in which emotions are gradually intensified due to background circumstances, the stage of explosion or overflowing, and the stage of escalation when violence becomes self-generating ('cycle of violence').

This schema is open to several elaborations. For instance, the Islamic religion is often regarded as a conduit that intensifies emotions and precipitates an explosion. Said (1981) quotes an article by the historian Michael Walzer which is entitled 'The Islam explosion'. In recent reports of the situation in the Gaza Strip, the religious movement Hamas is often said to make use of Islam to 'stir' the feelings of refugees. Other elaborations have been found in a study of Western popular fiction (van Teeffelen 1992; in press). Here the schema includes a dangerous (atomic) weapon and a conspiring leader who makes use of the explosive energy of individual terrorists or Islamic masses in order to pursue narrow or partisan interests. Also, the amplification stage of the process is elaborated to suggest a Western world at the brink of disaster. Such accounts were mirrored in media discourse during the Gulf War of 1990–91, when the Palestinians in the Occupied Territories and elsewhere were described as forming a rising 'mass' of emotions that could be exploited by Saddam Hussein. The inclusion into the schema of a conspiring leader or religious conduit allows blame for the violence to be attributed to a responsible source other than the occupation. In providing an agentless and dehumanized image of the West's others, the metaphors suggest people to be either extremely passive (the first stage) or extremely active (the second stage). This reflects the familiar stereotypes of Palestinians as refugees and terrorists.

Yet it is important also to recognize the flexibility of the schema. Not only does the parent frame allow for a great many variations, but it may also be the case that the context imputes different meanings to the same metaphor. Metaphors can serve divergent political functions in different contexts of controversy; their meaning is negotiable and never exactly the same. Despite their schematic nature, they may be appropriated to make a deviant argumentative point, as in the Bouman quotation.

Finally, an historical dimension can be introduced into the analysis by viewing the metaphors as functioning within a particular discourse, in this case the discourse of crisis or fear. In the Israeli discussion, crisis discourse was for a long time countered by other discourses which posed the possibility of control over the West Bank and the Gaza Strip, whether by the improvement of life through social engineering, or by the direct establishment of control by way of military repression or prevention. For the mainstream in Israeli politics and public opinion, these alternative discourses proved to be untenable. Gaza was abandoned and handed over to the PLO police and army. It is interesting, however, that the Gaza–Jericho solution still frames the problem in terms that are strongly reminiscent of the crisis discourse outlined above. Even in a mainstream Palestinian understanding, the Israeli withdrawal from Gaza can hardly be viewed as a fulfilment of the right to national self-determination. Predominant Israeli interpretations of the Gaza–Jericho agreement, which have strong international backing, put less emphasis on the question of political rights but instead foreground two factors that in general figure prominently in Israeli and Western crisis thinking on Middle Eastern politics: the military preservation of order and control, and economic and infrastructural development for dealing with adverse background circumstances to diminish the influence of the Islamic movement. In this view, the PLO's credibility hinges on its ability to meet the traditional concern of crisis discourse; namely, how to reinstate control over Gaza.

Acknowledgement

The theoretical part of this analysis draws from the findings of PhD research conducted in the programme of Discourse Analysis of the University of Amsterdam on the portrayal of the Israeli–Arab conflict in Western best-selling fiction. This research has been facilitated by a grant from the Netherlands Organization for Scientific Research (NWO).

References

Abu-Lughod, L. and C. Lutz 1990 'Introduction: emotion, discourse, and the politics of everyday life', in C. Lutz and L. Abu-Lughod (eds) *Language and the Politics of Emotion* Cambridge, Cambridge University Press.

Aya, R. 1979 'Theories of revolution reconsidered: contrasting models of collective violence', *Theory and Society* 8.

Billig, M. 1987 *Arguing and Thinking: Essays in Rhetorical Psychology* Newbury, Sage.

Farsoun, S.K. and J.M. Landis 1991 'The sociology of an uprising: the roots of the *intifada*', in J.R. Nassar and R. Heacock (eds) *Intifada: Palestine at the Crossroads* New York and Birzeit, Praeger and Birzeit University.

Fernandez, J.W. (ed.) 1991 *Beyond Metaphor: The Theory of Tropes in Anthropology* Stanford, Stanford University.

Grossman, D. 1988 *Over de Grens: Zoeklicht op de Westelijke Jordaanoever* (Beyond the Border: Focus on the West Bank) Utrecht/Antwerpen, Veen.

Haste, H. 1993 *The Sexual Metaphor* Harvester Wheatsheaf, Hemel Hempstead.

Jameson, F. 1980 *The Political Unconsciousness: Narrative as a Socially Symbolic Act* London, Methuen.

Kress, G. and R. Hodge 1979 *Language as Ideology* London, Routledge and Kegan Paul.

Lakoff, G. and M. Johnson 1980 *Metaphors We Live By* Chicago, University of Chicago Press.

Lakoff, G. and Z. Kovecses 1987 'The cognitive model of anger inherent in American English', in D. Holland and N. Quinn (eds) *Cultural Models in Language and Thought* Cambridge, Cambridge University Press.

Lee, D. 1992 *Competing Discourses: Perspective and Ideology in Language* London, Longman.

Lupton, D. 1994 *Moral Threats and Dangerous Desires: AIDS in the News Media* London, Taylor and Francis.

McKenzie, K. and T. van Teeffelen 1993 'Transcending the higher ground between Europe and Middle East', *Pragmatics* 5(3).

Moscovici, S. 1990 'The generalized self and mass society', in: H.T. Himmelweit and G. Gaskell (eds) *Societal Psychology* Hillsdale NJ, Sage.

Quinn, N. 1987 'Convergent evidence for a cultural model of American marriage', in D. Holland and N. Quinn (eds) *Cultural Models in Language and Thought* Cambridge, Cambridge University Press.

Said, E.W. 1981 *Covering Islam: How the Media and the Experts Determine How We See the Rest of the World* New York, Pantheon.

van Teeffelen, T. 1992 'Understanding political action as a script or a project: the representation of Palestinians in popular literature', *Journal of Narrative and Life History* 2(2).

van Teeffelen, T. 1994 'Racism and metaphor: the Palestinian-Israeli conflict in popular literature' *Discourse and Society* 5(3).

van Teeffelen, T. (in press) 'Popular fiction and Palestine', in A. Moors, T. van Teeffelen, I. Abou Ghazaleh and S. Kanaana (eds) *Discourse and Palestine* Amsterdam, Het Spinhuis.

Wetherell, M. and J. Potter 1992 *Mapping the Language of Racism: Discourse and the Legitimation of Exploitation* New York, Harvester/Wheatsheaf.

PART TWO

Imaginaries of cultural pluralism

8

'Mixed-bloods' and the cultural politics of European identity in colonial Southeast Asia

Ann Stoler

In contemporary Europe and the USA, students of postmodern society have identified the 'new racism' as a novel and nuanced phenomenon in which cultural markers are seen to replace the bolder physiological distinctions on which earlier racisms had so strongly relied (Hall 1980; Gilroy 1987; Barker 1981). The most compelling analyses of France's new racism are those that address its internal logic rather than dismiss its illiberalism out of hand. Pierre-André Taguieff, for one, points to the ability of the ultra-conservative National Front to harness widely shared popular feelings by linking specific cultural identities to human natures (Taguieff 1989). Le Pen's rhetoric positions immigrant groups as the 'foreign enemy within' with images of purity, cleanliness and contamination distinguishing the genuine 'French French' from their sullied psuedo-compatriots.

In England, cultural critics such as Paul Gilroy (1987: 43) argue that the 'novelty' of the new racism

> ... lies in the capacity to link discourses of patriotism, nationalism, xenophobia, Englishness, Britishness, militarism, and gender differences into a complex system which gives 'race' its contemporary meaning. These themes combine to provide a definition of 'race' in terms of culture and identity. ... 'Race' differences are displayed in culture which is reproduced in educational institutions and, above all, in family life. Families are therefore not only the nation in microcosm, its key components, but act as the means to turn social processes into natural, instinctive ones.

These formulations are surprising. Not because they do not make sense of what comprises racist thinking today, but because these 'new' braidings of race and culture are so resonant with earlier forms. Are these descriptions of the new racism meant to suggest that an earlier 'pure racism' once stood firmly on the belief in somatic difference and biology alone? Or that racist practice in its heightened form was not rooted in family life, identity politics, and gendered discriminations, but simply in race? Racisms have never existed in 'pure form'. As I argue here, they have always been 'displayed in culture', constituted through the management of sexuality and built upon a pyschology and politics of contamination that pervaded the home.

This chapter examines the importance of colonial regimes for under-standing the new cultural constructions of citizenship and national identity that emerged in late-nineteenth-century European nation-states. My claim is that these emergent constructions turned on two conflicting social agenda that placed discussions of parenting styles, domestic arrangements and sexual morality at their core. On one hand, the turn of the century was marked by a new liberal impulse for social welfare, humanitarianism and political representation. This was embodied in an inclusionary rhetoric, captured in the notion of a 'civilizing mission' directed at the educative transformation of both Europe's labouring poor and its colonized subjects. On the other hand, this period produced a newly refined set of ex-clusionary, discriminatory cultural practices that were written into the implementation of liberal reform. By focusing on those people who ambiguously straddled, crossed and threatened the divide marking colon-ized from colonizer, and subject from citizen, I explore how gender and class prescriptions shaped the family politics of citizenship and the cultural construction of race.[1]

I begin with a story about *métissage* (interracial unions) and the sorts of progeny to which it gave rise ('*métis*', 'mixed-bloods') in French Indochina at the turn of the century. It is a story whose multiple versions are about people whose cultural sensibilities, physical being, and political sentiments called into question the distinctions of difference that maintained the neat boundaries of colonial rule. Its plot and resolution reinforce the treatment of European nationalist impulses and colonial racist policies as inter-connected projects, since here it was in the conflation of racial category, sexual morality, cultural competence and national identity that the case was contested and politically charged. More broadly, it allows me to address one of the tensions of empire which this chapter only begins to sketch: between the rhetorics of inclusion (as in the Dutch 'Ethical Policy' of the turn of the century) and those exclusionary practices that were reactive to, coexistent with, and perhaps inherent in liberalism itself (see Mehta 1990).

Nowhere is this relationship between inclusionary impulses and ex-clusionary practices more evident than in the ways in which *métissage* was legally handled, culturally inscribed and politically treated in the contrasting colonial cultures of French Indochina and the Netherlands Indies. French Indochina was a colony of commerce, occupied by the military in the 1860s, settled by *colons* in the 1870s with a *métis* population which numbered no more than several hundred by the turn of the century.[2] The Netherlands Indies, by contrast, had been settled since the early 1600s; those of mixed descent or born in the Indies numbered in the tens of thousands by 1900, making up nearly three-quarters of those legally designated as European. Their Indies mestizo culture shaped the contours of this colonial society for its first two hundred years (Taylor 1983).

What is striking is that similar discourses were mapped onto such vastly different racial and political landscapes; that in both the Indies and Indochina, with their distinct demographics and internal rhythms, *métissage* was a focal point of political, legal and social debate, conceived as a dangerous source of subversion, a threat to white prestige, an embodiment of *European* degeneration and moral decay (Stoler 1991). I would suggest that both were so charged in part because such 'mixing' called into question the very criteria by which 'Europeanness' could be identified, citizenship should be accorded and nationality assigned. *Métissage* represented the dangers of foreign enemies not only at external national borders, but the more pressing affront for European nation-states, what the German philosopher Fichte so aptly defined as the essence of the nation, its 'interior frontiers' (Balibar 1991).

The concept of an 'interior frontier' is compelling precisely because of the contradictory connotations it implies. As Etienne Balibar has noted, a frontier locates a site of both enclosure and of contact, of surveilled passage and exchange. Coupled with the word 'interior', 'frontier' carries the sense of internal distinctions within a territory (or empire); at the level of the individual, it marks the moral predicates by which a subject retains her/his national identity despite location (outside the national frontier) and despite heterogeneity within the nation-state. For Fichte, an 'interior frontier' raised two problematics: that the 'purity' of the community was prone to penetration on its interior and exterior borders, and that the essence of the community was an intangible 'moral attitude', 'a multiplicity of invisible ties' (Fichte, quoted in Balibar 1991: 4). When we view late-nineteenth-century representations of a 'national essence' in these terms, *métissage* emerges as a powerful trope for internal contamination and challenge, morally, politically, and sexually conceived. Discussions of *métissage* trace the fault lines of colonial authority; in linking domestic arrangements to the public order, family to the state, sex to subversion, and national essence to racial type, it might be read as a metonynm for the biopolitics of empire at large.

In both Indochina and the Netherlands Indies, the rejection of *métis* as a distinct legal category only intensified how the politics of cultural difference were played out in other domains. In both colonies, the *métis/'indo'* problem produced a discourse in which facile theories of racial hierarchy were rejected, while the practical predicates of European superiority were confirmed at the same time. While the early Vietnamese and Indonesian nationalist movements created new sources of colonial vulnerability, the particular form that the securing of European privilege took was not shaped in the colonies alone.[3] The focus on moral unity, cultural genealogy and language joined the imagining of European colonial communities and metropolitan national entities in fundamental ways. Both visions embraced a moral rearmament, centring on the domestic domain and the family, as sites where state authority could be secured or irreparably undermined.

In both metropole and colony, the liberal impulse for social welfare, representation and protective legislation at the turn of the century focused enormous energy on domestic arrangements, sexual morality, parenting and more specifically the moral environments in which children lived

(Stuurman 1987; Fuchs 1984; Davin 1978). Education and upbringing were national projects, but not as we might expect, with a firm sense of national identity imported to the periphery from the metropolitan core. As Eugene Weber reminds us, in late-nineteenth-century France, 'patriotic feelings on the national level, far from instinctive, had to be learned' (1976: 114). Between 1871 and 1914, the French authorities were preoccupied with the threat of national diminishment and decline – external and interior frontiers were in question at home and abroad (Girardet 1983: 30), while the study of national character was a 'veritable industry in France' (Nye 1984: 140). France's declining natality, which accelerated in the 1880s, placed a premium on state strategies that would allow a wider membership in the French national community while protecting the cultural contours of what it meant to be French (Moses 1984: 20; Romein 1978: 6).

In the Netherlands, domestic and colonial anxieties over Dutch identity came together in a civilizing mission of social reform and a moral crusade for responsible citizenship, targeting the 'dangerous classes' in both locales – Holland's 'residuum' poor, and the Indies' impoverished whites, the majority of whom were Indo-European (De Regt 1982). While national anxieties were not at the same pitch as in France, there is evidence that at the turn of the century 'Dutch national feeling underwent something of a revival' (Schoffer 1978: 80). The domestic 'moralizing offensive' of the late nineteenth century, followed by the Boer War and a campaign for a 'Greater Netherlands' (embracing Flanders, South Africa and the Indies) make it clear that questions of national identity, family welfare and education were on the public agenda and intimately tied (Righart 1986: 195; Kuitenbrouwer 1985: 176). Thus the question of who might be considered 'truly' French or Dutch resonated from core to colony and from colony to core. In the Indies and Indochina, it was cultural milieu, both upbringing and education, that were seen to demarcate which *métis* children would turn into revolutionaries, patricides, loyal subjects or full-fledged citizens of the nation-state.

Cultural competence and *métissage*

In 1898, in the French Indochinese city of Haiphong, the nineteen-year-old son of a French minor naval employee, Sieur Icard, allegedly without provocation assaulted a German naval mechanic, struck his temple with a whip, attempted to crush his eye, and was sentenced by the tribunal court to six months in prison.[4] Spurred by the father's efforts to appeal for an attenuated prison term, some higher officials subsequently questioned whether the penalty was unduly severe. Clemency was not accorded by the Governor General and the boy, referred to by the court as 'Nguyen van Thinh *dit* Lucien' (called Lucien) was sentenced to serve out his full term. The apeal might have been less easily dismissed had the son not been *métis* (Eurasian), the child of a man who was a French citizen and a woman who was a colonial subject, his concubine and Vietnamese.

The ways in which the boy was referred to in the exchange of letters and reports between the Governor General, the father and the court imparted very different evaluations of his cultural identity, giving substance to their separate claims. For the Governor General, the boy was 'Nguyen van Thinh *dit* Lucien' (thereby invoking not only the double naming of the son, privileging first Nguyen van Thinh over Lucien, but suggesting the dubious nature of his cultural affinities – his *real* name was Nguyen van Thinh, although he answered to the name 'Lucien'). For the father, Icard, the boy was simply 'Lucien', (Nguyen van Thinh erased, thereby affirming the Frenchness of his son); and to an angry president of Haiphong's tribunal court, the boy was only 'Nguyen van Thinh' with Lucien dropping out altogether. Icard was named as his 'alleged father', a term putting the very kinship between the two in question.

Icard's plea for pardon was carefully conceived, invoking his own patriotic sentiments as well as those of his son. He protested that the tribunal had wrongly treated his son as a 'common Annamite' rather than as what he was: the legally recognized son a Frenchman who had been raised in a patriotic French household where Germans were held in 'contempt and disdain'. Icard emphasized that their home was full of drawings of the 1870 Franco–Prussian war and that like any impressionable [read 'French'] boy of his age, Lucien was intrigued and excited by these images.

The tribunal in its refusal to accept the appeal confronted and countered Icard's claims. At issue was whether Nguyen van Thinh *dit* Lucien could really be considered culturally and politically French, and whether he was sufficiently inculcated with the patriotic feelings and nationalist sentiments that might provoke a loyal French response. The tribunal argued that Icard was sailing too much of the time to impart such a love of *patrie* to his son, and that Icard's 'hate of Germans must have been of very recent origin, since he had spent so much time sailing with foreigners.' Furthermore, Lucien was illiterate and only knew a few words in French; since Icard himself 'spoke no Annamite', he had no language in common with his offspring.

While these counter-arguments may have been sufficient to convince the Governor General not to grant leniency, another vague but damning reason was invoked to deny the son's case and the father's appeal: namely, that 'immoral relations ... could have existed between the detainee and the one who declared himself his father'. Or, as put by the City Attorney in Haiphong charged with investigating Icard's appeal, the boy deserved no leniency because, first, 'his morality was always deplorable' and, second, the police reports permitted one 'to entertain the most serious suspicions concerning the nature of the relations which Nguyen van Thinh maintained with his alleged father'.[5]

Whether this was a coded allegation of homosexuality or a reference to a possibly illegal recognition of the boy by Icard (pretending to be his father) is unclear. Icard's case came up at a time when acts of 'fraudulent recognition' of native children were said to be swelling the French citizenry with a bastard population of native poor (Abor 1917: 25). What is clear is that immorality and nationalist sentiments were considered mutually exclusive categories. As in nineteenth-century Germany, adherence to a middle-class European sexual morality was one implicit requisite for full-fledged citizenship in the European nation-state (Mosse 1985).

But notwithstanding all these allusions to suspicious and duplicitous behaviour perhaps what was more unsettling in this case was another unspeakable story: namely, the power of the sentiment between father and son, the fact that Icard not only recognized his Eurasian son, but went so far as to plead the case of a boy who had virtually none of the exterior qualities (skin tone, language or cultural literacy) of being French – and therefore could have none at all of the interior qualities. What was scandalous and immoral in their relationship was that Icard could have shown such dedication and love for a child who was illiterate, ignorant of the French language, and spent most of his time in a cultural milieu that was much less French than Vietnamese. Under such circumstances, Icard's concern for Lucien was inappropriate and improper. Paternal love and responsibility were not to be disseminated arbitrarily as Icard had obviously done by recognizing his progeny but allowing him to grow up Indochinese. In denying the father's plea, sentence was passed both on the son and on Icard. Both were guilty of transgressing the boundaries of race, culture, morality and *patrie*. If Icard (whose penmanship, misspellings and profession belied his lower-class origins) was unable to raise his son in a proper French milieu, then, the court implied, he should have abandoned him altogether.

Métis children, native mothers and the racial politics of abandonment

The story invokes the multiple tensions of colonial cultures in Southeast Asia and would be of interest for that alone. But it is all the more startling because it so boldly contradicts the dominant formulation of the '*métis* question' at the turn of the century as a problem of 'abandonment', of children culturally on the loose, sexually abused, economically impoverished, morally neglected, and politically dangerous. The consequences of mixed unions were collapsed into a singular moral trajectory which, without state intervention, would lead to a future of Eurasian paupers and prostitutes – an affront to European prestige and a source of national decay.

If we look more closely at what was identified as 'abandonment' – and by whom – the cultural and historical peculiarities of this definition became more apparent. 'Abandonment' had several distinct meanings that diverged significantly from its European usage in the premodern period and at that time. In contrast to John Boswell's definition of abandonment as 'the *voluntary* relinquishing of control over children by their natal parents or guardians', in the colonies abandonment was not necessarily *voluntary*, nor participated in by *both* parents as Boswell implies (1988: 24). Second, whilst child abandonment in Europe was explicitly, though not always, associated with infanticide and child mortality, by contrast the colonial discourse rarely raises this concern, or addresses such an eventuality even obliquely.[6]

Social reform and moral debates over abandonment were about a specific class of children: primarily those of mixed-race unions between native women and European men who were either unable to afford or unwilling to raise their offspring in a European milieu. In this colonial context, the abandonment of *métis* children invoked a *social* death, not a biological one – a loss to European society, a forced banishment from the European cultural milieu in which these *métis* children could potentially thrive. 'Exposure' in the colonial context was not to the natural elements, but to the native milieu, and to that kind of native women whose debased character would have inclined them to succumb to a concubinary relationship in the first place.

If abandonment of *métis* offspring by European men was considered morally reprehensible, what was worse were the depraved motives of colonized women who categorically refused under any circumstances to give up their children to the superior environment of state institutions. Thus the president of the Hanoi Society for the Protection of Métis Youths noted in 1904 that 'numerous mothers refuse to confer their children to us ... under the *pretext* of not wanting to be apart from them, despite the fact that they may periodically visit them at school.'[7] But if maternal love obscured more mercenary quests to exploit their young for profits and pleasure, as was oftem claimed, why did so many women not only refuse to give up their children but reject any form of financial assistance for them?[8]

The portrait of abandonment and charitable rescue is seriously flawed; it misses the fact that the channelling of these children into special state institutions was part of a larger (but failed) imperial vision. These children were to be shaped into very special colonial citizens; according to one scenario, the bulwark of a future white settler population, acclimatized to the tropics but loyal to the state. As stated by the 1931 French Feminist National Assembly, if *métisse* young women were rescued in time, they could be educated in special institutions to become 'bonnes ménagères' (good housekeepers) of a settled Indochina, wives or domestics in the service of France (Etats-Généraux du Féminisme 1931: 139). While such proposals were never realized in the Indies or Indochina, the questions they entertained were as fundamental to colonial thinking as those reforms, such as the campaign against concubinage, that met with more success. What to do with this mixed population whose ambiguous positioning and identifications could make them either dangerous adversaries or effective partisans of the state was a pivotal question for the colonial project overall.

'Fraudulent recognitions' and other dangers of *métissage*

The question prompted a number of different responses, each of which hinged on whether *métis* should be classified as a distinct legal category subject to special education, or so thoroughly assimilated into French culture that they would pose no threat. In French Indochina, the model treatment of the Indo-European population in the Netherlands Indies was invoked at every turn. Reporting on a fact-finding trip to Java in 1901, Joseph Chailley-Bert, director of the *Union Colonial Française*, was immensely impressed and urged the government to adopt several Dutch practices among which that abandoned *métis* youth be assigned European status until proof of filiation was made, and that European standing should not be confined to those with the proper 'dosage of blood' alone.[9]

What is so curious about this and other appeals to Dutch wisdom is how little these accorded with conditions on the ground. At precisely the moment of Chailley-Bert's visit, a massive government investigation of European pauperism was under way, detailing the precarious economic conditions and political dangers of a population legally classified 'European' that was riddled with impoverished widows, indigent ex-soldiers, beggars, vagrants, and abandoned children most of whom were Indo-European. The investigating Pauperism Commission identified an 'alarming increase' of poor Europeans, born in the Indies or of mixed parentage, who could neither compete for civil service positions against the influx of 'full-blooded' Dutch educated in Europe nor against members of the native population who were willing to work for lower pay in the same jobs (*Rapport der Pauperisme-Commissie* 1902). Among the more than 70,000 Europeans in the Indies in 1900, nearly 70 per cent knew little Dutch or none at all (Veur 1968: 45).

The causes of the situation were found in the continued prevalence of concubinage not only among subaltern European military barred from legal marriage, but also among the more comfortable class of civil servants and European plantation personnel for whom marriage to European women was made an economically difficult option (Stoler 1991). Condemning the moral environment of Indies society, the Pauperism Commission targeted concubinage as the source of a transient 'rough' and 'dangerous pauper element' who lived off the native population, disgraced European prestige, and posed a financial burden to the state (*Encyclopedie van Nederlandsch-Indie 1919*: 367).

But Indo-European pauperism in the Indies was seen to derive from even more disturbing problems than inadequate education and sexual immorality. It was also attributed to a surreptious penetration of 'natives' into the legal category of 'European' (Kohlbrugge 1901: 26–8). Because European standing exempted men both from labour service and from the harsher penal code applied to those of native status, officials alleged that an underclass of European soldiers and civilians were engaged in a profitable racket: 'falsely recognizing' native children who were not their own for an attractive fee. The Pauperism Commission, among others, held that European impoverishment was far less widespread than the statistics indicated; not least because the European civil registers were inflated by lowlife mercenaries and, as in Indochina, by 'des sans-travail', who might register as many as thirty to forty children as their own. Among them were not only those of mixed descent, but also 'full-blooded natives' with no proper rights to Dutch or French citizenship at all (N.A. 1892: 8; *Rapport der Pauperisme Commissie* 1902; Koster 1922).

The discourse on 'fraudulent recognition' hinged on several related fears: that a lower class of European men were willing to facilitate the efforts of native mothers who sought such arrangements; and that children were being raised in cultural fashions that blurred the distinctions between ruler and ruled. Whether there were as many 'fraudulent recognitions' of *métis* children in Indochina, or '*kunstmatig gefabriceerde Europeanen*' ('artifically fabricated Europeans') in the Indies as was claimed, is really not the point. The repeated reference to 'fictitious', 'fraudulent', and 'fabricated' Europeans expressed an underlying preoccupation of the colonial authorities, shared by many in the European community as well; that illicit incursions into the Dutch and French citizenry were far more pervasive than those cases labelled as such would suggest. We should remember that the condemnation of 'Nguyen van Thinh *dit* Lucien' was never explicitly argued on the basis of his suspicious parentage, but instead on the more general basis that his behaviour had to be understood as that of a *indigène* in disguise, rather than of a citizen of France.

Colonial officials wrestled with their belief that the Europeanness of *métis* children could never be assured, despite a rhetoric affirming that education and upbringing were transformative processes. Social reforms might refer to abandoned *métisse* daughters as '*les filles françaises*' when arguing for their redemption, or alternately, by those who supported segregated education, as 'the fruits of a regrettable weakness' (Mazet 1932); youths were described as physically marked and morally marred with 'the faults and mediocre qualities of their [native] mothers' (Douchet 1928). Such children represented not only the sexual excesses and indiscretions of European men, but also the dangers of a subaltern class 'lacking paternal discipline' – of a world in which mothers took charge (Kohlbrugge 1901: 23). *Métis* children undermined the inherent principles upon which national identity thrived – those 'invisible bonds' that all *men* shared and that so clearly and comfortably marked off *pur sang*, French and Dutch, from those of the generic colonized.

The rejection of *métis* as a legal category, on the explicit grounds that it would infest the colonies with a 'destructive virus', in no way diminished the concern about them (Mazet 1932: 37, 42). On the contrary, it produced an intensified discourse in which cultural markers of racial difference were to be more finely honed and carefully defined. French citizenship was never open to all *métis*, but granted only after a scientific and moral investigation proved that the child was '*non-indigène*' (Mazet 1932: 90). As we have seen in the case of 'Nyugen van Thinh *dit* Lucien', the name 'Lucien', the paternity acknowledged by Icard, and the patriotic ambiance of the household were sufficient only for the child to be legally classified as French, not for him to be treated as French by a court of law.

Inclusionary laws had written into them an implementation based on exclusionary principles and practices.

The moral outrage against abandonment was related to another underlying dilemma: how to educate *métis* youths to feel French without fostering the desire for privileges above their station simply because French or Dutch blood flowed in their veins. The aim of the Hanoi Society for the protection of Métis Youths was 'to inculcate them with our sense of honour and integrity, while only suggesting to them modest tastes and humble aspirations'.[10]

Similarly, in the Indies, Indo-European pauperism was commonly attributed to the 'false sense of pride' of Indos who refused to do manual labour or take on menial jobs, who did not know that 'real Dutchmen' in the Netherlands worked with their hands (Geuns 1904: 4). The assault was doubled-edged: it blamed those impoverished for their condition, and it suggested more subtly that if they were really Dutch in spirit and drive, they would have never fallen into pauperism.

The cultural frontiers of the national community

Concern over white impoverishment was tied to a more general fear: that European men living in concubinary relations with native women would themselves lose their Dutch or French identity, become degenerate and *décivilisé*. Central to this logic was a notion of cultural, physical and moral contamination, the fear that those Europeans who did not subscribe to Dutch middle-class conventions of respectability would not only compromise the cultural distinctions of European authority but waver in their allegiances to the metropolitan state. Such fears focused on 'mixed-bloods', but not on them alone. On the crest of the moment of liberal reform, a prominent Indies doctor warned that Europeans born and bred in the colonies lived in surroundings that stripped them of their 'pure' European sensibilities, and that 'could easily lead them to metamorphize into Javanese' (Kohlbrugge 1907). These allusions had specific colonial coordinates; they were directed at poor whites who *chose* to live on the cultural borderlands of the *echte* European community, at *some* European men who married native women, at *all* European women who chose to marry native men, and at both European and Indo-European women who co-resided with non-Europeans and chose not to marry at all.

What underwrites this discourse is a new tension between race and culture; as race dropped out of certain legal discriminations, it re-emerged, marked out by specific cultural criteria, in other domains. The concept of cultural 'surroundings' (*'milieu'* in French, *'omgeving'* in Dutch) became crucial to the new legal stipulations on which racial distinctions and national identity were based. Questions of 'milieu' permeated both science and colonial policy with respect to education, health, labour and sexual relations (compare Rabinow 1989). Medical guides for the colonial tropics warned that Europeans could lose their physical health and cultural bearings if they stayed too long. Debates over whether European children should be schooled in France or the Netherlands rather than in the colony equally attended to this 'habitus' theme (see Bourdieu 1984). They drew not so much on Darwin as on a popular neo-Lamarckian understanding of environment in which racial and national essences could be secured or altered by the physical, psychological, climatic and moral surroundings in which one lived. It was, however, in the colonial legal discourse on the criteria for European status that the issue of 'surroundings', and the linkages between national, racial and cultural identities, were carefully inscribed. While the laws themselves self-consciously disclaimed racial difference, a racist cultural logic underpinned the legal arguments.

J.A. Nederburgh, one of the principal architects of Indies colonial law writing in 1898, engaged with the question of national identity and membership more directly than many of his contemporaries. He argued that in destroying racial purity, colonialism had made obsolete the criteria of *jus soli* (place of birth) and *jus sanguinis* (blood descent) for determining nationality. Colonial *'vermenging'* (mixing/blending), he contended, had produced a new category of 'wavering classes', large groups of people whose places of birth and mixed genealogies called into the question the earlier criteria by which rights to European citizenship and the designation 'colonial subject' had once been assigned. Taking the nation to be those who shared 'morals, culture and perceptions', 'feelings that unite us without one being able to say what they are', Nederburgh concluded that one could not determine who had these sensibilities by knowing birthplace and kinship alone. He concluded that 'surroundings' had an 'overwhelming influence', with 'the power to neutralize almost entirely the effects of descent and blood' (Nederburgh 1898a: 87). By his account, Europeans who remained too long in the Indies 'could only remain *echte-Europeesch* [really European] in thought and deed with much exertion', and that children were particularly susceptible, being 'exposed' at a tender age to native influence in school and native servants at home. Nederburgh proposed that the state provide support for all European children in the Indies to be brought up in Holland (Nederburgh 1898a: 90). Others made the more radical recommendation that all schools of higher education should be closed in Batavia, and replaced with state-subsidized education in Holland. Both proposals derived from the same assumption: that it was 'impossible for persons raised and educated in the Indies to be bearers of Western culture and civilization'.

Attention to upbringing, surroundings and milieu did not disengage personal potential from the physiological fixities of race. Appeals to difference on the basis of *'opvoeding'* (upbringing) and milieu coded racial distinctions by naturalizing cultural differences in the legal, educational and medical domains. I have discussed elsewhere how the turn-of-the-century shift in the colonies to white endogamy and away from concubinage, to an intensified surveillance of native servants, to a sharper delineation of the social space in which European children could be brought up and where and with whom they might play, not only marked out the cultural borders of the European community, but also indicated how much state power was seen to reside in the choices of residence, language and cultural style that individuals made (Stoler 1991).

In 1884, access to European-equivalent status in the Indies included as a legal requirement 'complete suitability [*geschiktheid*] for European society' defined by (1) belief in Christianity, (2) fluency in spoken and written Dutch, (3) training in European morals and ideas (Mastenbroek 1934: 70). In the absence of an upbringing in Europe, district authorities were charged with evaluating whether the concerned party was 'brought up in European surroundings *as* a European' (Prins 1933: 677). But European equivalence was not granted simply on the display of a competence and comfort in European norms; it required that the candidate should 'no longer feel at home' in native society and should have already 'distanced' himself from his 'native being' (*Inlander-zijn*) – in short that s/he should neither identify nor retain inappropriate senses of belonging or longings for the milieu from which s/he came. It was the *mental* states of potential citizens that were at issue, not material assets alone. How could such evaluations be made? Who were to be the arbitrators? 'Suitability' to which European society and to which Europeans? The questions are disingenuous because the coding is clear; cultural competence displayed in family form, language and a middle-class morality became the salient new criteria for marking different kinds of participation and placement in the nation-state. As European legal status and its equivalent became accessible to an ever broader population, the cultural criteria of privilege were more carefully defined. As we will see, *some* European women were made the custodians of the new morality – those who subscribed to the social prescriptions that included white endogamy, not the 'fictive' European women who rejected those norms.

The mixed marriage law of 1898

The mixed marriage law of 1898 and the legal arguments that surrounded it are a special set of documents on several counts: nowhere in the Dutch colonial record is the relationship between gender prescription, class membership, and racial category so contentiously debated and so clearly defined. Nowhere is the danger of *certain kinds* of mixing so linked to national image while references to race are so carefully denied. Hailed in later years as the paragon of liberal 'ethical' thinking, the mixed-marriage debate sets out the cultural criteria of exclusion in no uncertain terms.

When the Indies civil code was established in 1848 it followed the Napoleonic code with one curious omission, namely, that upon marriage a woman's legal status should automatically follow that of her husband's. As Dutch jurists were to argue half a century later, since mixed marriages had then been overwhelmingly between Europen men and native women, who was to follow whom could be easily assumed. This, however, was no longer the case in the 1880s, when Indies colonial officials noted two troubling phenomena: first, that more women classified as European were choosing to marry non-European men, and, second, that concubinage continued to remain the domestic arrangement of choice over legal marriage. This was despite a growing official consensus that concubinage was destroying the moral fibre of the colony, and the European community, and abetting the pauperization of its middling members (Prins 1933: 665).[11]

Colonial lawyers were thus faced with a conundrum: how to implement a ruling that would facilitate certain kinds of mixed marriages (over concubinage) and condemn others. Agreed that the unity of the family was essential to state security and could only be assured by its unity in law, jurists posed two possible solutions: either that superior European standing should determine the legal status of husband and wife or, alternatively, that the patriarchal principle should determine that a woman should follow the legal status of her husband (regardless of race) (Nederburgh 1898: 17). Those who argued that a European woman should retain her European legal standing when married to a native man did so on the grounds that her subjection to native conjugal and penal law would put her in a vulnerable if not humiliating position and reflect poorly on European prestige at large (Nederburgh 1898b: 20).

Those who argued the counter-case contended that finer distinctions needed to be made; that the quality of women classified as European was highly varied, and that those who chose to marry non-European men were from a class of women who neither properly belonged in the category of 'European' nor actually lived in its community. They were 'outwardly and inwardly indistinguishable from natives', in short 'fictive' Europeans not warranting the protection of European law (Nederburgh 1898b: 13).

Such arguments rested on an interior distinction within the category 'European', between 'real' Dutch women and those of whom it was said 'very little European blood actually flowed in their veins'. Claims that such women had already fallen from cultural and racial grace had their 'proof' in the 'fact' that a 'real European woman' would never 'take a step that was so clearly humiliating and debasing'. Such legislation defined a 'real' European woman in sharply racist terms; not by her own character but by her choice of (non-native) husband and, second, by her maternal obligation to guard her progeny's European standing, lost to her children should she marry a non-European under the new law. Finally, this appeal to patriarchical supremacy prevented the entry into the Dutch citizenry of native men who might otherwise not have access to it (Nederlandsch-Indische Juristen-Vereeniging 1887: 40). Here again, as in the case of 'fraudulent recognitions' of *métis* children, the mixed-marriage law was designed to deter 'persons who would only be European in name' (Nederburgh 1898b: 64).

By reinvoking the Napoleonic civil code, colonial jurists assured that the 'invisible bonds' of nationality remained intact for European men, regardless of legal partner. European women, on the contrary, were summarily disenfranchized from their national community on the basis of conjugal choice alone.[12] While the new ruling effectively blocked the naturalization of native adult males through marriage, it granted a new generation of *métis* children European standing by affixing their nationality to that of their fathers. Could such legal measures really assure that this next generation would be severed from their native mothers' roots? The persistent vigilance with which concern for their surroundings, domestic upbringing and education were discussed in the 1920s and 1930s suggests that there were resounding doubts.

Between place and race: how Indo-Europeans identified themselves

The slippage between race and culture, as well the intensified discussions of racial membership and national identity, were not invoked by the 'echte Europeesche' population alone. The moral geography of the colonies defined certain 'mixed-bloods' as a class apart, with the word 'Indo' reserved for those who were *'verindische'* (Indianized) and poor. But what are less clear are the cultural, political and racial criteria by which those of mixed descent identified themselves. The contradictory and changing criteria that were used by the various segments of the Indo-European movement at the turn of the century highlight how contentious and politically contingent these deliberations were. It is no accident that the term 'Indo-European' is difficult to define. It applied to those of mixed descent, to Europeans born in the Indies of Dutch nationality, and to those 'pur sang' Europeans born elsewhere for whom the Indies was a 'second home' (Blumberger 1939: 5). The semantics of 'mixing' included the criteria of blood, place and cultural belonging to different degrees and at different times.

When the Indo-European movement emerged in the late nineteenth century, it coalesced around a population of mixed-bloods and 'pureblood' Dutch of Indies origin whose distinct economic interests, cultural style and legal positioning produced equivocal loyalties to the colonial state. The voice of the movement manifested itself in two ways: by its cultural rooting in the Indies rather than the Netherlands, and by an ambiguous appeal to the notion of race. At a time when the native nationalist project was just under way, the Indo-European press articulated a new notion of an 'Indies fatherland'. It contested the popular terms of Indonesian nationalism, but was opposed to the economic and political hegemony of the Dutch-born elite.

Between 1898 and 1903 various Indo-European associations rose, fell and reassembled as they each sought viable programmes that would embrace the 'uplifting' of the Indo-European poor *without* linking the fate of well-situated and educated families of mixed descent to the impoverished and 'nativized' Indo-European population. Their bids for political and economic empowerment invoked Eurasian racial superiority to 'natives' while at the same time denouncing any racial criterion for judging their status vis-à-vis European-born Dutch. The Indisch Bond formed in 1898, for example, was led by an Indies-born European constituency that spoke for the Indo poor, but whose numbers were not represented in their ranks. Even the Indische Partij, whose motto 'Indies for the Indiers' revealed a strong populist bent, failed to form a platform that could unite the native and poor Indo constituency on a common political ground (Blumberger 1939; Veur 1968). By the 1920s, when the Indo-Europeesch Verbond had more than 10,000 members, its platform remained committed to the cause of the Indo poor while retaining its loyalty to the state (Blumberger 1939: 50).

Questions of cultural, racial and national identity were particularly charged around the proposals for Indo-European agricultural settlements (Veur 1966). These utopian projects for white settler colonies, proposed in both the Indies and Indochina, were to be peopled by those of mixed descent. Despite their widely differing political persuasions, spokesmen for the government and for the Indo movement equally argued that native blood ties would make those of mixed descent easily acclimatized to tropical agriculture while their European heritage would provide them with the reason and drive for success. Thus brawn and brains, tropical know-how and European science, government assistance and private initiative, were to produce an economically self-sustaining, morally principled and Dutch-sympathetic *volk*.

The vision of turning potential patricides into pastoral patriots never worked, but its discussion raised critical national issues for different constituencies: from the state's perspective, the poor Indo population was *déraciné*, rootless and therefore dangerous; to the Indo-European associations, it was clear that they could not claim a fatherland without territorial rights and roots within it. For the fascist-linked Vaderlandse Club, rural settler colonies in the 1930s were part of a wider project: to create a solid defence against Japanese invasion, while alleviating overpopulation 'at home'. An unlikely alliance between it and the Indo-European constituency to support the settler schemes and to oppose the 'unwhitening' of the Indies did not last long (Drooglever 1980: 285). For the Indo-European movement, their *vaderland* was to be a new one, independent of the Netherlands, whereas for the colonial right the goal was to bring the Netherlands and the Indies into a 'Greater Netherlands' as a single state.[13] Both projects collided with that of the Indonesian nationalists, who rejected these racially inspired visions and territorial claims.

With 'rootedness' at centre-stage of the nationalist discourse, the notion of 'rootlessness' captured a range of dangers about *métissage* (see Malkki 1992, and Taguieff 1989). Abandoned *métis* youths were generically viewed as vagrants in Indochina, as intinerant beggars in the Indies, as *de facto* stateless subversives without a *patrie* (Braconier 1917). While private and government poor relief programmes created a barrage of institutions to alternately incorporate them into or insulate them from the European citizenry, the image of rootlessness stuck to a wider population of mixed descent, not only those who were abandoned.

As late as 1938, French authorities in Hanoi conducted a colony-wide inquiry to monitor the physical and political movements of the *métis* population. The Resident of Tonkin recommended a massive state-sponsored social rehabilitation programme that would give *métis* youths the means to function as real *citoyens* using the argument that with 'French blood prevailing in their veins', they already 'manifested an instinctive attachment to France'.[14] But many French in Indochina must have been more equivocal about their 'instinctive' patriotic attachments. The fear that *métis* might revert to their 'natural inclinations' persisted, as did a continuing discourse on their cultural lability and susceptiblity to the 'native milieu', where they might relapse to the immoral and subversive states of their mothers. But the perceived danger of *métis* 'rootlessness' – of ambiguous cultural affinities and locations – may have expressed deeper political anxieties on the part of those who ruled. The fear of 'mixed-bloods' may not have been about their burden to the state as so often claimed, but about the *empowerment* that cultural hybridity conferred; about groups that straddled and disrupted cleanly marked social divides and whose diverse membership exposed the arbitrary logic by which the taxonomies of control were made.

Métissage was so heavily politicized because it threatened to destabilize both national identity and the Manichean categories of ruler and ruled. The turn of the century represents one major break point in the nature of colonial morality and in national projects. In both the Indies and Indochina, a new humanitarian liberal concern for mass education and representation was coupled with newly recast social prescriptions for maintaining separatist and exclusionary cultural conventions regarding how, where and with whom European colonials should live.

As such, these colonial discourses about *métissage* revealed strange twists in the texture of cultural hegemony: the tension between a form of domination predicated on both incorporation and distancing at one and the same time (Sider 1987). 'The *métis*/Indo problem' expressed that dilemma in quintessentiel form: some *métis* were candidates for incorporation. To others it was categorically denied. In either case, the decision that a person labelled *métis* should be granted citizenship or subject status could not be made on the basis of blood alone, since some degree of European descent was, by definition, what all *métis* shared. The criterion of cultural competence served as the protean and porous measure of appropriate affiliation in the matters of nation and race.

Virtually all of these differentiating practices were worked through a psychologizing and naturalizing impulse that embedded gender inequalities, sexual privilege, class priorities and racial superiority in a tangled political field. The new terms for defining nationality opened up the possibilities of representation for some while it stipulated a finely delimited moral posture that partially closed those possibilities down. At the core of these deliberations were gender and class issues that made these 'laboratories of modernity' unwieldy sites (Wright 1987: 297). The experiments were re-worked by their subjects, challenged by women who refused poor relief and European training for their children, women and men who chose cohabitation over marriage. On the borderlands of European bourgeois society there existed women and men in the colonies whose culturally hybrid lifestyles intercepted nationalist and racist visions. Without romanticizing their impoverishment, we might consider the possibility that their choices expressed a domestic subversion, a rejection of the terms of the 'civilizing mission'. For those who did not adhere to European bourgeois prescripts, cultural hybridity may have affirmed new measures of civility of their own.

In 1987, E.D. Hirsch, an English professor at the University of Virginia, argued (in a book that fast became a national bestseller) that 'cultural literacy', namely, the concrete cultural knowledge that one needs to operate appropriately in mainstream culture, is

> ... the only available ticket to full citizenship. Getting one's membership card is not tied to class or race. Membership is automatic if one learns the background information and the linguistic conventions that are needed to read, write and speak effectively. Although everyone is literate in some local, regional, or ethnic culture, the connection between mainstream culture and the national written language justifies calling mainstream culture *the* basic culture of the nation. (Hirsch 1987: 22)

Such a statement could have been written by anyone of the colonial authorities in French Indochina or the Netherlands Indies who contended and wrote into the legal system that a cultural fluency was an essential requisite for European citizenship rights. Cultural literacy was part of the ticket to full citizenship in colonial Southeast Asia, but it was never (nor is it now) unfettered knowledge, dissociated from relations of power, dissociated from the exclusionary practices that restricted access and use of that knowledge by gender, race and class. Nor was cultural literacy a compendium of 'facts' and implicit conventions that one needed to know. In the hands of subaltern groups, such as Indochina's *métis* and the Indies' Indos, too much European cultural literacy was dangerous, perceived by colonial elites as the illicitly acquired cultural accoutrements of a potentially subversive population with no proper entitlements to that knowledge at all. But for most of the mixed-blood and native population it was an unattainable goal. Not only because educational facilities were severely restricted but, more important, because cultural competence entailed dispositions and psychological sensibilities that those not of 'pure-blood' European descent could allegedly never possess.

Cultural literacy and full citizenship are intimately related, but not in the unproblematic erasure of class and racial discriminations that Hirsch suggests. On the contrary, as I have tried to suggest here, the very notion of cultural literacy in written or spoken French or Dutch in the late nineteenth century, or in mainstream US written and spoken English today, entail deeper cultural commitments, conventions of upbringing and education that are exclusionary to the core. In tracing the genealogical link between culture, race and the making of citizens, we can begin to pivot our attention from the public to the private countenance of race, from its visual to its more potent intangible coordinates, and to the domestic domain as a crucial site where racial categories are made and national identities formed.

Finally, this foray into the changing terms of cultural hybridity in a colonial context should make us wary of the postmodern conceit that fragmented and fluid identities are the signature of the contemporary postcolonial world. Such arguments not only buy into a foundational colonial script that Manichean categories of ruler and ruled were unproblematic. They undermine any effort to identify the historical construction and subversions of those categories themselves. An effective colonial history of the present does not rest on some generic distinction between the rigid taxonomies of the colonial state and postcolonial disruptions to them, but on attention to the scrambled categories in which people lived, to the rejection of those taxonomies, and to the ruptures and reinscriptions of them today.

Notes

1. This is a much-shortened and revised version of a paper entitled 'Sexual affronts and racial frontiers: European identities and the cultural politics of exclusion in colonial Southeast Asia' that appeared in *Comparative Studies in Society and History* 34(3) in July 1992.

2. Cochinchine's European population was 3,000 in 1900 (Meyer 1985: 70): in the Netherlands Indies the European population was over 70,000 in the same year.

3. Anti-colonial challenges in Indochina, contrary to the discourse that characterized the *métis* as a potential subversive vanguard, was never predominantly led, nor peopled, by them. In the Indies on the other hand, where persons of mixed descent made up a potentially powerful constituency, the bids they made for economic, social and political reform were more often made in contradistinction to the demands of the native population, not in alliance with them.

4. The following account is drawn from letters housed in the Archives d'Outre-Mer, Protectorat de l'Annam et du Tonkin, File 39127, No. 1506, 17 December 1898.

5. Archives d'Outre-Mer, No. 1792, 12 December 1898.

6. One important difference between social reform movements in Europe and in the colonies at the turn of the twentieth century was reflected in the attitudes and policies toward the mothers of abandoned children: public policy under the Third Republic in France no longer treated such mothers as 'social deviants' but as victims, whereas in the Indies and Indochina, native mothers of mixed-blood children continued to be considered as deviants and beyond redemption, necessitating the rapid removal of children from their care. See Fuchs 1984: especially pp. 57–9.

7. Archives d'Outre-Mer, No. 164, 11 May 1904, my emphasis.

8. Cases of such refusal were not uncommon. In 1903 the Haiphong court admonished a *métisse* mother who was herself 'raised with all the exterior signs of a European education' for withdrawing her daughter from a government school 'for motives which could not be but base given the mother's character'; in 1904, Thi-Ba, the seventeen-year-old *métisse* daughter of an Annamite woman and a French man who herself was cohabiting with a native man, declared she 'voluntarily' accepted and preferred her own situation over what the Society for the Protection of Métis Youths could offer her (Archives d'Outre-Mer, letter no. 151, 29 February 1904).

9. Archives d'Outre-Mer, Amiraux 7701, Report on Métis in the Dutch East Indies (1901).

10. Statutes of the 'Société de protection des enfants métis,' 18 May 1904, Article 37.

11. Why some women might choose cohabitation over legal mixed marriage is not addressed. Colonial and contemporary historians usually assume that all forms of 'cohabitation' were concubinary arrangements, and that it was the woman who was 'kept', as the latter term implies. Several passing comments in the Pauperism Commission report, suggesting that it was European men who 'lived off' native women, not the other way around, might challenge this account. At the very least they suggest that this issue needs further investigation.

12. A woman who had contracted a mixed marriage could, upon divorce or the death of her husband, declare her desire to reinstate her original nationality so long as she did so within a year. However, a native woman who married a European man and subsequently married and divorced a man of non-European status could not recoup her European status.

13. *Verbond Nederland en Indie*, No. 3, September 1926, p. 3. By the late 1920s this publication was subtitled 'A Fascist Monthly'.

14. Enquête sur Métissage, Archives d'Outre-Mer, Amiraux 53.50.6.

References

Abor, Raoul 1917 *Des Reconnaissances frauduleuses d'enfants naturels en Indochine* Hanoi, Imprimerie Tonkinois.

Balibar, Etienne 1991 'Fichte et la frontière interieure: A propos des *Discours à la nation allemande*', *Cahiers de Fontenay* (?).

Barker, M. 1981 *The New Racism* London, Junction Books.

Blumberger, Petrus 1939 *De Indo-Europeesche Beweging in Nederlandsch-Indië* Haarlem, Tjeenk Willink.

Boswell, John 1988 *The Kindness of Strangers: the Abandonment of Children in Western Europe from Late Antiquity to the Renaissance* New York, Pantheon.

Bourdieu, Pierre 1984 *Distinction* Cambridge, Harvard.

Braconier. A. de 1917 'Het Pauperisme onder de in de Nederlands Oost-Indie levende Europeanen', *Nederlandsch-Indie* Baarn, Hollandia-Drukkerij.

Davin, Anna 1978 'Imperialism and motherhood', *History Workshop* 5: 9–57.

De Regt, Ali 1984 *Arbeidersgezinnen en beschavingsarbeid: Ontwikkelingen in Nederland 1870–1940* Amsterdam, Boom.

Douchet 1928 *Métis et congaies d'Indochine* Hanoi.

Drooglever, P. 1980 *De Vaderlandse Club 1929–1942* Franeker, Wever.

Encyclopedie van Nederlandsche-Indië 1919, s'Gravenhage, Nijhoff and Brill.

Etats-Généraux du Féminisme 1931 Exposition Coloniale Internationale de Paris 1931, rapport général présenté par le Gouverneur Général Olivier Paris, Imprimerie Nationale.

Fuchs, Rachel 1984 *Abandoned Children: Foundlings and Child Welfare in Nineteenth Century France* Binghamton, SUNY.

Geuns, M. van 1904 'De karaktervorming der Indo's', *Weekblad voor Indie*, 25 December 1904: 4.

Gilroy, Paul (ed.) 1987 *There Ain't No Black in the Union Jack* London, Hutchinson.

Girardet, Raoul 1983 *Le Nationalisme français* Paris, Seuil.

Hall, Stuart 1980 *Race, Articulation and Societies Structured in Dominance* UNESCO Sociological Theories, Race and Colonialism, Paris, UNESCO.

Hirsch, E.D. 1987 *Cultural Literacy: What Every American Needs to Know* New York, Vintage.

Kohlbrugge, J.F. 1901 'Prostitutie in Nederlandsch-Indië', *Indische Genootschap* 19: 26–8.

Kohlbrugge, J.F. 1907 'Het Indische kind en zijne karaktervorming', *Blikken in het zielenleven van den Javaan en zijner overheerschers* Leiden, Brill.

Koster, G.H. 1922 'Aangenomen Kinderen en Staatsblad Europeanen', *De Amsterdammer*, 15 July 1922.

Kuitenbrouwer, M. 1985 *Nederland en de opkomst van het modern imperialisme: kolonien en buitenlandse politiek, 1870–1902* Amsterdam/Dieren, de Bataafsche Leeuw.

Malkki, Liisa 1992 'National Geographic: the rooting of peoples and the territorialization of national identity among scholars and refugees', *Cultural Anthropology* 7(1): 24–44.

Mastenbroek, W.E. van 1934 *De Historische Ontwikkeling van de Staatsrechtelijke Indeeling der Bevolking van Nederlandsch-Indië* Wageningen, Veenam.

Mazet, Jacques 1932 *La Condition juridique de métis* Paris.

Mehta, Uday 1990 'Liberal strategies of exclusion', *Politics and Society* 18(4): 427–54.

Meyer, Charles 1985 *De Français en Indochine, 1860–1910* Paris, Hachette.

Moses, Claire Goldberg 1984 *French Feminism in the Nineteenth Century* Binghamton, SUNY.

Mosse, George 1985 *Nationalism and Sexuality* Madison, University of Wisconsin.

N.A. 1892 'Ons Pauperisme', *Mededeelingen der Vereeniging 'Soeria Soemirat'* 2: 8.

Nederburgh, J.A. 1898a *Wet en Adat* Batavia, Kolff.

Nederburgh, J.A. 1898b *Gemengde Huwelijken: Staatsblad 1898 No. 158* Batavia.

Nederlandsch-Indische Juristen-Vereeniging 1887 *Verslag van het Verhandelde in de Bijeenkomsten der Nederlandsche-Indische Juristen-Vereeniging* (25, 27 and 29 June 1887), Batavia.

Nye, Robert 1984 *Crime, Madness and Politics in Modern France: the Medical Concept of National Decline* Princeton, Princeton University.

Prins, W.F. 1933 'De Bevolkingsgroepen in het Nederlandsch-Indische Recht', *Koloniale Studien* 17: 652–88.

Rabinow, Paul 1989 *French Modern* Cambridge, MIT.

Rapport der Pauperisme-Commissie 1902. Batavia, Landsdrukkerij.

Righart, Hans 1986 'Moraliseringsoffensief in Nederland in de periode 1850–1880' in H. Peeters (ed.) *Vijf Eeuwen Gezinsleven* Nijmegen, SUN, pp. 194–208.

Romein, Jan 1978 *The Watershed of Two Eras: Europe in 1900* Wesleyan, Wesleyan University.

Schoffer, I. 1978 'Dutch "expansion" and Indonesian reactions: some dilemmas of modern colonial rule (1900–1942)', in H. Wesseling (ed.) *Expansion and Reaction* Leiden, Leiden University, pp. 78–99.

Sider, Gerald 1987 'When parrots learn to talk, and why they can't: domination, deception and self-deception in Indian–White relations', *Comparative Studies in Society and History* 29(1): 3–23.

Stoler, Ann Laura 1991 'Carnal knowledge and imperial power', in Micaela di Leonoardo (ed.) *Gender at the Crossroads: Feminist Anthropology in the Postmodern Era* Berkeley, University of California, pp. 51–101.

Stoler, Ann Laura 1992 'Sexual affronts and racial frontiers: European identities and the cultural politics of exclusion in colonial Southeast Asia', *Comparative Studies in Society and History* 34(1): 514–52.

Stuurman, Siep 1987 *Verzuiling, Kapitalisme en Patriarchaat: aspecten van de ontwikkeling van de moderne staat in Nederland* Nijmegen, SUN.

Taguieff, Pierre-André 1989 'The National Front in France', *New Political Science* 16/17: 29–70.

Taylor, Jean 1983 *The Social World of Batavia* Madison, University of Wisconsin.

Veur, Paul van de 1966 'The Eurasians in Indonesia: a problem and challenge in colonial history', *Journal of Southeast Asian History* 9(2): 191–207.

Veur, Paul van de 1968 'Cultural aspects of the Eurasian community in Indonesian colonial society', *Indonesia* 6: 38–53.

Weber, Eugene 1976 *Peasants Into Frenchmen* Stanford, Stanford University.

Wright, Gwendolyn 1987 'Tradition in the service of modernity: architecture and urbanism in French colonial policy, 1900–1930', *Journal of Modern History* 59: 291–316.

9

Patterns of exclusion: imaginaries of class, nation, ethnicity and gender in Europe

Jan Berting

The advent of modern 'Europe' and patterns of exclusion

The advent of modern Europe, so much discussed in the context of 'Europe 1992', implies a process of economic enlargement of scale, the formation of a European state and the rethinking of the emerging socio-cultural order by the populations concerned. This transformation goes together with changing representations of nation-states, class structures, ethnicity, religion and gender. The present transformation of Europe marks the end of a long struggle among its leading nations to impose their particular model of development. Which Europe will emerge from this transformation? Since the relations between Western and Eastern Europe will be characterized by a high degree of instability for many years to come, it is too early to answer this question. And our present models of development fail in the face of these turbulent developments. There is increased awareness of the problems that Europe's development presents. Different images of Europe and the West come to the fore in public debates. As a consequence of the rapid political transformations in Eastern Europe, most attention is paid to the relations between Western Europe, especially the European Community (EC), and Eastern Europe. With respect to Europe's eastern boundaries, there is a plurality of conceptions. In the long run, the North–South relations between Europe and the world outside are likely to become more important on different levels (for example, cultural openness, migration, cooperation). An analysis of the imageries of Europe's futures will contribute to our clarification.

When we analyse Europe's transformation we observe patterns of exclusion based on class, ethnicity, religion and gender which, in spite of many changes in other respects, such as increasing social and spatial mobility and enlargement of the scale of information systems, are highly persistent. Patterns of exclusion and inclusion seem to be related to collective representations of the world around us and are to a large extent stereotypical.

In this contribution my main aim is to analyse patterns of exclusion and inclusion, related to representations of class, nation, ethnicity and gender among the populations of Europe. Moreover, it is important to pay attention to the ways in which these representations are interrelated. I will look back on the model of development that had an enormous impact on European development in the past, the Enlightenment model of industrial development, and discuss the assumptions of this model with respect to distinctions within populations on the basis of class, gender, ethnicity and nation. My next step is to consider current developments in Europe that pertain to patterns of exclusion and social factors that may be responsible for their persistence or change. Finally, I will briefly discuss whether it is possible to influence developments in this domain by adopting specific policy-oriented measures.

The Enlightenment model and industrial development

The advent of industrial society was accompanied by the expectation that the distribution of economic rewards would be increasingly based on universalistic and individualistic achievement principles. This expectation was and remains part of a powerful image of the coming society as an open one.

The emerging social order was interpreted in terms of social progress in which everyone's position is ideally based on individual achievement and on his or her position in the emerging division of labour. In this new order, everyone contributes according to his or her skills and receives remuneration according to the market value of this contribution. This development was thought to be based on the rise of industrial society, in which economic growth depends on industrial production propelled by science and technology. It depends on open, worldwide markets and the adequate use of individual talents. This image of society implies increased individual occupational and social mobility together with a growing equality of educational opportunities, a fading away of traditional class differences, a growth of the middle classes as a consequence of the increasing demand for skilled and professional workers and, consequently, a decrease of collective forms of antagonism, especially class struggle. In this perspective, the exigencies of industrialization will in the long run everywhere generate the same type of social order, which will ultimately merge in an encompassing world system.

The ideals of the Enlightenment are closely interwoven with this perspective, since development is thought to be primarily dependent on the forward march of rationality, resulting from the enquiring human mind that follows the rules of positivist, logico-empirical science, while analysing the physical and social world in the pursuit of truth. Moreover, this leads to the development of new technologies, as applications of the growth of knowledge. The motor of development is science and technology, in combination with open international markets which compel industry to adapt quickly to available technologies. Failure to do so by an enterprise or branch of industry or nation would result in quick deterioration of its international competitive position (Berting 1988).

With reference to our theme – images of collectivities and patterns of exclusion – it is important to note that the rise of the industrial society and the image of social progress are closely related to the birth of human rights. Although the idea of human rights has deep historical roots, and not exclusively in the Western world, human rights as formulated in documents such as the Bill of Rights and the Déclaration des droits de l'homme et du citoyen are very much the product of both the Enlightenment and the rise of the industrial society. As such, the concept of human rights is associated with individualism, rationalism and universalism. Dumont states that the adoption of the Déclaration marks the triumph of the individual (1983: 102). This connection between the birth of human rights and the rise of a new liberal, democratic order – or at least the development of a powerful image of such a coming order – affected the concept of human rights as individual, universal rights. The origin of human rights sheds some light on the model of 'man' traditionally associated with those who favour civil rights. This model is, in Campbell's words, of a person somewhat beyond the norm in the sense of normal: an active, rational, entrepreneurial person equipped with a certain degree of self-expression, self-help and self-defence: a person who has the opportunity to possess and manage property, to communicate views and pursue happiness along individually chosen lines, to share in government and freely go about everyday activities without interference of officials and prohibitions of the state beyond those strictly necessary for the defence of the rights of others (Campbell 1986: 126).

Human rights, then, are tied to a view of society that combines individualism with rationalism, universalism and cosmopolitanism and as such opposes particularism, collectivism and traditionalism. Human rights refer to the individual and go beyond his or her particular social relations or roots. This primacy of reason, universalism and the individual appears to be essential in solving problems related to human rights as it has developed in international law today (Haarscher 1987: 21; Berting 1990: 189).

In this image of social development there is no conflict between technological and economic development and human rights. On the contrary, industrialization leads to liberation from traditional social and cultural bonds and thus from ignorance. Industrial development reduces class antagonism and state repression, enhances opportunities for individual choice and for the solution of future problems, including those caused by industrial development itself. This optimism is grounded in a confidence that logico-empirical science will always find new technologies to handle present and future problems.

The development of industrial society could not have taken place without the rise of the modern nation-state. Industrialization is a process of modernization in which the development of economic power goes together, although not always in a harmonious manner, with nation building: local autonomy has to be broken down to a certain extent (Galtung 1983: 1). This development led to a twofold distinction: between the leading elites of the emerging nation states and the social categories (classes, regions, ethnic groups, and so on) that were reluctant to follow the rules of the 'civilization of modernity'; and between 'leading nations' and those peoples and countries, especially colonized peoples outside Europe, that were considered to be laggards by the elites and by some other segments in the dominating or leading nations.

Between the leading modernizing nations and those that aspired to leadership, fierce competition ensued in order to maintain or achieve a position of dominance. No wonder they tended to accentuate the differences among themselves. This was surely the case in the retarded nation-state Germany, which put more emphasis on its own identity, in opposition to Enlightenment values, than England, the USA or France. These rivalries were ideologically embedded in social Darwinism and, after the defeat of France in 1870, by biologist (racist) theories, such as those of Gobineau (1853–55) and LaPouge, and geopolitical ideologies. These 'theories' can be considered as efforts to legitimize the domination of leading modernizing nations over subjugated populations or over nations with an inferior status in the international ranking order. Leading nations claimed the right and duty ('white man's burden') to dominate 'inferior' peoples. In this period many stereotypes of nations and peoples became imbued with racist connotations. The same applies to stereotypes held by higher classes in modernizing society with respect to lower classes.

The Enlightenment model of development and stereotypes of collectivities

The Enlightenment model of development implies a gradual fading away of structural differences in modernizing societies. Ongoing individualization and rationalization of social life will, in the long run, destroy collective antagonisms and distinctions based on class, ethnicity, religion and gender. In this image of modernization, men and women figure as autonomous individuals who occupy their place in society on the basis of their individual qualifications, not as members of a collectivity.

As we know, the actual development of modern societies has not led to the disappearance of such distinctions, although modern societies have become more open in several respects in comparison with the preceding types of social organization. Why have distinctions between (traditional) collectivities persisted, why have antagonisms between classes and ethnic groups not withered away? And why do we continue to draw a distinction between those who belong to our in-group and 'strangers' or enemies (Kristeva 1988: 9)?

The Enlightenment model, with its emphasis on social progress, did draw a sharp distinction between modernizing in-groups and others, in spite of its universalistic values. This model contains universal values that its adherents, the in-group, express to the highest degree, while from their point of view the behaviour and ideas of the 'others' represent aberrations. Here we are confronted with the phenomenon of ethnocentrism. The ethnocentric individual, also as an adherent of the universalistic model of development, thinks that his values 'sont les valeurs, et cela lui suffit: il ne cherche jamais véritablement à le prouver. ... L'ethnocentriste a donc deux facettes: la prétension universelle, d'une part, le contenu particulier (le plus souvent naturel), de l'autre' (Todorov 1989: 19–20). This is a key to the understanding of patterns of exclusion and the role of stereotypes of class, nation, ethnicity and gender in modern Europe.

The Enlightenment model as an ideology of modernizing elites contributed to a sharp distinction between, on the one hand, the universalistic orientation of these elites and, on the other, their assessment of the lifestyles of peoples and cultures they encountered while expanding their economic and political systems. During the eighteenth century and later, the myth of the lazy native developed, a stereotype that reflects the values of the dominant colonial strata and the effects of colonial rule on the dominated peoples (Alatas 1977).

This model of development also created distinctions among the nation-states that were competing for world leadership. Instead of merging culturally, the elites of those nations each accentuated their own specific interpretation of modernization as 'universal', as is shown in Elias's analysis of the sociogenesis of the concepts of culture and civilization. Elias points out that the French and British concepts of civilization emphasize universalism, that which all men have – or should have – in common as participants in this common culture, and express the consciousness of nations with an established position as leading nations which have known economic, political and cultural expansion over a long period. The German concept of culture emphasizes the specificity and uniqueness of German culture (Elias 1939: 4; Berting and van de Braak 1990: 33) and opposes the Enlightenment model on the basis of cultural identity. Already in the eighteenth century the modernization trend was severely criticized by Herder, who introduced the idea of 'Volksgeist', which emphasizes the uniqueness of peoples and cultures. He rejected the idea of universal timeless principles of truth, justice, beauty, and argued that all norms originate within a specific cultural context on which they depend for their further development.

The Enlightenment model also legitimizes the role of modernizing elites. Modernizing elites lead their country to a better future – an orientation that creates a sharp distinction between the 'universal values of modernity' and the traditional values and institutions that have to be replaced: the classic opposition between *Gesellschaft* and *Gemeinschaft*.

The modernizing elites tend to impose upon the lower classes their 'universal' values and individualistic achievement orientation, according to which individual achievements should be rewarded in such a way that individuals are aware of a clear connection between, on the one hand, their 'investments' in terms of initiative, risk-taking based on calculation, education etcetera and, on the other, their rewards in terms of income, social prestige and influence. In this image of society, success in occupational life and social esteem depend on a rational utilization of opportunities by individuals. The modernizing elites in industrializing countries tend to regard the lower classes as the bearers of collectivistic or fraternalistic ideas and as having a 'natural' resistance to change which has to be broken by the tools of modern management. The lower classes in industrializing societies have indeed strongly resisted the imperatives of the achievement society, not because of a 'natural' resistance to change but because they resisted becoming victims of divide-and-rule policies of the elites. They tended to favour, in contrast to the emerging middle classes, Marxist and reformist models of development. The individualistic achievement principle as a pivotal element of the liberal Enlightenment model was never accepted by major segments of the blue-collar workforce. Although in our time the working classes have become fully incorporated into civic society and by now show an allegiance to the individualistic achievement principle, their interpretation deviates both from the 'classical' interpretation and from those to which the professional categories subscribe.

As has become obvious during the rise of socialist societies, the ruling elites in these systems tended to have similar attitudes towards those who do not accept their model of development as the liberal ruling elites. In fact, both have their roots in the Enlightenment tradition.

The image of the lower classes as inclined to resist change is reinforced in relation to migrant workers from non-Western countries who settle in the West. Their sense of belonging and identity contrasts with the universalistic values of modern societies. This produces a paradoxical situation. The modern state embodies a strong tension between communalist and universalist principles. In certain respects universalist values are used as an instrument of exclusion. Modern nations often fail to provide full citizenship to members of allochtonous ethnic minorities. 'Moreover,' Dench remarks, 'it is the dominant group who still holds the best cards. They can easily dissemble in order to exploit ambiguities to their own advantage. When lines of conflict are kept complex and confused, the status quo is more readily maintained. The fate of minority communities is to be suspended between two principles of collectivism' (Dench 1986: 36) – between the communalist universalism of the state and that of the ethnic community. The autochtonous lower classes are confronted with the same opposition between principles and, moreover, with a fragmentation of their 'traditional' life world.

What about the role of gender in relation to the Enlightenment model? Social inequality related to gender differences is part and parcel of this model of development. In this developmental perspective, the highest rewards go to those who occupy the leading positions, the leaders of large enterprises, scientists and engineers, high-ranking political innovators. In a paternalistic society, the overwhelming majority of these positions are occupied by men; women, not being participants in the core activities of development, have a rather low status. Thus the image of gender difference cannot be detached from the image of development.

I have shown that stereotypical images of class, nation, ethnicity and gender are clearly related when they are analysed from the developmental perspective. The Enlightenment model presents an image of a new Europe and its others that, on the one hand, is still powerful in shaping the future, as it remains the leading model of the economic and political elites, and, on the other, is considered obsolete and inadequate by many both inside and outside Europe and the West. The struggles between bearers of different models and images of the future are important as they pertain to patterns of exclusion and inclusion based on the dominance of an institutionalized Enlightenment model and to efforts to oppose these patterns and to formulate alternatives to them. New ways of thinking about the future in opposition to the industrial convergence model could mean the end of the 'traditional' patterns of exclusion and the real beginning of the decolonization of the imagination in the domains of class, ethnicity, nation and gender.

This task is not easy. In spite of many important socioeconomic changes in the everyday conditions of most people, changes that often do not fit with the dominant model of development, images of class, ethnicity, nation and gender do not change as rapidly. Images of collectivities are clearly not solely epiphenomena of structural socioeconomic conditions. Stereotypical images of collectivities have a strong resistance to change. At the end of this contribution I will return to this problem and offer a theoretical framework for analysis.

European culture and stereotypes of collectivities

Models of development, such as the Enlightenment model, impact on social development when they provide frames of reference for the actions of modernizing elites. The advent of 'modern' Europe confronts us with the urgent question of whether the making of Europe depends primarily on quasi-autonomous economic and technological forces or whether it also depends on choices related to different images of Europe's future. The present EC does not offer us signs of cultural imagination with respect to the future. This may be a consequence of the fact that the EC is run by technocrats and Eurocrats who try to promote the interests of their own countries first. One of the architects of the EC, Jean Monnet, once remarked: 'Si c'était à refaire, je commencerais par la Culture.' If this refers to the need to think about different ways in which we can arrange the relations between collectivities in Europe, and change stereotypes of collectivities (nations, ethnic groups, gender distinctions, class structures), I agree. Our future is too precious to leave to the 'autonomous' development of technological and economic forces.

The problem is, however, that at present a real debate on the cultural shaping of Europe is lacking. International political documents such as the Final Act of Helsinki (1975), the Concluding Document of the Vienna Meeting of the CSCE (1989) and the Charter of Paris of the Conference on Security and Cooperation in Europe (1990) only give some indications of a rather vague 'consciousness of cultural identity' (Berting 1992: 115ff.).

The analysis of some major political documents concerning European cooperation demonstrates the necessity to distinguish between different 'levels' and conceptions of 'European culture' and 'cultures of Europe' and to analyse their interrelations and relations to stereotypes of collectivities (ethnic groups, classes, and so on). Ideas about 'European culture' are strongly dependent on the Enlightenment image of development: culture is regarded as something to be protected and cultivated (for example, against the standardizing forces of modernization), or as values and habits that are functional for modernization's unique path. My analysis presents us with five different images of European culture(s), each of which can be related to patterns of exclusion/inclusion. I will refer to them briefly and contrast them with other ideas about culture formulated by opponents of the dominant European model of development. I distinguish among the following:

1. *Europe as a common heritage and cultural identity.* The Concluding Document of the Vienna Meeting of the CSCE remarks that efforts are needed towards the identification of common elements of the European cultural heritage. In an analysis of the concept of Europe up until the nineteenth century, Bochmann concludes (1990: 51–63) that at the end of the nineteenth century the concept of Europe was 'complete' and that in our time there is an *opinio communis* that acknowledges the following components, at least with respect to Europe's most positive achievements: (1) a cultural and spiritual common heritage consisting of Graeco-Roman antiquity, Christianity, the Renaissance and humanism, the political thinking of the Enlightenment and the French Revolution and all types of socialism; (2) a rich and dynamic material culture that has been extended to all other continents; (3) a conception of the individual expressed by respect for legal guarantees of individual liberty and human rights; (4) a plurality of states with different political orders which are condemned to live together in one way or another; (5) respect for the peoples, states and nations outside Europe.

2. *Europe as a totality of 'national cultures'* in the sense of the cultures of nation-states, in which a nation is 'a large collection of men [*sic*] such that its members identify with the collectivity without being acquainted with its other members, and without identifying in any important way with sub-groups of that collectivity' (Gellner 1987: 6). Such nation-states are the result of nation-building, a process in which a preindustrial structure is replaced by an industrial one. In this way also the culture is changed.

3. *Europe as a totality of 'cultures'.* This concept is broader than the preceding one as it comprises also the minority cultures that survived the standardizing forces of nation-building. At present, as national borders lose part of their significance as a consequence of the development of European political institutions, we are witnessing a revival of these 'preindustrial cultures' in Europe and of concomitant regionalism crosscutting national borders both in Western and Eastern Europe. In Western Europe these cultures may be interpreted as manifestations of declining nationalism; in Eastern Europe there are indications of a revival of strong nationalist sentiments, at least for the time being.

4. *Europe as a modern culture in the making.* This notion emphasizes, in contrast to the concept of 'European culture', the dynamics of ongoing modernization and the interplay between socioeconomic and cultural changes. The rise of industrial society requires, as Gellner states, that 'members of such a society be able to communicate in speech and writing, in a formal, precise, context-free manner – in other words they must be educated, literate and capable of orderly, standardised presentation of messages. The consequence of all this is the necessity of universal literacy and education, and a cultural homogeneity or at least continuity.' The general profile of modern society is, then, 'literate, mobile, formally equal with a merely fluid, continuous, so to speak atomised inequality, and with a shared, homogeneous, literacy-carried, and school-inculcated culture' (Gellner 1987: 15). In the nineteenth and twentieth centuries nation-states, emphasizing the importance of national culture, provided the framework for socioeconomic development. By now, the ongoing processes of modernization have made these national frameworks obsolete in certain respects. The changing socioeconomic structure of Europe and the advent of a European state imply important changes on the cultural level: the making of a European culture.

5. *Europe's 'culture areas'.* Some cultural dividing lines cannot be accounted for under the preceding concepts of culture. In his study of European culture, Delmas observes that Europe is divided by strong ancient cultural boundaries. One of these separates the countries of northwestern Europe from eastern countries. The second runs between the Mediterranean and the Byzantine European countries. In this way we can distinguish cultural families: the northwestern, Slavic and Mediterranean culture areas (Delmas 1980: 9–22). Scardigli remarks that the technico-economic development of Europe is accompanied by cultural diversity and a reinforcement of cultural differences between areas, produced by an increasing confrontation of values and practices. The cultural differences between northern Europe (Scandinavia, the United Kingdom, the Netherlands, Flanders, Luxembourg and Germany) and Mediterranean Europe (south, west and central France, Italy, Spain, Portugal and Greece) are considerable with respect to the degree of autonomy of women, the role of sociability, satisfaction with life,

confidence accorded to fellow men, and trust in technological development (Scardigli 1988: 115). These cultural differences seem to be rather persistent. They pertain to conceptions of the nature of hierarchy within organizations and their fellow workers (D'Iribarne 1989; Hofstede 1980), the awareness of time, punctuality with respect to the fulfilment of agreements and appointments, intellectual styles (Berting 1987c) and citizens' perceptions of the central tasks of their states (Enzensberger 1989). Perhaps these differences have a stronger effect than linguistic differences, although it is evident that language families partly coincide with culture areas.

Patterns of exclusion in Europe and sociocultural policy

Only the fourth of these images of European culture has a dynamic character, and this is strongly tied to modernization according to the Enlightenment imagery. Those who tend to be excluded or marginalized in the process of modernization react to this image of development with its emphasis on universalism, individualism, rationalism in different ways. One reaction is to try to protect cultural (ethnic) differences by arguing that the (ethnic) community is the primary source of a person's dignity. Against the universalism and individualism of the dominant model of modernization, the particularistic character of one's own culture or religion is emphasized. Modernization is considered to be a source of degradation of one's own specific way of life. This emphasis on the specific identity of minorities is interwoven with the idea that modern societies are multicultural and that ethnic or cultural communities should have collective rights enabling them to preserve their specific character. The idea of collective rights in relation to cultural identity is not without problems, as they may be used by minority elites to force individuals to comply with their exigencies. A society made up of ethnic or religious communities may lead to a system of neo-apartheid in which each individual is strongly connected with one community without the opportunities for individual choice available in a modern society.

A second strategy of the victims of exclusion processes is not the search for isolation, but the systematic effort to change the character of the one-sided image of modernization by reinterpretating the major values of modernization. The standard image of modernization is replaced by one in which the values of feminist social movements or other social movements (for example, in the Third World) play a major role. This strategy – fighting for changing values and for the inclusion of others – seems much more promising than the former, which is based on an unrealistic image of modernization, and especially of cultural development. It accepts some major general developments as inevitable while at the same time seeking to elaborate diversities – old and new – within the general process of modernization. This strategy is not *a priori* in opposition to the Enlightenment programme since it is easy to recognize that the Enlightenment ideals are not being realized in the actual process of modernization. People experience a massive loss of control and autonomy as workers and citizens, also in the most advanced countries, a degradation in everyday life that is not compensated by sufficient reward, and increasing anxiety about the risks engendered by the system of production.

Stereotypes of groups and patterns of exclusion have to be studied from a developmental perspective. As such, our analysis proceeds on two levels: that of the (implicit) models of development of elites and major interest groups in societies; and that of the technological, organizational, social-structural changes that are partly the result of the implementation of these models and social reactions to them.

The interrelations between stereotypes and patterns of exclusion are complex and persistent. They have to be elucidated theoretically, especially the ways in which patterns of exclusion change. Questions pertaining to Europe's cultural development are of strategic importance with respect to stereotypes and patterns of exclusion, in particular those regarding the definition of 'Europe' and of Europe's 'outside world'.

The major task for 'Europe' is to avoid a development in which either the individualist–universalist or the communalist perspective predominates. The former could lead to a European society in which the richness of cultural diversity is lost, which would not only be a loss for the minorities concerned but would also impoverish European culture and deprive it of an essential source for its future development. The latter perspective could easily lead to a Balkanization of Europe and hence to the stagnation of its economic and political development. This opposition between perspectives is, of course, not specific to Europe. However, our obligation is to work out European strategies, which will keep this tension as the focus of our attention in the field of cultural development.

This developmental perspective on European culture/s implies several tasks. First, European cultural diversity cannot be left to the forces of modernization, especially of the market, without the introduction of measures to protect 'minor' cultures (including minor languages). A model of development in which individuals and cultures are regarded primarily as 'human resources' is not acceptable. The logic of technological and economic development is not the final answer to cultural problems, although it requires specific cultural developments. But 'European culture' is a very stratified phenomenon and it requires an ongoing effort to understand its 'cultural archaeology'. Second, there is a necessity for the development of policies designed to heighten awareness of European culture/s and the role of exclusion patterns. This should be directed at the common elements of Europe's cultural heritage, the contributions from various sources (also from outside Europe), the role of continuing diversity, and the dynamics of European culture. In this area the role of education and the mass media is pivotal. The development of a European educational programme from a developmental perspective must include the analysis of stereotypes of other peoples and the role they play in international relations, and the possibilities for altering stereotypes and other sources of lack of respect for other cultures, especially lack of respect for the achievements of so-called 'minor' cultures and languages.

How do stereotypes of collectivities change?

Most scientific analyses of the nature of stereotypes are rather one-sided. In this section a model is presented that may be useful for interdisciplinary research in this domain. The social sciences oscillate between two perspectives on social and cultural life which seem to exclude each other (Berting 1989: 8–23). These are the *rationalist* perspective, in which social and cultural life are seen as objective realities and the task of social science is to develop methods that will explain 'how society works'; and the *historicist* approach, which holds that the understanding of social life can only be compelling for a time. Historical conditions change, and along with them the facts and their contexts, as well as the scholars with their interests and methods (Bendix 1984: 8).

This opposition coincides largely with the opposition between 'objectivism' and 'subjectivism'. It is phrased well by Bourdieu:

> On the one hand, it can 'treat social facts as things', according to the old Durkheimian precept, and thus leave out everything that they owe to the fact that they are objects of knowledge, of cognition – or misrecognition – within social existence. On the other hand, it can reduce the social world to the representation that agents have of it, the task of social sciences consisting then in producing an 'account of the accounts' produced by social subjects. (Bourdieu 1989: 14–15)

A second opposition that plays an important role in the social sciences pertains to the level of explanation. Structuralists assert that all interesting and important social phenomena can be explained by the operation of supra-individual factors, that is, at the level of analysis of social structures and/or aggregations of some form. Structuralist approaches often represent social holistic types of explanation. In contrast, methodological individualists assert that the most important and interesting social and cultural problems can be explained in terms of the operation of intra-individual factors (the capacity for rational choice, for example) in relation to inter-individual factors (for example, social interaction and its unintended consequences or other social phenomena emerging from interaction processes).

Stereotypes provide a good vantage point for analysing the relations between these perspectives on social reality. On the one hand, stereotypes are 'images' or 'representations' of an 'objective world' in that those who have stereotypes as 'pictures in the mind' assume some correspondence between their image of reality and the objective world out there (characteristics of nations, peoples, ethnic groups, and so on). A stereotype is not purely imagination or fiction, it somehow reflects an objective world. Moreover, stereotypes have a collective character. They are collective representations that pertain to 'out-groups' and individuals as representatives of these out-groups. Stereotypes endure from generation to generation. Stereotypes have a strong persistence, although the way elements of a stereotype are evaluated may change rapidly when the nature of interactions between groups changes.

On the other hand, it can be argued that stereotypes are commonsense constructs which are used to handle the complexities of social life. In contrast to the first approach, in which the social scientist tries to discover and to explain the links between an objective reality and the stereotypes, in the second approach no appeal can be made to an outside world: the social scientist can only make 'constructs of ("commonsense") constructs'. Directly observable social reality is the result of the enactment of social constructs (as hidden cultural codes). This can be represented schematically as follows:

Schema A

Rationalist		Historicist	
Structuralist approach (A)	Individualist approach (B)	Structuralist approach (C)	Individualist approach (D)

Within each of these four approaches, the analysis of stereotypes follows different assumptions and the concept of stereotype carries different meanings. In the rationalist/structuralist approach, stereotypes are considered as products – in the minds of individuals – of external social conditions. Stereotypes – and other cultural products – reflect social reality from the specific position that an individual or group occupies in a social structure. A social structure is an ensemble of invisible relations: a social space in which individuals and groups stand in a specific relation to each other (proximity, distance, hierarchy, same level, etcetera). In this approach the social and cultural world is a world of signs, of semiotic codes such as myths, ideologies and marriage rules, as Lévi-Strauss has observed (1949; 1967: 61).

The significance of social and cultural phenomena cannot be found in the consciousness of actors but has to be discovered at another level than conscious representation. The hidden codes of the social and cultural world are like the syntax of a language which structures speech but is not a set of rules to which a person, while speaking, conforms in a conscious way. The code 'determines' the structuration of cultural phenomena.

In the rationalist/individualist approach, the emphasis is on the analysis of the characteristics of personality structures and the tendency of individuals with a specific constellation of personality characteristics to view the social and cultural world in terms of stereotypes (for example, the work of Adorno on the authoritarian personality). Such personality characteristics may be the result of a specific type of socialization (Adorno) and/or related to genetic individual differences (Pareto).

The historicist/structuralist approach is, in some respects, the reverse of the rationalist/structuralist view. This approach emphasizes the ways in which cultural systems develop and perpetuate themselves, 'express' themselves in artifacts and social arrangements (for example, Sorokin, Parsons). Stereotypes are analysed as elements of the cultural systems from which they derive their meaning (stereotypes as elements of life orientation, for example).

In the historicist/individualist approach, researchers are primarily interested in the ways in which social life is produced or 'created' in everyday life (Weber, Schütz, Mead, and others). The interactions between individuals are analysed as processes of actor interpretations in which stereotypes are used to label, to stigmatize, to exclude, to include, and so on (Berting 1987).

This schema (Schema A) demonstrates the different ways stereotypes can be approached. On the theoretical level these approaches are mutually exclusive, but viewed from a wider perspective they may be complementary. This is the way Williams looks at the relationship between rationalism and historicism. Williams distinguishes two conceptions of culture: (a) an emphasis on the 'informing spirit' of a whole way of life which is manifest over the whole range of activities but is most evident in specifically cultural activities – language, styles of art, intellectual work; and (b) an emphasis on 'a whole social order' within which a specific culture, in styles of art and types of intellectual work, is seen as the direct or indirect product of an order primarily constituted by other social activities. The first, 'idealist' approach implies as its major method the clarification of the informing spirit. The second, 'materialist' approach is concerned with extrapolation from the known or discoverable general social order to specific forms taken by its cultural manifestations.

According to Williams, a new convergence is coming to the fore in contemporary research, in which cultural practices and production are considered as major elements in the construction of social order. In this convergence, culture is viewed as 'the signifying system through which necessarily (though among other means) a social order is communicated, reproduced, experienced and explored' (Williams 1981: 13).

Bourdieu argues that these two major approaches stand in a dialectical relationship:

> ... on the one hand, the objectivist structures that the sociologist constructs, in the objectivist moment, by setting aside the subjective representations of the agents, form the basis for these representations and constitute the structural constraints that bear upon interactions; but, on the other hand, these representations must also be taken into consideration particularly if one wants to account for the daily struggles, individual and collective, which purport to transform or to preserve these structures. (Bourdieu 1989: 15)

I will not try to overcome the rifts between these four approaches but use all of them to highlight the main elements of stereotypes before addressing the main theme of this chapter: societal change and changing stereotypes. Major elements and characteristics of stereotypes – as representations of groups or categories that go together with positive or negative value judgements and specific sentiments – are as follows:

1. They are social constructions of reality.
2. They are shared by (most) members of a certain group and transmitted from generation to generation.
3. Stereotypes are related to the personality structure of individuals in at least two ways: (a) persons with a personality structure in which rigidity is a dominant trait (fixed habits, accuracy, irritation when daily routines are broken, sticking to decisions when circumstances change, and so on) are more prone to stereotypical thinking than persons with a flexible, open mind; (b) persons with such a personality structure will cling to the stereotypes current in the group culture to which they belong.
4. Stereotypes are not isolated items but elements of a collective life orientation (according to the historicist approach).
5. Stereotypes are related to social and economic conditions (group interests).
6. Stereotypes are the concrete manifestations of a common code that structures relationships between groups in a 'mental map', and as such structure perceptions of out-groups.
7. Stereotypes are manifestations of 'closed thinking': persons who cling to stereotypes do not confront their constructs with reality (no reality testing). Evidence that runs counter to the social construct does not destroy or change it; on the contrary, it is declared an exception ('some of my best friends are Jews').
8. Stereotypes are an expression of collectivistic thinking. Individualistic types of thinking are not easily reconciled with stereotypes which are related to groups.
9. Stereotypes are durable and persistent with respect to the ascription of traits to groups, but not in terms of value judgements. Changing circumstances may influence judgements of some 'objective' trait ('assiduity', for example, may be regarded as a positive trait in one period and as a threat in another; militant behaviour may be seen as valour, or as aggressiveness).

These elements are to a large extent congruent with the definitions proposed by Schaff (1980: 86–7) and Villain-Gandossi (1990). Villain-Gandossi adds that cognitive, emotional and pragmatic aspects may be distinguished. The pragmatic functions of stereotypes are 'socialement intégrante, défensive, idéologico-créative et politique'.

The main conclusion from this analysis is that stereotypical images of class, nation, ethnicity and gender do not merely change because socioeconomic conditions are changing. Images of collectivities are not solely epiphenomena of structural conditions of social life. Structural changes may have an indirect impact on stereotypical images (through changing socialization patterns). Moreover, it is important to take account of the historicist approaches which indicate that it matters how we imagine the development of social life and which values are accorded prominence in the interactions between collectivities. 'Culture' – our values, models, stereotypes, images, imagination – does not come to the fore after the fulfilment of technoeconomic, socio-structural and political conditions, but is a dynamic force and determining factor of the quality of life in the coming European society.

References

Alatas, S.H. 1977 *The Myth of the Lazy Native* London, Frank Cass.

Bendix, R. 1984 *Force, Fate and Freedom: on Historical Sociology* Berkeley, University of California Press.

Berting, J. 1987 'Cultural barriers in international and comparative research in the social sciences', in L. Hantrais and S. Mangen (eds) *Doing Cross-National Research: Language and Culture on Cross-National Research* Birmingham, Aston University.

Berting, J. 1988 'Goals of development in developed countries', in *Goals of Development*. Paris, UNESCO, pp. 140–81.

Berting, J. 1989 'Structures, actors and choices', in J.H.G. Klabbers et al., *Simulation-Gaming: on the Improvement of Competence in Dealing with Complexity, Uncertainty and Value Conflicts* Oxford, Pergamon, pp. 8–23.

Berting, J. 1990 'Social change, human rights and the welfare state in Europe', in J. Berting et al., *Human Rights in a Pluralist World – Individuals and Collectivities* Westport and London, Meckler.

Berting, J. 1992 'La Culture Européenne; les objectifs, les auteurs, les moyens', in F. Marti (ed.) *Droits culturels des peuples en Europe* Barcelona, Centre Unesco de Catalunya, pp. 115–48.

Berting, J. and H. van de Braak 1990 'L'identité culturelle de la "Grande Europe": mythe ou réalité?', in C. Villain-Gandossi et al. (eds), *Le Concept de l'Europe dans les processus de la CSCE* Tübingen, Gunter Narr Verlag.

Bochmann, K. 1990 'L'idée d'Europe jusqu'au XXe siècle', in C. Villain-Gandossi et al., *Le Concept de l'Europe dans les processus de la CSCE* Tübingen, Gunter Narr Verlag.

Bourdieu, P. 1989 'Social space and symbolic power', *Sociological Theory* 7 (1).

Campbell, T. 1986 'The rights of the mentally ill', in T. Campbell, D. Goldberg, S. McLean and T. Mulem (eds), *Human Rights: from Rhetoric to Reality* Oxford, Basil Blackwell.

Delmas, C. 1980 *La Civilisation européenne* Paris, Que sais-je?

Dench, G. 1986 *Minorities in the Open Society: Prisoners of Ambivalence* London, Routledge and Kegan Paul.

D'Iribarne, P. 1989 *La Logique de l'honneur. Gestion des entreprises et traditions nationales* Paris, Seuil.

Dumont, L. 1983 *Essais sur l'individualisme, une perspective anthropologique* Paris, Seuil,

Elias, N. 1939 *Über den Prozess der Zivilisation: Soziogenetische und psychogenetische Untersuchungen* Basel, Haus zum Falken.

Enzensberger, H.M. 1989 *Europe, Europe: Forays into a Continent* New York, Pantheon.

Galtung, J. 1983 'On the possible decline and fall of Japan: limits of transcendence of contradictions', *International Review of Economic, Political and Social Development*, Vol. 1.

Gellner, E. 1987 *Culture, Identity and Politics* Cambridge, Cambridge University Press.

Gobineau, A. de 1853–1855 *Essai sur l'inégalité des races humaines* Paris (four volumes).

Haarscher, G. 1987 *Philosophie des droits de l'homme* Bruxelles, Editions de l'Université de Bruxelles.

Hofstede, G. 1980 *Dimensions of National Culture: Value Systems in Organizations in Forty Countries* Beverly Hills, Sage

Kristeva, J. 1988 *Etrangers à nous-mêmes* Paris, Gallimard.

Lévi-Strauss, C. 1949 *Les Structures élémentaires de la parenté* Paris, Presses Universitaire de France.

Lévi-Strauss, C. 1967 *Structural Anthropology* New York, Anchor.

Maurice, M., F. Sellier and J.J. Silvestre 1982 *Politique d'éducation et organisation industrielle en France et Allemagne* Paris, Presses Universitaire de France.

Scardigli, V. 1988 *L'Europe des modes de vie* Paris, Editions du CNRS.

Schaff, A. 1980 *Stereotypen und das menschliche Handeln* Vienna, Europa Verlag.

Todorov, T. 1989 *Nous et les autres: La réflexion française sur la diversité humaine* Paris, Seuil.

Villain-Gandossi, C. et al., 1990 *Le Concept de l'Europe dans les processus de la CSCE* Tübingen, Gunter Narr Verlag.

Williams, R. 1981 *Culture* London, Fontana.

10

Culture wars in the United States: closing reflections on the century of the colour line

Ronald Takaki

The twentieth century, W.E.B. DuBois observed at its beginning, would be dominated by the colour line. In 1990, *Time* published a cover story on 'America's Changing Colors'. 'Someday soon,' the magazine announced, 'white Americans will become a minority group.' How soon? By 2056, most Americans will trace their descent to 'Africa, Asia, the Hispanic world, the Pacific Islands, Arabia – almost anywhere but white Europe' (Henry 1990: 28–31). This changing social reality in the USA is readily apparent. Currently, one third of the people of the USA do not trace their origins to Europe; in California, minorities are fast becoming a majority. They already predominate in major cities across the country: New York, Chicago, Atlanta, Detroit, Philadelphia, San Francisco, and Los Angeles.

Now, in the final decade of the twentieth century, we are offered two closing reflections. What we are witnessing, Francis Fukuyama claims, is the 'end of history'. Liberal democracy, he trumpets, remains 'the only coherent' political ideology. Capitalism with its 'free market' has succeeded in producing new levels of material prosperity in the industrially developed countries and also in many Third World countries (Fukuyama 1992: xviii, xiii). Traditional identities of tribe and ethnicity are being replaced by rational forms of social organization based on efficiency and natural rights. John Lukacs, however, is not so sanguine. 'The twentieth century is now over,' he observes. 'It was a short century. It lasted seventy-five years – from 1914 to 1989.' Its end is being accompanied by explosions of 'tribalisms' throughout the world (Lukacs 1993: 1, 262). What are we witnessing – a new world order or new chaos in the world?

Racial inscriptions of the 1992 LA riots

As it turns out, DuBois was wrong in one crucial respect: the twentieth century has become one of colour line*s*, a reality recently revealed in Los Angeles. Suddenly, in April 1992, television images beamed from Los Angeles stunned viewers around the world. Immediately after four police officers were found not guilty of brutality against Rodney King, rage exploded. During the nightmarish rampage, scores of people were killed, two thousand were injured, twelve thousand were arrested, and a billion dollars of property destroyed. Entire sections of Los Angeles resembled a bombed city.

This violence and destruction unshrouded a larger crisis in America. 'South central Los Angeles is a Third World country,' declared a young African American. 'There's a south central in every city, in every state.' Describing the desperate conditions in his community, he continued: 'What we got is inadequate housing and inferior education. I wish someone would tell me the difference between Guatemala and south central.' Another resident of the area explained that the uprising was 'not a riot – it was a class struggle. [It] ain't just about Rodney King. He was the lighter and it blew up.' (Lewis 1992; Lynch 1992)

What exploded was economic despair. Plants and factories had been moving out of south central Los Angeles into the suburbs as well as across the border into Mexico and even overseas to countries such as South Korea. Many factories in the area were shut down, boarded up like tombs. In terms of manufacturing jobs, south central Los Angeles had become a wasteland. Many young black men and women nervously peered down the corridor of their futures and saw no possibility of full-time employment paying above minimum wages, or no jobs at all. The unemployment rate was 50 per cent – higher than the national rate during the Great Depression. 'Once again, young blacks are taking to the streets to express their outrage at perceived injustice,' Newsweek reported, 'and once again, whites are fearful that The Fire Next Time will consume them.' But this time, the magazine noticed, the situation was different from the earlier riot: the recent conflict was not just between blacks and whites. 'The nation is rapidly moving toward a multiethnic future,' Newsweek reported, 'in which Asians, Hispanics, Caribbean islanders, and many other immigrant groups compose a diverse and changing social mosaic that cannot be described by the old vocabulary of race relations in America' (Newsweek 1992).

The colour lines were crisscrossing, colliding: racial minorities were fighting against one another, especially African-Americans and Korean-Americans. At the street level in south central Los Angeles, black community organizer Ted Watkins commented: 'This riot was deeper, and more dangerous [than the 1965 Watts riot]. More ethnic groups were involved.' Similarly, social critic Richard Rodriguez reflected: 'The Rodney King riots were appropriately multiracial in this multicultural capital of America.' Old and traditional dichotomies such as whites versus blacks now seem dated; race relations theories such as assimilationism and internal colonialism now seem punctured (Rimer 1992; Rodriguez 1992).

But the Los Angeles conflagration would not have shaken Fukuyama's view of the end of history. Capitalism is capable of the inclusion of blacks in its progress, he argues. The problem of the black underclass is clear: young blacks growing up in the ghetto lack 'a home environment capable of transmitting cultural values needed to take advantage of opportunity'. They fail to acquire 'internalized moral values', and welfare programmes only undercut the family and increase its members' dependency on the state (Fukuyama 1992: 292–3). For Lukacs, on the other hand, the Los Angeles explosion would confirm the thesis that history has not ended and that the ethnic and nationalistic antagonisms and conflicts of the past are intensifying.

But neither Fukuyama nor Lukacs illuminate the reality of Los Angeles. The celebrator of history's end merely echoes a simplistic theory of cultural deficiency that blames underclass blacks for their own condition, while the historian of the past as future offers mainly a description rather than an explanation for the particular situation in the United States.

The last three decades have witnessed radical economic transformations and the growth of a black underclass – what William Julius Wilson describes as 'the truly disadvantaged' (Wilson 1987). At the core of this new group has been the dramatic rise of black families headed by single women: between 1960 and 1980, the percentage of such families doubled, reaching 40 per cent of all black families. This development can be measured in terms of black welfare enrolment. While blacks composed only 12 per cent of the American population in 1980, they constituted 43 per cent of all welfare families.

Why has there been this growth of the black underclass? Charles Murray (1984) blames the welfare system, but his analysis is both misleading and mistaken. As Wilson has shown, welfare mainly provided the necessary support for families in desperate need because of economic changes.

One of these changes has been the suburbanization of production. The movement of plants and offices to the suburbs has isolated inner city blacks in terms of employment: in 1980, 71 per cent lived in central cities whereas 66 per cent of whites resided in suburbs. Illustrating this dynamic interaction of economic relocation, unemployment and welfare, Chicago lost 229,000 jobs and enrolled 290,000 new welfare recipients in the 1960s, while its suburbs gained 500,000 jobs. Trapped in inner cities, many unemployed blacks were unable to find new employment as easily as white workers living in suburbs, where the economy continued to expand.

Meanwhile, blacks also suffered from the devastating effects of the 'deindustrialization of America'. US corporations operate in a globalized economy and are no longer dependent on domestic labour. Tens of millions of American workers have lost their jobs in consequence of the relocation of production in low-wage countries such as South Korea and Mexico. In the ranks of this new army of displaced workers has been a disproportionately large number of blacks. The decline of employment in manufacturing industries such as automobile and steel production has had a particularly severe impact on black workers. A 1986 study by the Congressional Office of Technology Assessment reported that 11.5 million workers lost jobs because of plant shutdowns or relocations between 1979 and 1984, and that 60 per cent of them found new jobs in that period. But of the displaced black workers, only 42 per cent were able to find new employment. 'Blacks have been severely hurt by deindustrialization,' Wilson explained, 'because of their heavy concentration in the automobile, rubber, steel, and other smokestack industries' (Wilson 1987: 72–92).

But what made these economic changes especially damaging to blacks was also racism in the form of 'American apartheid'. In their important study of residential racial discrimination, Douglas Massey and Nancy Denton argue that housing segregation has contributed significantly to the making of the black underclass:

> For the past twenty years, this fundamental fact [of segregation] has been swept under the rug by policymakers, scholars, and theorists of the urban underclass. Segregation is the missing link in prior attempts to understand the plight of the urban poor.

They disagree with Wilson:

> Although rates of black poverty were driven up by the economic dislocations Wilson identifies, it was segregation that confined the increased deprivation to a small number of densely settled, tightly packed, and geographically isolated areas.

The existence of this desperately poor and alienated group of blacks in the inner cities has generated images of menacing blacks and fears among many middle-class whites, which, in turn has driven the latter to the suburbs for security and made them even more determined to erect walls of residential segregation. Here we have a modern example of what Gunnar Myrdal called the 'vicious cycle' (Massey and Denton 1993: 3, 8).

But Wilson as well as Massey and Denton overlook yet another factor – a very crucial one – in the formation of the black underclass. This is the Cold War. For the last fifty years, the US economy has been organized around the needs of the national security state in the pursuit of the strategy of containing Soviet communism. Consequently, much of US research and development have been focused on the designing and building of strategic nuclear weapons. Mega-corporations such as Martin-Marietta, Grumman, Hughes Aircraft, Rockwell International, and Northrup have been producing 'smart' bombs. Meanwhile, Japan and Germany have been producing 'smart' consumer goods. These developments have contributed to the US trade imbalance and the decline of the US economy with its resulting job losses, especially in manufacturing in US cities.

Thus the structural economic changes described by Wilson, the apartheid pattern analysed by Massey and Denton, and also the decline of the USA's manufacturing base caused by the Cold War – all of these factors together – have led to what can be called the economic hollowing out of America's inner cities.

Together they have pushed US society into an era of new racial crisis: the issue is no longer whether inner city blacks are employable or can become employable, but whether they are even needed in the US economy of the late twentieth century. Many of them are conscious of their grim employment prospects, and their despair has given rise to what Cornel West has described as the 'nihilism that increasingly pervades black communities' (West 1993: 14).

The end of the Cold War has presented a new peril: the US economy has become so dependent on federal military spending that budget cuts for defence contractors has led to a downturn in the economy. This crisis has intensified racial antagonisms: Asian-Americans have been associated with the 'invasion' of Japanese cars, Hispanics have been viewed as undocumented workers taking jobs away from Americans, and blacks have been blamed for their dependency on welfare and the special privileges of affirmative action.

Backlash against cultural pluralism

Within the context of these economic problems and racial tensions, an intellectual backlash against peoples of colour has been under way. Conservative foundations have been financing projects to promote their own political agenda on campuses across the USA, and the National Association of Scholars has been attacking the movement for cultural pluralism by smearing it with the brush called 'political correctness'. Under the banner of intellectual freedom, Eurocentric conservatives have been imposing their own intellectual orthodoxy by denouncing those who disagree with them as 'the new barbarians' (D'Souza 1992).

Allan Bloom, author of *The Closing of the American Mind*, has emerged as a leader of this backlash. In his view, students entering the university are 'uncivilized', and the faculty have the responsibility to 'civilize' them. Bloom claims he knows what their 'hungers' are and 'what they can digest'. Noting the 'large black presence' in major universities, he laments the 'one failure' in race relations – black students have proven to be 'indigestible'. They do not 'melt as have all other groups'. The problem, he contends, is that 'blacks have become blacks': they have become 'ethnic'. This separatism has been reinforced by an academic permissiveness that has befouled the curriculum with 'Black Studies' along with 'Learn Another Culture'. The only solution, Bloom insists, is 'the good old Great Books approach' (Bloom 1987: 91–3, 340–41, 344).

Similarly, E.D. Hirsch worries that the USA is becoming a 'Tower of Babel', and that the multiplicity of cultures is threatening to tear its social fabric. He, too, longs for a more cohesive culture and a more homogeneous USA: 'If we had to make a choice between the one and the many, most Americans would choose the principle of unity, since we cannot function as a nation without it.' The way to correct fragmentization, Hirsch proposes, is to acculturate 'disadvantaged children'. What do they need to know? 'Only by accumulating shared symbols, and the shared information that symbols represent', Hirsch answers, 'can we learn to communicate effectively with one another in our national community.' Though he concedes the value of multicultural education, he quickly dismisses it by insisting that it 'should not be allowed to supplant or interfere with our schools' responsibility to ensure our children's mastery of American literate culture'. In *Cultural Literacy: What Every American Needs to Know*, Hirsch offers a long list of terms that excludes much of the history of minority groups (Hirsch 1987: xii, xvii, 1, 18, 96).

Recently, Arthur Schlesinger has joined the backlash against multiculturalism. In *The Disuniting of America*, this old-time liberal historian denounces what he calls 'the cult of ethnicity' – the shift from assimilation to group identity, from integration to separatism. The issue at stake, he argues, is the teaching of 'bad history under whatever ethnic banner'. After acknowledging that US history has long been written in the 'interests of white Anglo-Saxon Protestant males', he describes the enslavement of Africans, the seizure of Indian lands, and the exploitation of Chinese railroad workers. But his discussion on racial oppression is perfunctory and parsimonious, and he devotes most of his attention to a defence of traditional history. 'Anglocentric domination of schoolbooks was based in part on unassailable facts,' Schlesinger declares. 'For better or worse, American history has been shaped more than anything else by British tradition and culture.' Like Bloom, Schlesinger utilizes the metaphor of eating. 'To deny the essentially European origins of American culture is to falsify history,' he explains. 'Belief in one's own culture does not require disdain for other cultures. But one step at a time: no culture can hope to ingest other cultures all at once, certainly not before it ingests its own.' Defensively claiming to be an inclusionist historian, Schlesinger presents his own credentials : 'As for me, I was for a time a member of the executive council of the Journal of Negro History. ... I have been a lifelong advocate of civil rights' (Schlesinger 1992: 2, 24, 14, 81–2).

What happens when people of colour define their civil rights in terms of cultural pluralism and group identities? They become targets of Schlesinger's scorn. This 'exaggeration' of ethnic differences, he warns, only 'drives ever deeper the awful wedges between races', leading to an 'endgame' of self-pity and self-ghettoization. The culprits responsible for this divisiveness are the 'multicultural zealots', especially the Afrocentrists. Schlesinger castigates them as campus bullies, distorting history and creating myths about the contributions of Africans (Schlesinger 1992: 58, 66).

What Schlesinger refuses to admit or is unable to see clearly is how he himself is culpable of historical distortion: his own omissions in *The Age of Jackson* (1945) in effect erased what James Madison had described then as 'the black race within our bosom' and 'the red on our borders'. Both groups were entirely left out of Schlesinger's study: they do not have headings in the index. Moreover, there was no mention of two marker events: the Nat Turner insurrection and Indian Removal, which Andrew Jackson himself would have been surprised to find omitted from a history of his era. Unfortunately, Schlesinger fails to meet even his own standards of scholarship: 'The historian's goals are accuracy, analysis, and objectivity in the reconstruction of the past' (Schlesinger 1992: 20).

Behind Schlesinger's cant against multiculturalism is fear. What will happen to our national ideal of 'e pluribus unum?' he worries. Will the 'center' hold, or will the Melting Pot yield to the Tower of Babel? For answers, he looks abroad. 'Today,' he observes, 'the nationalist fever encircles the globe.' Angry and violent 'tribalism' is exploding in India, the former Soviet Union, Indonesia, Guyana, and other countries across the world. 'The ethnic upsurge in America, far from being unique, partakes of the global fever.' Like Bloom, Schlesinger prescribes individualism as the cure. 'Most Americans', he argues, 'continue to see themselves primarily as individuals and only secondarily and trivially as adherents of a group.' The dividing of society into 'fixed ethnicities nourishes a culture of victimization and a contagion of inflammable sensitivities'. This danger threatens the 'brittle bonds of national identity that hold this diverse and fractious society together'. The Balkan present, Schlesinger warns, may be America's prologue (Schlesinger 1992: 2, 21, 64).

Diversity and its discontents

But Schlesinger's very attack indicates that the cultural terrain is being contested. Many Americans of colour have been challenging traditional and dominant notions regarding nationality. They have been asking: How should America and Americans be defined? Whose history is it? One focus of their struggle has been education, and they have been demanding a more inclusive, culturally pluralistic curriculum. Institutions of learning have been responding to their pressures. In 1990, the Task Force on Minorities for New York emphasized the importance of a culturally diverse education. 'Essentially,' the *New York Times* commented, 'the issue is how to deal with both dimensions of the nation's motto: "E pluribus unum" – "Out of many, one"' (Fiske 1990). Universities from New Hampshire to Berkeley have established American cultural diversity graduation requirements. 'Every student,' explained University of Wisconsin's chancellor Donna Shalala, 'needs to know much more about the origins and history of the particular cultures which, as Americans, we will encounter during our lives' ('University of Wisconsin' 1988). Even the University of Minnesota, located in a state that is 98 per cent white, requires its students to take ethnic studies courses. Asked why multiculturalism is so important, Dean Fred Lukermann answered that as a national university, Minnesota had to offer a national curriculum – one that included all of the peoples of America. He added that after graduation many students move to cities like Chicago and Los Angeles and thus need to know about racial diversity (Lukermann 1987).

But, despite the efforts of cultural pluralists, most Americans are still unable to understand how they, representing an immense diversity of peoples, are connected to a larger narrative of the United States. 'We can get along, we can work it out,' Rodney King declared during the days of rage in Los Angeles (King 1992). But how do we get along, how do we work it out, unless we, as Americans, learn about one another? Here we remain largely strangers to each other.

While the primary reason for this ignorance continues to be the hegemony of a Eurocentric culture, the failure also reflects some shortcomings of the cultural pluralists themselves. In their critique of domination, they frequently focus exclusively on culture, and hence overlook the material basis of racial inequality. Hence, they do not help different groups understand the economic context of their subordination and exploitation. In the case of the United States, our racial diversity grew out of the development of our capitalist economy and the need for geographical expansion as well as imported groups of labourers from many different countries. During the nineteenth century, for example, industrialization connected a diverse assemblage of Americans. Irish immigrants worked in New England factories manufacturing textiles from cotton cultivated by enslaved blacks on lands taken from Indians and Mexicans. Different groups of labourers were pitted against each other to break strikes and discipline workers – blacks against the Irish, the Chinese against blacks, Mexicans against the Japanese. Ours was a diversity by design. This economic reality is often overlooked by many cultural pluralists, or it is sometimes merely referenced.

Part of the problem is the influence of certain aspects of postmodernist theory. This approach has been extremely useful in terms of helping our scholarship develop a critical epistemology as well as an alertness to conditions of complicity and ambiguity of language. But frequently the analysis of some cultural pluralists is so abstract and their writings so excessively elusive in language that they render their critical scholarship remote from the very subaltern communities they are seeking to help empower. What this body of writings offers is a debate over scholarly representations of other scholarly representations of the original representations – feasts of intellectual delights detached from the reality of poverty, racism, greed, theft, chicanery and exploitation. Such scholarship is anti-political, even reactionary, in effect, presented as the similacrum of something radical. Theory is crucial, but the purpose of theory is to guide our reaching for understanding of reality. Here we need not only theoretical discussions about the importance of dense description, but we need also to do it. In the end, what we may have that really matters is the narrative to explain the world and who we are.

But sometimes instead, we are offered studies of representations that end up inadvertently serving racial hierarchy, while trying to challenging it. For example, the deconstructing of colonial ideology contains the study of people of colour as the 'Other'. Thus the critique of domination becomes complicit in the 'Othering' of racially oppressed groups. Here, feminist scholarship can be helpful. Feminist criticism calls attention to the 'Tootsie trope' – the failure of a scholarly study to allow its feminist intentions to alter its male-centred mode of signification (Hutcheon 1989:

159). A similar 'orientalist trope' continues to centre Western culture by exclusively examining the West and its manufacture of the 'oriental Other'. The members of the stereotyped groups remain faceless and voiceless; their subordination is reinforced, albeit inadvertently. Thus 'orientals' remain 'Orientalized' (Said 1978).

This very action of representing is freighted with responsibility, for multicultural scholarship, like the traditional body of knowledge it seeks to oppose, has been engaged in meaning-making through representation. The critical issue is not only whose history is to be told but also who should be doing the telling. One problem here is the reality that the scholars in the universities are predominantly not members of the oppressed racial groups they are studying and representing. This might account for the continued marginalization of the 'Other' as object rather than subject; it also contributes unintentionally to the reproduction of the exclusion of racial diversity within the academy. The 'Others' cannot represent themselves; hence, they must be represented.

But regardless of who does the telling, much of what is presented as multicultural scholarship also tends to fragment US society by separately studying specific groups such as African-Americans or Hispanics. Inter-group relationships become invisible, and the big picture is missing. This decontextualizing only reinforces the bewilderment already separating racially and ethnically diverse Americans from one another. We are left with shards of a shattered mirror of our diversity. The very search for the voices of people has sometimes reinforced this fragmentation by focusing on specific texts of individuals, which are examined in isolation from larger social and economic contexts. Sometimes, this focus on a single group leads to extremes of nationalistic scholarship. All of this particularizing only burdens socially concerned intellectuals in carrying out their task of not only comprehending but also transforming the world.

At a deeper level there is a lack of new theoretical work capable of analysing a multiracial reality. Cultural pluralist scholars continue to operate largely within the river banks of two major theories: the assimilationist theory seeking to explain race relations in terms of the incorporation of minorities into the white mainstream versus the internal colonialist theory contending that peoples of colour in the USA represent colonized groups. Both paradigms assume the existence of a racial hierarchy in terms of white and black, or white and people of colour. But they become woefully inadequate to explain tensions between different groups of colour such as the antagonism between African-Americans and Korean-Americans. Crucial to any effort to address this need for new theory and new multicultural analysis is the re-visioning of history. Scholars need to approach the past from a broad and comparative perspective in order to comprehend the dynamic, dialectical process in which different groups came together from different shores to create a new society in North America.

This need for an understanding of the making and meaning of a multicultural United States is especially crucial during the closing decade of DuBois's century of the colour line. Contrary to Fukuyama, we have not reached the end of history. In order for democracy to emerge in a country, Fukuyama notes, its citizens must share a strong sense of national unity and accept one another's rights. This made democracy possible in Britain, France, and the United States. Thus democracy is linked to national identity. Actually, in the United States, rights and nationality have not been extended to all groups. Liberal democracy and capitalism must still address the continuing economic and racial inequality in America itself. The American ideal of human rights and dignity still remains for many citizens of colour a dream deferred; the material abundance of the 'free market' continues to be enjoyed by a privileged group. Fukuyama argues that the problem of racial inequality is not 'insoluble on the basis of liberal principles' (Fukuyama 1992: 216, xxi). But his optimism does not resonate reassurance to a society witnessing escalating racial tensions and conflicts. Indeed, Fukuyama's very celebratory insistence that history has ended only shrouds the explosive reality Lukacs describes as 'tribalism': identities and interests based on ethnicity.

References

Bloom, A. 1987 *The Closing of the American Mind: how Higher Education Has Failed Democracy and Impoverished the Souls of Today's Students* New York, Simon and Schuster.

D'Souza, D. 1992 'The Visigoths in tweed', in Patricia Aufderheide (ed.) *Beyond PC: Towards a Politics of Understanding* St Paul, MI, Graywolf, pp. 11–13.

Fiske, E. 1990 'Lessons', *New York Times* 7 February.

Fukuyama, F. 1992 *The End of History and the Last Man* New York, Free Press.

Henry, W., III 1990 'Beyond the melting pot,' in 'America's changing colors', *Time* 135(15) (9 April): 28–31.

Hirsch, E., Jr 1987 *Cultural Literacy: What Every American Needs to Know* Boston, Houghton Mifflin.

Hutcheon, L. 1989 *The Politics of Postmodernism* London, Routledge.

King, R. 1992 statement to the press 2 May 1992, in *New York Times*: 6.

Lewis, G. 1992 'LA riot area likened to Third World nation', *San Francisco Examiner* 31 May.

Lukacs, J. 1993 *The End of the Twentieth Century and the End of the Modern Age* New York, Ticknor and Fields.

Lukermann, F. 1987 interview, University of Minnesota.

Lynch, A. 1992 'Southland's hopes turn to ashes: promise eroded by recession, ethnic tensions', *San Francisco Chronicle* 22 May.

Massey, D. and N. Denton 1993 *American Apartheid: Segregation and the Making of the Underclass* Cambridge, MA, Harvard University Press.

Murray, C. 1984 *Losing Ground* New York, Basic.

Newsweek (18 May 1992) 'Beyond black and white', p. 28.

Rimer, S. 1992 'Watts organizer feels weight of riots, and history', *New York Times* 24 June, p. A9.

Rodriguez, R. 1992 'Horizontal city', *San Francisco Chronicle* 24 May, p. 16.

Said, E. 1978 *Orientalism* New York, Vintage.

Schlesinger, A., Jr 1945 *The Age of Jackson* Boston, Little, Brown and Company.
Schlesinger, A., Jr 1992 *The Disuniting of America: Reflections on a Multicultural Society* Knoxville, TN, Whittle.
'University of Wisconsin-Madison: the Madison Plan', 9 February 1988.
West, C. 1993 *Race Matters* Boston, Beacon.
Wilson, W. 1987 *The Truly Disadvantaged: the Inner City, the Underclass, and Public Policy* Chicago, University of Chicago Press.

Teaching for the times

Gayatri Chakravorty Spivak

This chapter was originally written for the Annual Convention of the Midwestern Modern Language Association in the United States.[1] I have not removed the signs that show that I am speaking to fellow teachers; in other words, it is a practical piece. I have also kept its local flavour. I think these signs and marks can be of some interest to readers from various parts of the world, if only because they might then produce some effort to work out how, in their contexts, the teaching of literature can be transnational.

The word 'transnational' now bears the weight of the untrammelled financialization of the globe in the recent post-Soviet years. I will not offer a detailed discussion of this abundantly discussed phenomenon here, except to remark that, in this dispensation, the integrity of particular states has become much more fluid, especially in the South, and especially since capitalism is being reterritorialized as 'democracy'. It seems obvious that the always precarious hyphen between nation and state is now rather more so; and that this hyphen is being inhabited by multifarious mobilizers of identity politics. It is within this broad context that the words were first uttered; the exhortation was for new immigrant American college and university teachers of English to locate themselves in it: and that effortful location was called transnational literacy.[2] It would, I think, be less useful to read 'transnational' only by the rules of an older lexicon, where it stands for a globality in conflict with the nation-state, although that lexicon is by no means obsolete.

It should also be kept in mind that we are speaking here of college and university teaching of English, not of subaltern projects of literacy, or pedagogy of the oppressed. In an effort to understand how diversified yet related transnational teaching must be, I have attempted to travel the course, starting from rural or specifically aboriginal literacy under different national circumstances, all the way to international conferences – again under various national determinations, with situations of national(ized) education systems somewhere in the middle. If it has taught me anything, it is that nothing applies everywhere. I speak of the invention of unity for the new immigrant teacher in the body of the piece. That is a strategic unity. I do not believe we can have any more globalized a vision within the boundaries of the varieties of academic practice.

When I wrote the piece, we in the United States were still caught between 'liberal multiculturalism' on the one hand and white cultural supremacy – the anti-'politically correct' (PC) – on the other.[3] If the reader wishes to tease out a presupposition from the following pages, here is one: at a certain limit, the two sides of the debate feed each other. The lines have now become somewhat blurred in this fast-moving arena. 'Contingency' has invaded 'unity' talk on the other side: 'Our task is to combine due appreciation of the splendid diversity of the nation with due emphasis on the great unifying Western ideas of individual freedom, political democracy, and human rights' (Arthur M. Schlesinger Jr).[4] 'Recognition both of the complexity and the contingency of the human condition thus underlines the *political* need for shared moral consensus in the increasingly congested and intimate world of the twenty-first century' (Zbigniew Brzezinski).[5] One is writing with rousing confidence in the American Dream, the other with alarm about the world. Now more than ever it seems right for good teaching to turn from emphasis upon our contingent histories to the invention of a shared and dynamic present – as the continuous unrolling of an ungraspable event with consequences that might as well be called 'global' in its minute detail.[6]

Another item about the effort to teach multicultural English in the United States might be of interest here. Among many of the participants in that effort, teachers and students, there is talk of something called postcolonialism. These pages may be seen as an elaboration of a response to that trend: given the role of the United States in what has been called 'recolonization', if there is to be a US postcolonial*ism*, it can only be a transnational literacy; for postcolonial*ity* is a failure of decolonization. Is decolonization possible? In the broadest possible sense, once and for all, no; but this is what it shares with everything else.[7] Yet, given the situation of the self-representation of multicultural teaching of literature in the United States, it seems more canny to stop (or start) with prospects for decolonization, presumably a condition before *post*coloniality (or *post*colonialism) can be declared. As far as I can tell, and for all practical purposes, a general condition of postcoloniality is a future anterior, something that will have happened, if one concerned oneself with the persistent crafty details of the calculus of decolonization, in the sphere in which one is contractually engaged, not excluding tacit affective contracts, of course.

Since its inception, the United States has been a nation of immigrants. The winner among the first set of European immigrants claimed, often with violence, that the land belonged to them, because the Industrial Revolution was in their pocket. And the story of its origin has been represented as an escape from old feudalism, in a general de Tocquevillian way. It is well-known that in the Founders' Constitution, African slaves and the Original Nations were inscribed as property in order to get around the problem of the representation of slaves as wealth: 'The key slogan in the struggle against the British had been "no taxation without representation." … The acceptance that slaves as wealth should entitle Southern voters to extra representation built an acknowledgement of slavery into the heart of the Constitution.'[8]

Here we have extreme cases of marginalization where the term itself gives way: dehumanization, transportation, genocide. I will not begin in that scene of violence at the origin, but rather with the phenomenon that has gradually kicked us – marginal voices – from opposition to become the perceived dominant in the US cultural space: New Immigration in the New World Order.

Let us rewrite 'cultural identity' as 'national origin validation'. Let us not use 'cultural identity' as a permission to difference and an instrument for disavowing that Eurocentric economic migration (and eventually even political exile) persists in the hope of justice under capitalism. That unacknowledged and scandalous secret is the basis of our unity. Let us reinvent this basis as a springboard for a teaching that counterpoints these times. This is what unites the 'illegal alien' and the aspiring academic. I am arguing that this is all the more important because 'we' – that vague, menaced, and growing body of the teachers of culture and literature who question the canon – are not oppositional any more. We are being actively opposed because what used to be the dominant literary–cultural voice – the male-dominated, white Eurocentric voice – obviously feels its shaping and moulding authority slipping away. We seem to be perceived as the emerging dominant. What is the role and task of the emerging dominant teacher? Since one of the major functions of professional organizations in the United States is to facilitate employment, let us also consider the problems of educating the educators of the emerging dominant field: in other words, let us consider both the undergraduate and the graduate curriculum.

Access to the universal/national origin validation on the undergraduate curriculum

In a powerful paper entitled 'The campaign against political correctness: what's really at stake', Joan Wallach Scott lays bare the shoddy techniques of what was the opposition at the beginning of the nineties:[9]

> Serious intellectuals have only to read the self-assured, hopelessly ill-informed, and simply wrong descriptions of deconstruction, psychoanalysis, feminism, or any other serious theory by the likes of D'Souza, Richard Bernstein, David Lehman, Roger Kimball, Hilton Kramer, George Will – and even Camille Paglia – to understand the scam. ... [T]heir anger at the very scholars they long to emulate ... seems to have worked in some quarters. That is partly because the publicists have assumed another persona beside that of the intellectual: they pretend to represent the common man – whom, as elitists, they also loathe.[10]

This brilliant and shrewd paper focuses on the contemporary US scene. And as such its writer shows that the opposition is desperately claiming a 'universality' that, in my view, has already slipped out of their grasp. She quotes S.P. Mohanty who 'calls for an alternative to pluralism that would make difference and conflict the center of a history "we" all share'. She quotes Christopher Fynsk as offering 'the French word *partage* [meaning] ... both to divide and to share', as an informing metaphor of community. I will keep these suggestions in mind in this first section, most specifically confined to the undergraduate curriculum in the United States.

Emergence into an at best precarious dominant does not for a moment mean that our battle for national-origin validation in the USA is over. First, we as new immigrants must rethink the battle lines. Since the 'national origins' of new immigrants, as fantasized by themselves, have not, so far, contributed to the unacknowledged and remoter historical culture of the United States, what we are demanding is that the United States recognize *our* rainbow as part of its history of the present. Since most of our countries were not *territorially* colonized by the USA, this is a transaction that relates to our status as New Americans, not primarily to the countries of our origin. (In this respect our struggle is similar to as well as different from that of the new European immigrants.) Second, we must realize that, in the post-Soviet post-Fordist world, we as a specific part of the collective of marginals are currently fighting from a different position. We face the need to consolidate ourselves in new ways, which I have tried to indicate in my opening words. Being reactive to the dominant is no longer the only issue. I agree with Scott's and Mohanty's and Fynsk's general point: conflict, relationality, divide and share. In the US context these are good marching orders. But difference and conflict are hard imperatives. Difference becomes competition, for we live and participate – even as dissidents – within institutions anchored in a transnational capitalist economy. Our 'limited physical supply of what is at stake makes it easy to overlook the fact that the functioning of the economic game itself presupposes adherence to the game and *belief in the value of its stakes*'.[11]

The stakes in question are not just institutional but generally social. Eurocentric economic migration as a critical mass is based on hope for justice under capitalism. The task of the teacher is as crucial as it is chancey, for there is no guarantee that to know it is to be able to act on it (especially since our self-representation as marginal in the US might involve a disavowed dominant status with respect to our countries of national origin). To continue with the quotation above:

> ... how is it possible to produce that minimal investment which is the condition of economic production without resorting to competition and without reproducing individuation? As long as the logic of social games is not explicitly recognized (and even if it is ...), even the apparently freest and most creative of actions is never more than an encounter between reified and embodied history ... a necessity which the agent *constitutes* as such and for which [s]he provides the scene of action without actually being its subject.

'Reified history' is in this case our monumentalized national–cultural history of origin combined with ideas of a miraculated resistant hybridity;

'embodied history' our disavowed articulation within the history of the present of our chosen new nation-state.[12] This 'encounter' does not translate to the scene of violence at the origin – slavery and genocide, black and red – that I laid aside at the opening of my speech.

In the US classroom I spend some time on Bourdieu's caution: 'and even if it is [recognized] ...' I draw it out into the difference between knowing and learning. Without falling into too strict an adherence to the iron distinction between the constative and the performative, I still have to hang onto a working difference between knowing about something and learning to do something. The relationship between knowing and learning is crucial as we move from the space of opposition to the menaced space of the emerging dominant.

An anthology piece in an international collection will not allow the meditative tempo of the classroom. Let me therefore ignore Bourdieu's parenthesis and emphasize the point Bourdieu makes, keeping myself, for the moment, confined to our role within the academic institution. I will return to the more general social point of new-immigration-in-capitalism later.

So long as we are interested, and we *must* be interested, in hiring and firing, in grants, in allocations, in budgets, in funding new job descriptions, in publishing radical texts, in fighting for tenure and recommending for jobs, we are *in* capitalism and we cannot avoid competition and individuation. Under these circumstances, essentializing difference, however sophisticated we might be at it, may lead to unproductive conflict among ourselves. If we are not merely the opposition any more, we must not lose the possibility of our swing into power by crumbling into interest groups in the name of difference. We must find some basis for unity. It is a travesty of philosophy, a turning of philosophy into a direct blueprint for policy making, to suggest that the search for a situational unity goes against the lesson of deconstruction. If we perceive our emergence into the dominant as a situation, we see the importance of inventing a unity that depends upon that situation. I am not a situational relativist. No situation is saturated. But imperatives arise out of situations and, however unthinkingly, we act by imagining imperatives. We must therefore scrupulously imagine a situation in order to act. Pure difference cannot appear. Difference cannot provide an adequate theory of practice. 'Left to itself, the incalculable and giving idea of justice [here as justice to difference] is always very close to the bad, even to the worst, for it can always be reappropriated by the most perverse calculation.'[13]

In the interest of space I am collapsing a good few philosophical moves needed to make this argument acceptable. I can only ask you to take it on trust that those moves can be made.[14] What is important for me, in order, later, to pass into the second part of my remarks, is simply the conviction: We, the new immigrant teachers of so-called oppositional discourses in the USA, must today find a practical basis for unity at this crucial moment.

Consider this good passage from Jonathan Culler, also quoted by Joan Scott:

> A particular virtue of literature, of history, of anthropology is instruction in otherness: vivid, compelling evidence of differences in cultures, mores, assumptions, values. At their best, these subjects make otherness palpable and make it comprehensible without reducing it to an inferior version of the same, as a universalizing humanism threatens to do.[15]

I repeat, good words, words with which we should certainly claim alliance. Yet, today in particular, we must also ask: Who speaks here? Who is the implied reader of this literature, the researcher of this history, the investigator of this anthropology? For whose benefit is this knowledge being produced, so that he or she can have *our* otherness made palpable and comprehensive, without reducing it into an inferior version of *their* same, through the choice of studying literature, history, and anthropology 'at their best'? Shall we, today, be satisfied with the promise of liberal multiculturalism that these disciplines will remain 'at their best', with a now-contrite universal humanism in the place of the same, and us being studied as examples of otherness? Or should we remind ourselves of Herbert Marcuse's wise words in the sixties? I will speak of our difference from the sixties in a while, but Marcuse's words are still resonant over against the promises of liberal multiculturalism: 'Equality of tolerance becomes abstract, spurious. ... The opposition is insulated in small and frequently insulated groups who, even when tolerated within the narrow limits set by the hierarchical structure of society, are powerless while they keep within these limits.'[16]

This does not mean that we should be opposed to small victories: it is certainly important that some Third World literature job descriptions – 'global' rather than 'insular' English – now appear on the job lists issued by our national professional organization, the Modern Language Association of America. Yet it is possible that we will remain powerless collaborators in repressive tolerance if, in higher education in the humanities, we do not rethink our agency. Predictably, my agenda in the end will be the persistent and shifting pursuit of the global history of the present.

Other voices are asking questions similar to mine. I would cite here Aihwa Ong's article 'Colonialism and modernity: feminist re-presentations of women in non-Western society', which ends with these important words: 'We begin a dialogue when we recognize other forms of gender- and culture-based subjectivities, and accept that others often choose to conduct their lives separate from our particular vision of the future.'[17] To claim agency in the emerging dominant is to *recognize* agency in others, not simply to comprehend otherness.

A distorted version of this recognition is produced in liberal multiculturalism. Yet we have to claim some alliance with it, for on the other side, as the article by Joan Scott that I have already cited will make abundantly clear, are the white-supremacist critics of 'political correctness,' a major phenomenon on the US scene. It is no secret that liberal multi-culturalism is determined by the demands of contemporary transnational capitalisms. It is an important public relations move in the apparent winning of consent from developing countries in the dominant project of the financialization of the globe. (I am arguing that, having shifted our lives from those nations to this, we become part of the problem if we continue to disavow its responsibility.) Procter and Gamble, a large US multinational corporation, sends students specializing in business administration abroad to learn language and culture. Already in 1990, the National Governor's Association Report queried: 'How are we to sell our product in a global economy when we are yet to learn the language of the customers?' If we are to question this distorting rationale for multi-culturalism while utilizing its material support, we have to recognize also that the virulent backlash from the current *racist* dominant in the USA is out of step with contemporary geopolitics. We are caught in a larger struggle where one side devises newer ways to exploit transnationality through a distorting culturalism and the other knows rather little what transnational script drives, writes, and operates it. It is within this ignorant clash that we have to find and locate our agency, and attempt, again and again, to unhinge the clashing machinery.

What actually happens in a typical liberal multicultural classroom 'at its best'? On a given day we are reading a text from one national origin. The group in the classroom from that particular national origin in the general polity can identify with the richness of the texture of the 'culture' in question, often through a haze of nostalgia. (I am not even bringing up the question of the definition of culture.) People from other national origins in the classroom (other, that is, than Anglo) relate sympathetically but superficially, in an aura of 'same difference'. The Anglo relates benevolently to everything, 'knowing about other cultures' in a relativist glow.

What is the basis of the sympathy and the feeling of 'same difference' among the people from various national origins in such a best-case scenario? Here the general social case writes our script. To pick up on my earlier argument, the basis for that feeling is that we have all come with the hope of finding justice or welfare within a capitalist society. (The place of women within this desire merits a separate discussion.)[18] We have come to avoid wars, to avoid political oppression, to escape from poverty, to find opportunity for ourselves and, more important, for our children: with the hope of finding justice within a capitalist society. Strictly speaking, we have left the problems of postcoloniality, located in the former colony (now a 'developing nation' trying to survive the ravages of colonialism), only to discover that the white-supremacist culture wants to claim the entire agency of capitalism – re-coded as the rule of law within a demo-cratic heritage – only for itself; to find that the only entry is through a forgetfulness, or a museumization of national origin in the interest of class mobility. In the liberal multicultural classroom we go for the second alternative, thinking of it as resistance to forgetfulness, but necessarily in the long-term interest of our often disavowed common faith in democratic capitalism: 'a necessity [as Bourdieu reminded us] which the agent *constitutes* as such and for which [s]he provides the scene of action without actually being its subject'. This necessity is what unites us and unless we acknowledge it ('and even if we do ...') we cannot hope to undertake the responsibility of the emerging dominant.

Let me digress for a moment on a lesson such an acknowledgement can draw from history. If by teaching ourselves and our students to acknowledge our part and hope in capitalism we can bring that hope to a persistent and principled crisis, we can set ourselves on the way to intervening in an unfinished chapter of history that was mired in Eurocentric national disputes.

'The Law is the element of calculation, and it is just that there be Law, but justice is incalculable, it requires us to calculate with the incalculable.'[19] Now that the Bolshevik experiment has imploded, we cannot afford to forget that the incalculable dreams of the vestiges of Second International communism (rather than the overt history of its demise in national competition), placed within the calculus of the welfare state, are daily eroded by the forces of what is politely called 'liberalization' in the Third World and the new Second World (the old Eastern bloc) – and by privatization in the First.

In the first version of this essay, delivered in the United States and addressed to teachers of the humanities, I used the term 'Second International' in rather a loose way. In a European and social-scientific context, the steps leading to this loose use should be spelled out.

In *Imperialism*, Lenin writes: 'The boom at the end of the nineteenth century and the crisis of 1900–03. Cartels become one of the foundations of the whole of economic life. Capitalism has been transformed into imperialism.'[20] The description sounds old-fashioned in its terms precisely because the transformation has moved into spectacular determinations. The post-Soviet world order is an example of the timeliness of Lenin's harsh proposition. His scathing critique of Kautsky and the Second International in the same text, on the other hand, has lost some of its point precisely because of the astuteness of his judgement that imperialism does not resemble its nineteenth-century lineaments today. Today the US left turns toward 'radical democracy' rather than socialism because the project is a transformation of capitalist imperialism everywhere, not a claim to the culture or postcoloniality in the multicultural United States of Europe and America.[21] When liberalism claims its revolution in the name of capitalism in the social sciences [see my discussion of Ackerman in note 6], it is time for us, humanist academics marked by recent other-national origin but integrated into developed civil societies, to take note; for we teach a large sector of the growing electorate the uncertain grounds of choice: the singular and unverifiable witnessing of literature.

I will quote Immanuel Wallerstein because the narrative here is conveniently put together, not because I necessarily subscribe to his position on world systems or movements of ethnic identity. I should also mention that the invocation of specifically the *Second* International was to distinguish myself from those academic leftists in the USA who were concentrating on a Trotskyist critique of the Soviet system, precisely because such a concentration did not seem productive of a specific plan of action for the new immigrant academic. Given the absence of a serious state-level Left in the United States, I must confess I did not see the need, in a hortatory piece, to distinguish carefully between the Second International, as such, and the specific party positions and histories of social democracy and democratic socialism. It should be also be remembered that the closest thing to a serious left party in the United States had been the Democratic Socialists of America under the leadership of Michael Harrington. With regard to new immigrants the point is that, whereas the original Second International socialist movement had come to an end in European nationalisms, and the Third International communist movement now shows itself to have had, in many respects, the lineaments and problems of a species of colonialism in the name of internationalism, this particular US group, with what I am calling its 'negotiable' national sentiments straddling the periphery and the centre, can, especially through its contingent of radical humanist teachers, teach not only for a nostalgic culturalism but also for a progressivist socialism. Here is the passage from Wallerstein:

> during the period between the First and Second World Wars [there] exist[ed] ... two rival and fiercely competitive Internationals, the Second and the Third, also known as the conflict between Social Democrats and Communists. ... It is less that the social-democratic parties came to be seen as one of the alternating groups which could legitimately govern than that the main program of the social democrats, the welfare state, came to be accepted by even the conservative parties [of Northwestern Europe], even if begrudgingly.[22]

I now return to the original essay.

The calculations with the incalculable dream of communism are concealed in many passages of the later Marx, the most memorable being the long paragraph at the end of the chapter entitled 'The illusion created by competition' in *Capital*, Vol. 3, where, in a series of five massive ifs (the rhetorical bulwark of the element of calculation), Marx comes to the conclusion: '... *then* nothing of these [capitalist] forms remains, but simply those foundations of the forms that are common to all social modes of production.'[23] If, if, if, if, if. The line between 'democratic' capitalism and democratic socialism is here being undone, with a certain set of impossible conditions. Persistent critique is being replaced by blueprint. The new immigrant ideologue today acts out the impossibility of that blueprint. It is in the face of that impossibility that she must persistently investigate the possibility of the push from democratic capitalism into a globally responsible democratic socialism; the only struggle that fits the post-Soviet scene.[24] It is no secret that, in the developing countries, it is the forces of feminist activism and the non-Eurocentric ecology movement that are attempting to regenerate the critical element into that dream of displacement from capitalism to socialism. Ethnicity, striking at the very heart of identity, is the incalculable and mystical principle that is open for the 'most perverse calculation' in that larger field. The role and agency of the US-based marginal movement and its claims to ethnicity are therefore up for reinvention. That is indeed my theme. But by sounding this motif too soon, I am short-circuiting into my second movement, in which I will speak of educating the educators. Let us return to the undergraduate classroom.

In spite of our commonsense estimation of the best-case scenario, national-origin validation in the general multicultural classroom remains crucially important, for the various national origins, if only to undermine the symbolic importance, out of all proportion to its content and duration, of the test in 'American History and Civilization' administered by the Immigration and Naturalization Services for new citizens, which establishes that, from now on, the history of the racial dominant in the United States is the migrant's own.

I have already suggested that the place of women within the desire for justice under capitalism may be different. Amy Tan's controversial *Joy Luck Club* animates this difference in every possible way.[25] The competitive difference among marginal groups, the difference between economic migration (to the USA) and political exile (in China), the necessity and impossibility of representation of the 'culture of origin', culture as negotiable systems of representation between mothers and daughters, the role of university and corporatism in 'moving West to reach the East' (T205), the extreme ungroundedness of identity in the obsessive pursuit of perspectives, all thematized in this first novel, can be used for political pedagogy in the invention of unity.

Let me indicate the inaugural staging of the economic argument, rehearsed many times in the novel:

> After everybody votes unanimously for the Canada gold stock, I go into the kitchen to ask Auntie An-mei why the Joy Luck Club started investing in stocks. … 'We got smart. Now we can all win and lose equally. We can have stock market luck. And we can play mah jong for fun, just for a few dollars, winner take all. Losers take home leftovers! So everyone can have some joy. Smart-hanh?' (T18)

Contrast this egalitarian Joy Luck by way of investment to the original Joy Luck Club, four women attempting to contain political exile by force of spirit. This is the frame narrator remembering the reminiscence of her recently dead mother. They are refugees from the Japanese, in Kweilin:

I knew which women I wanted to ask. They were all young like me, with wishful faces. ... Each week we could forget past wrongs done to us. We weren't allowed to think a bad thought. We feasted, we laughed, we played games, lost and won, we told the best stories. And each week, we could hope to be lucky. That hope was our only joy. ... I won tens of thousands of *yuan*. But I wasn't rich. No. By then paper money had become worthless. Even toilet paper was worth more. And that made us laugh harder, to think a thousand-*yuan* note wasn't even good enough to rub on our bottoms. (T10, T12)

In this perspectivized field of identity, only the Polaroid produces the final ID. Here is the last scene of the novel, where the Chinese-American frame narrator meets her long-lost Chinese half-sisters. No attempt is made to provide interior representations of their memories:

I look at their faces again and I see no trace of my mother in them. Yet they still look familiar. ... The flash of the Polaroid goes off and my father hands me the snapshot. ... The gray-green surface changes to the bright colors of our three images, sharpening and deepening all at once. And although we don't speak, I know we all see it: Together we look like our mother. Her same eyes, her same mouth, open in surprise to see, at last, her long-cherished wish. (T331–332)

It is at her peril that the reader forgets the authoritative cherished wish that is given in the opening epigraphic tale:

The old woman remembered a swan she had bought many years ago in Shanghai for a foolish sum. This bird, boasted the market vendor, was once a duck that stretched its neck in hopes of becoming a goose. ... When she arrived in the new country, the immigration officials pulled her swan away from her, leaving the woman ... with only one swan feather for a memory. ... For a long time now the woman had wanted to give her daughter the single swan feather and tell her, 'This feather may look worthless, but it comes from afar and carries with it all my good intentions.' And she waited, year after year, for the day she could tell her daughter this in perfect American English. (T3–4)

Tan's risk-taking book offers us a timely concept–metaphor: the dead mother's voice achieves perfect American English in the regularizing graph of the Polaroid. It is left to us to decode the scandal with sympathy and responsibility.

The earlier scene

Since Reconstruction, the first major change in the Constitution after the Civil War, the various waves of immigrants have mingled with one of the supportive, original agents of the production of American origins: the African-American (not the Original Nations). But even here, the emphasis on assimilation given in the melting-pot theory followed the pattern of Anglocentrism first, and a graduated Eurocentrism next, with the lines of dominance radiating out of that presumptive centre. Indeed, this is why the older immigrant elements in the multicultural classroom may or may not strengthen the undermining of the INS [Immigration and

Naturalization Service – eds] test, if the issue is the invention of unity rather than difference. This is the pedagogic imperative, the persuasive force field of the classroom, to change the 'may not' to 'may' among the descendants of the older white immigrants, in the interest of a different unity. We are not disuniting America. If we are not aware of this as participating agents, the tremendous force of American ethnicity can be used in the service of consolidating the New World Order out of the ashes of the Soviet Union, simply by re-coding capitalism as democracy.

I have so far put aside the uprooting of the African and the redefining of the Original Nations in the interest of the new (and old) immigrants. Also to be placed here is the itinerary of the Chicano/Latino, unevenly straddling the history of two empires, the Spanish and the US, one on the cusp of the transition to capitalism, the other active today.

For me, an outsider who came to the United States in 1961, the voice that still echoes from the civil rights/Black Power movement is from the Ocean Hill-Brownsville School District Struggle of 1968.[26] I had received my PhD the previous year. My own schooldays in India, a newly independent country attempting to decolonize its curriculum, were not far behind. Perhaps this is why words from that less famous struggle have been retained by the force of my memory. I am not even sure who it was that said them. It may have been the Reverend Galamaison: 'This is a struggle against educational colonization.' The other day I caught a voice on television, of a little African-American girl who was then a student in that school district, now a mature woman who spoke of her experience and remarked: 'We became Third World. We became international.'

Let me propose what may at first sight seem odd: in the struggle against *internal* colonization, it is the African-American who is *post*colonial in the United States. To imply that postcoloniality is a step beyond colonialism is the new immigrant's reactive and unexamined disavowal of the move (however justified) away from the postcolonial scene to embrace the American dream – the civilizing mission of the new colonizing power. In its own context, postcoloniality is the achievement of an independence that removes the legal subject status of a people as the result of struggle, armed or otherwise. In terms of internal colonization, Emancipation, Reconstruction, civil rights is just such an achievement. Furthermore, postcoloniality is no guarantee of prosperity for all, but rather a signal for the consolidation of recolonization. In that respect as well, the condition of the African-American fits the general picture of postcoloniality much more accurately than the unearned claims of the Eurocentric well-placed migrant. Paradoxically, the rising racist backlash is an acknowledgement of this. In the so-called postcolonial countries, postcoloniality is not a signal for an end to struggle, but rather a shifting of the struggle to the persistent register of decolonization. Here, too, the situation of the African-American struggle offers a parallel. The second wave of backlash rage is on the rise. With an awareness of that register Joan Scott asks her astute question and makes her judgements in terms of class:

... the special treatment that came with high social status never seems to have been seen as a compromise of university standards. (One has to wonder why it was that, for example, the test scores of blacks are stolen from the admissions office at Georgetown Law School and published by disgruntled conservatives, while those of alumni children of influential politicians were not. One can only conclude that the call for a return to a meritocracy that never was is a thinly veiled manifestation of racism.)[27]

I am claiming postcoloniality for the African-American, then, not because I want to interfere with her self-representation, but because I want to correct the self-representation of the new immigrant academic as postcolonial, indeed as the source of postcolonial theory.

In terms of internal colonization in the United States, the original three groups have not emerged equally into postcoloniality. If I read the signs right (and I may not), the Latino/Chicano segment has, on one side, been moving for some time toward a recognition, in literary–cultural studies, of 'our America' in the entire (North–Central–South) American continental context, not contained within *internal* US colonization, as the African-American must be. The *différence* of unity and difference between African and African-American Pan-Africanism is the authoritative text here. The Latino/Chicano move toward 'our America' may be read as a move toward globality. This is particularly interesting today because, given US economic policy toward Latin America, 'illegal immigration', especially in the case of Mexico, *is* transnationality. On that level – the level of the subaltern *as* 'illegal immigrant' under limited surveillance by the border patrol – the local *is* the global.[28] By contrast, specifically the Chicano engagement in the restoration of the major voices within internal colonization belongs within diasporic discourse studies.[29]

The thought of sublating internal colonization (another description of postcoloniality) is articulated differently in the context of the Original Nations.

At a recent conference on the literature of ethnicity, John Mohawk anguished that Native American writing was not yet stylistically competitive with the kind of sexy postmodernism that some of our best-known colleagues celebrate in the name of postcoloniality.[30] The embattled phrase 'stylistically competitive' was not his. But I will use that phrase again before I end.

Since the Native American voice has been most rigorously marginalized even within marginality, I want to spend some time on the work of a Native American scholar, Jack D. Forbes, who is claiming a new unity with African-Americans. Unity in this sphere cannot be based on an initial, often disavowed, *choice* for justice under capitalism, as in the case of the new immigrants; but rather in the investigation of the institution of the so-called origins of the white-supremacist United States: a sublation of internal colonization.[31] Before making the claim to this divided unity, Forbes lays bare the mechanics of constructing another unity, in another political interest. He gets behind dictionaries to capture the elusive lexical space in-between meaning shifts, by sheer empirical obstinacy. He teases out usage to show the emergence of juridico-legal practice and rational classification. This is an invaluable quarry, on the level of aggregative apparatuses (power) and of propositions (knowledge), for a future Foucauldian who will dare to try to take these further below, into the utterables (*énoncés*) that form the archival ground level (not ground) of knowledge and the non-symbolizable force field that shapes the shifting ground levels of power.[32] I cannot readily imagine such a person, for the *pouvoir-savoir* (ability-to-make-sense) in question involves

> ... 300 to 400 years of intermixture of a very complex sort, [and] varying amounts of African and American ancestry derived at different intervals and from extremely diverse sources – as from American nations as different as Naragansett or Pequot and the Carib or Arawak, or from African nations as diverse as the Mandinka, Yoruba, and Malagasy. (F270–71)

For the perceptive reader, then, Forbes's book at once opens the horizons of Foucault's work, shows the immense, indeed perhaps insuperable complexity of the task once we let go of 'pure' European outlines, and encourages a new generation of scholars to acquire the daunting skills for robust cultural history. This work is rather different from the primitivist patronage of orality. It is in the context of this complexity that a new 'unity' is claimed:

> In an article published in the *Journal of Negro History* [James Hugo] Johnston remarked: 'Where the Negro was brought into contact with the American Indian the blood of the two races intermingled. The Indian has not disappeared from the land, but is now part of the Negro population of the United States.' The latter statement might offend many Indians today, who still survive, of course, in great numbers as Native Americans, but nonetheless the significance of Johnston's thesis as regards the extent of Native American-African intermixture remains before us. (F191)

This point of view is to be contrasted with the persuasive and representative usual view of the substitution of one collective identity by another: that the Indian population dwindled, was exported, and was replaced by Africans and imported slaves from the West Indies.[33] It is in the pores of such identity-based arguments that Forbes discovers the survival of the Native American, in the male and female line. By focusing on the vast heterogeneity and textuality of the description of mixed groups, Forbes shows that the emergence of the 'other', as the Other of the white, may be, at best, an unwitting legitimation by reversal of the very dominant positions it is supposed to contest. My argument thus is a corollary of that of Forbes. Forbes points out what we caricature by defining ourselves as the 'other (of the white dominant in metropolitan space)':

> It would appear that both Americans and Africans began to appear in exotic pageants and entertainments staged in London during the seventeenth century. It is not always possible to clearly ascertain the ethnicity of the performers,

since Africans were sometimes dressed up as Americans, or perhaps vice versa. (F56)

In the discontinuous narrative of the development of racism, how are we to compute the relationship between that usage and the 1854 California State Supreme Court statement that 'expresses a strong tendency in the history of the United States, a tendency to identify two broad classes of people: white and non-white, citizen and non-citizen (or semi-citizen)' (F65)? Are we, once again, to become complicitous with this tendency by identifying ourselves, single ethnic group by group, or as migrant collectivity, only as the 'other' of the white dominant? Shall we, 'like so many Europeans, [remain] utterly transfixed by the black–white nexus either as "opposites" or as real people' (F172)? Given that, in the literally post-colonial areas like Algeria or India, white racism is no longer the chief problem, Forbes's historical reasoning is yet another way of bringing together the intuitions of global resistance.[34]

Yet even in this work, where isolationist concerns broaden out into global decolonization of scholarship, one must note the absence of a feminist impulse. The Native American woman, being legally free, was often the enslaved man's access to 'freedom' in the USA. And slavery itself is 'matrilineal'. These two facts provide the motor for a great deal of Forbes's narrative of interaction. Yet *Black Africans and Native Americans*, so resourceful and imaginative in probing the pores of the hide of history, never questions the gender secrets hidden in them. It is correctly mentioned that Native American practices included the thought of 'individual freedom and utopian socialism' (F266). But it is not noticed that there is feminism in those practices as well. What is it to define as 'free', *after* enslavement, genocide, colonization, theft of land, tax imposition, women who had, before these acts (masquerading today as social cohesion), been culturally inscribed as 'freer'? What is it to become, then, a passageway to freedom after the fact? What is the 'meaning' of matrilineage-in-slavery, mentioned in parentheses – '(generally slavery was inherited in the female line)' (F240) – where lineage itself is devastated?[35]

The global field/transnational literacy on the graduate curriculum

With the name of woman I pass from the heading 'Access to the Universal' into 'The Global Field', of uneven decolonization, and make an appeal to decolonize feminism as it studies feminism in decolonization. With plenty of help from feminist historians and social scientists, I teach myself to teach a course on 'Feminism in Decolonization'. From personal experience, then, I know how much education an educator (in this case myself) needs in this venture. 'Feminism in Decolonization' is a political rewriting of the title 'Women in Development'. I am encouraged to see that a critique of the metropolitan feminist focus on women in development is one of the main premisses of the article by Aihwa Ong that I have already cited (see note 17). This gives me an opportunity to recite once again that, in this effort, we have to learn inter-disciplinary teaching by supplementing our work with the social sciences and supplementing theirs with ours.

It is through the literature of ethnicity that we customarily approach the question of globality within literary–cultural studies when they are defined along humanist disciplinary lines. The Greek–English Lexicon tells us that the word *ethnos* meant 'a number of people accustomed to live together' – one's own kind of people, in other words – and therefore, after Homer, 'nation'. Side by side with the Greek word *ethnos* was the word *ethnikos* – other people, often taken to mean 'heathen, pagan, foreign'. It is not hard to see how the New Testament would use these already available words to mean 'all but Jews and Christians'. Like many ideas belonging to Christianity, these words were pressed into pejorative service in English, to mean 'other (lesser) peoples', in the Age of Conquest. In the nineteenth century, as conquest consolidated itself into imperialism, the word becomes 'scientific', especially in the forms 'ethnography' and 'ethnology'. We are aware of the debates between the British ethnologist-ethnographers on the one hand, and anthropologists on the other, as to whether their study should be based on language or on physical character-istics. In the event, the discipline concerned itself, of course, with ideas of race, culture, and religion. The connections between national origin and 'ethnicity' are, at best, dubious, and, at worst, a site of violent contestation. In the cultural politics of the United States, they are now firmly in place without question.

I think the literature of ethnicity writes itself between *ethnos* – a writer writing for her *own* people (whatever that means) without deliberated self-identification as such – and *ethnikos*, the pejoratively defined other reversing the charge, (de)anthropologizing herself by separating herself into a staged identity. The literature of ethnicity in this second sense thus carries, paradoxically, the writer's signature as divided against itself, for the staging of the displacing of the dominant must somehow be indexed there. A woman's relationship to a patriarchal or patriarchalized ethnicity makes her access to this signature even more complex.

The standard world-systems estimation of ethnicity, not unrelated to the failures of systemic communism, is something like the following: 'Seen in long historical time and broad world space, [nations and ethnic groups] fade into one another, becoming only "groups". Seen in short historical time and narrow world space, they become clearly defined and so form distinctive structures.'[36] Although I am in general sympathy with the resistance to 'the intellectual pressure to reify groups', I cannot work with this world-system view of ethnicities in globality. The long view and the broad space are so perspectivized that to learn to acquire them in order to produce correct descriptions may be useful only if supplemented unceasingly, not just by way of the popular US T-shirt slogan 'think globally act locally', although it is not bad for a start.

Sublimation (and what Lacan calls the symbolic circuit) stands over against what Freud represents as cultural–ethical pathogenic repressions that may be represented as movements against the individual or social psychic system. On the literary-critical side, Fredric Jameson represents such representations. And therefore he has been reading Third World literary works for some time now as *allegories* of transnational capitalism. It is because I agree with Jameson in a general way that I would like to insist here upon a different definition of allegory, not just a symbolic order of semiosis. Otherwise, caught between accusations of political correctness and liberal multiculturalism, we are denied the right to say 'Heresy by itself is no token of truth.'[37]

I take as my motto the opening words of *Abarodh-bāshini* (Lady Prisoner), a critique of veiled female life published by Rokeya Sakhawat Hossain, an Indian Muslim woman, between 1915 and 1917. She shows that not only the signature of the writer of ethnicity, but also the signature of the patriarchally imprisoned woman, is self-separated:

> We have become habituated after living for so long in prison; therefore, against the prison we, especially I myself, have nothing to say. If the fishwife is asked, 'Is the stink of rotten fish good or bad?' what will she respond? Here I will make a gift of a few of our personal experiences to our reader-sisters, and I hope they will be pleased.'[38]

Rokeya Hossain allows me to produce a more responsible sense of allegory: the fishwife-as-feminist who, like Hossain, admits to being unable to distance herself from her own imprisonment 'admits', in other words, 'to the impossibility of reading [her] own text ...' can only produce, as she herself says, fragmentary instances 'against the inherent logic which animate[s] the development of the narrative, [of imprisonment], and disarticulates it in a way that seems perverse. ...'[39] On that model, since *we* are imprisoned in and habituated to capitalism, we might try to look at the *allegory* of capitalism not in terms of capitalism as the source of authoritative reference but as the constant small failures in and interruptions to its logic, which help to recode it and produce our unity. 'Allegory', here, 'speaks out with the referential efficacy of a *praxis*.'

Learning this praxis, which may produce interruptions to capitalism from within, requires us to make future educators in the humanities transnationally literate, so that they can distinguish between the varieties of decolonization on the agenda, rather than collapse them as 'postcoloniality'. I am speaking of transnational *literacy*. We must remember that to achieve literacy in a language is not to become an expert in it. I am therefore not making an impossible demand upon the graduate curriculum. Literacy produces the skill to differentiate between letters, so that an articulated script can be read, reread, written, rewritten. Literacy is poison as well as medicine. It allows us to sense that the other is not just a 'voice', but that others produce articulated texts, even as they, like us, are written in and by a text not of our own making. It is through transnational literacy that we can invent grounds for an interruptive praxis from within our disavowed hope in justice under capitalism.

If we were transnationally literate, we might read sectors that are stylistically noncompetitive with the spectacular experimental fiction of certain sections of hybridity or postcoloniality with a disarticulating rather than a comparative point of view. Native American fiction would then allegorically intervene in reminding us of the economic peripheralization of the originary communist precapitalist ethnicities of the Fourth World. We can link it to the fact that, even as we admire the sophistication of Indian writing in English, we have not yet seen a non-Christian *tribal* Indo-Anglian fiction writer in English.[40] And we will also discover that all stylistically noncompetitive literature cannot be relegated to the same transnational allegory in the crude sense.

Take, for example, the case of Bangladesh. You will hardly ever find an entry from Bangladesh on a course on postcolonial or Third World literature. Bangladesh is stylistically non-competitive on the international market. The UN has written it off as the lowest on its list of developing countries, its women at the lowest rung of development. Our students will not know that, as a result of decolonization from the British in 1947, and liberation from West Pakistan in 1971, Bangladesh had to go through a double decolonization; that as a result of the appropriation of its language by the primarily Hindu Bengali nationalists in the nineteenth century, and the adherence of upper-class Bangladeshis to Arabic and Urdu, the Bangladeshis have to win back their language inch by inch. Some of this may be gleaned from Naila Kabeer's essay on Bangladesh in Deniz Kandiyoti's *Women, Islam, and the State.*[41] But apart from a rather mysterious paragraph on 'progressive non-government organizations' which would be incomprehensible to most graduate students of modern languages, there is no mention of the fact that, because of the timing and manner of Bangladesh's liberation, the country fell into the clutches of the transnational global economy in a way significantly different from the situation both of the Asian-Pacific *and* the older postcolonial countries.[42] The transnationally illiterate student might not know that the worst victim of the play of the multinational pharmaceuticals in the name of population control is the woman's body; that in the name of development, international monetary organizations are substituting the impersonal and incomprehensible State for the older more recognizable enemies-cum-protectors: the patriarchal family; it is a substitution broadly comparable, in women's history, to the transition from feudalism to capitalism.[43] In this situation, the most dynamic minds are engaged in alternative development work, not literary production. And class-fixed literary production as such in Bangladesh is not concerned with the place of the nation in transnationality, but rather with a nation-fixed view which does not produce the energy of translation.[44]

About twelve years ago, in an essay that was allegedly refused entry into the Norton Critical Edition of *Jane Eyre* because it was too oppositional, I wrote these words:

A full literary reinscription cannot easily flourish in the imperialist fracture or discontinuity, covered over by an alien legal system masquerading as Law as such, an alien ideology established as only Truth, and a set of human sciences busy establishing the 'native' as self-consolidating Other. ... To reopen the fracture without succumbing to a nostalgia for lost origins, the literary critic must turn to the archives of imperial governance.[45]

Over the last decade, I have painfully learned that literary reinscription cannot easily flourish, not only in the inauguration of imperialism, but also in the discontinuity of recolonization. The literary critic and educator must acquire and transmit transnational literacy in a system that must be allegorized by its failures. There is a mad scramble on among highly placed intellectuals to establish their 'colonial origins' these days. Such efforts belong with the impatience of world-systems literary theory, with portmanteau theories of postcoloniality, with the isolationism of both multiculturalism and antiracism; they cannot keep the fracture or wound open. This is the infinite responsibility of the emergent dominant engaged in graduate education in the humanities. Otherwise we side with the sanctimonious pronouncement of a Lynn Cheney: of course I support multicultural education. I want each child to know that he can succeed.[46] Woodrow Wilson, I believe, suggested at some point that he wanted each American to be a captain of industry! Faith in capitalism gone mad in the name of individualism and competition.

Over against this super-individualist faith, let me quote the Declaration of Comilla (1989), drawn up in Bangladesh by the Feminist International Network of Resistance to Reproductive and Genetic Engineering, under the auspices of UBINIG, a Bangladesh Development Alternative collective, proposing once again an interruptive literate practice within development:

> We live in a limited world. In the effort to realise [the] illusion [of unlimited progress leading to unlimited growth] within a limited world, it is necessary that some people [be] exploited so that others can grow; Woman is exploited so that Man can grow; South is exploited so that North can grow; Animals are exploited so that people can grow! The Good Life of some is always at the expense of others. Health of some is based on the disease of others. Fertility of some is based on the infertility of others. ... What is good for the ruling class should be good for everybody?[47]

I can just hear world-systems theorists murmuring, 'moralism'. But then, the unexamined moralism of liberal multiculturalism allows us to forget these women's admonition. Like the fishwife, we cannot tell if the stink of rotten fish is good or bad when we disavow our own part or hope in US capitalism.

I heard a colleague say recently, only half in jest, that the newest criticism no longer considered the 'literary' part of literature to be that important. On the contrary. We expand the definition of literature to include social inscription. Farida Akhter intervening angrily against 'the agenda of developing countries enforcing population policies on others' at the Third Plenary of the World Women's Congress for a Healthy Planet on 11 November 1991 has something like a relationship with the absence of classy postcolonial women's literary texts from Bangladesh on the US curriculum. If those of us who write dissertations and teach future teachers still peddle something called 'culture' on the model of national-origin validation (crucial to the general *undergraduate* curriculum), we have failed to grasp the moment of the emerging dominant, to rend time with the urgency of justice. Indeed, in the era of global capital rampant, it is the new immigrant intellectual's negotiable nationality that might act as a lever to undo the nation-based conflict that killed the Second International.

Conclusion

I close with two passages I often quote these days, from Assia Djébar's novel, *Fantasia.*[48] Algeria, like India, is an older postcolonial state. The old modes of decolonization at the time of national liberation are crumbling in both. Transnational literacy allows us to recognize that we hear a different *kind* of voice from these countries, especially from singular women, from Mahasweta, from Assia Djébar.

In the case of Djébar, that crumbling can be staged as a profound critique of Fanon's false hopes for unveiling expressed in *A Dying Colonialism.* Here are Fanon's famous words:

> There is the much discussed status of the Algerian woman ... today ... receiving the only valid challenge: the experience of revolution. Algerian woman's ardent love of the home is not a limit imposed by the universe. ... Algerian society reveals itself not to be the woman-less society that had been so convincingly described.'[49]

And here is Djébar, in *Fantasia.* Staging herself as an Algerian Muslim woman denied access to classical Arabic, she gives a fragmented version of the graph-ing of her biography in French, of which I quote the following fragments:

> The overlay of my oral culture wearing dangerously thin ... . Writing of the most anodyne of childhood memories leads back to a body bereft of voice. To attempt an autobiography in French words alone is to show more than its skin under the slow scalpel of a live autopsy. Its flesh peels off and with it, seemingly, the speaking of childhood which can no longer be written is torn to shreds. Wounds are reopened, veins weep, the blood of the self flows and that of others, a blood which has never dried. (D156; 178)

Identity is here exposed as a wound, exposed by the historically hegemonic imperial languages, for those who have learned the double-binding 'practice of [their] writing' (D181). This double bind, felt by feminists in decolonizing countries rather than in Eurocentric economic migration, is not ours. The wound of our split identity is not this specific wound, for this wound is not necessarily, indeed rarely, opened by a hope in Anglo–US–EEC-based capitalism.

One of the major motifs of *Fantasia* is a meditation upon the possibility that to achieve autobiography in the double bind of the practice of the conqueror's writing is, not for the well-placed marginal to 'tell her own story', but to learn, to learn to be taken seriously by the gendered subaltern, the woman in radical disenfranchisement, who has not had the chance to master that practice. And therefore, hidden in the many-sectioned third part of the book, there is the single episode where the central character speaks in the ethical singularity of the *tu-toi* to Zohra, an eighty-year-old rural *mujāhida* (female freedom fighter) who has been devastated both by her participation in the nationalist struggle and by the neglect of woman's claims in decolonized Algeria. The achievement of the autobiographer-in-fiction is to be fully fledged as a storyteller to this intimate interlocutor. Telling one's own story is not the continuist imperative of identity upon the privileged feminist in decolonization.

Rokeya Sakhawat Hossain, an upper-class Indian woman, had not kept a journal, but spoken as the fishwife. Djébar's French-educated heroine attempts to animate the story of two nineteenth-century Algerian prostitutes, Fatma and Meriem, allegorically interrupting Eugène Fromentin's *Un Été au Sahara*, a masterpiece of orientalism. She succeeds, for Zohra's curiosity flares up:

> 'And Fatma? And Meriem?' Lla Zhora interrupted, catching herself following the story as if it were a legend recounted by a bard. 'Where did you hear this story?' she went on, impatiently.

The 'I' (now at last articulated because related and responsible to 'you') replies simply thus:

> 'I read it!' I retorted. 'An eye-witness told it to a friend who wrote it down.' (D166)

This unemphatic short section ends simply: 'I, your cousin, translate this account into the mother tongue, and report it to you. So I try my self out, as ephemeral teller, close to you little mother, in front of your vegetable patch' (D167). The central character shares her mother tongue as instrument of translation with the other woman.

In the rift of this divided field of identity, the tale shared in the mother tongue forever interrupts (in every act of reading) and is forever absent, for it is in the mother tongue. The authority of the 'now' inaugurates this absent autobiography in every 'here' of the book. The fleeting framed moment undoes the 'blank [*blanc*] in the memory' of the narrator's *personal* childhood, which only yields the image of an old crone whose muttered Quranic curses could not be understood (D10).

The final movement of *Fantasia* is in three short sections, what remains of an autobiography when it has been unravelled strand by strand. First, a tribute to Pauline Rolland, the French revolutionary of 1848, exiled in Algeria, as the true ancestress of the *mujāhidāt*.[50] Revolutionary discourse for women cannot rely upon indigenous cultural production. If the tale told to Zohra is a divided moment of access to autobiography as the telling of an absent story, here autobiography is the possibility of writing or giving witing to the other identifiable only as a mutilated metonym of violence, as part object. The interrupted continuous source is, once again, Eugène Fromentin. There is one unexplained Arabic word in the following passage, a word that means, in fact, 'pen':

> Eugène Fromentin offers me an unexpected hand – the hand of an unknown woman he was never able to draw. He describes in sinister detail: as he is leaving the oasis which six months after the massacre is still filled with its stench, Fromentin picks up out of the dust the severed hand of an anonymous Algerian woman. He throws it down again in his path. Later, I seize on this living hand, hand of mutilation and of memory, and I attempt to bring it the *qalam.* (D226)

Everything in this chapter has been a meditation upon the possibility that, at this divided moment, we should not only work mightily to take up the pen in our own hands, but that we should also attempt to pick up the *qalam* offered us in uneven decolonization, and, with the help of our Polaroid, attempt to figure forth the world's broken and shifting alphabet.

Notes

1. I thank Thomas W. Keenan for reading the first, and Vincent Cheng for reading the final versions, respectively.

2. As always, by 'new immigrant' I mean the continuing influx of immigrants since, by the 'Immigration and Nationality Act of 1 October 1965', Lyndon Johnson 'swept away both the national-origin system and the Asia-Pacific Triangle' – precisely the groups escaping decolonization, one way or another. 'That the Act would, for example, create a massive brain drain from developing countries and increase Asian immigration 500 per cent was entirely unexpected' (Maldwyn Allen Jones, *American Immigration*, Chicago, University of Chicago Press, 2nd edn, 1992, pp. 266, 267). For purposes of definition, I have repeated this footnote in other writing.

3. Darryl J. Gless and Barbara Herrnstein Smith (eds), *The Politics of Liberal Education* (Durham: Duke University Press, 1992), gives a sense of the debate.

4. Arthur M. Schlesinger Jr, *The Disuniting of America* (New York, Norton, 1992), p. 138.

5. Zbigniew Brzezinski, *Out of Control: Global Turmoil on the Eve of the Twenty First Century* (New York, Scribner's, 1993), p. 231.

6. As I revise the essay for publication, the issue of multiculturalism has become visible in the high waters of the academic mainstream, as witness Charles Taylor, *Multiculturalism and 'The Politics of Recognition': An Essay* (Princeton, Princeton University Press, 1992), Bruce Ackerman, *The Future of Liberal Revolution* (New Haven, Yale University Press, 1992), John Rawls, *Political Liberalism* (New York, Columbia University Press, 1993). These important books can obviously not be discussed in a footnote. Here suffice it to say that the three texts have something like a relationship with the civilizing mission of imperialism seriously credited. Ackerman's position is so musclebound with learning as to be least examined, and it is not surprising that, at the 1994 Pacific American Philosophical Association Convention,

he advanced his position as a justification both for foreign aid and for the emancipation of the women of developing nations. His book is specifically addressed to the needs of the New World Order: 'The meaning of 1989' (pp. 113–23) is one of his chapters. Charles Taylor reduces the value of his thoughtful study by deducing the subject of multiculturalism (difficult for me to imagine as a unity) from the 'European' historical narrative of the emergence of secularism. And John Rawls, by far the most astute of the three, recognizes the limits of liberalism as politics in order to save it as philosophy. 'The hearts of innumerable men and women respond … with idealistic fervour to [t]his clarion, because it [goes] … without saying that it would be good for … anywhere … to be made [American]. At this point it might be useful to wonder which of the ideals that make our hearts beat faster will seem wrong-headed to people a hundred years from now' (Doris Lessing, *African Laughter: Four Visits to Zimbabwe*, New York, Harper Collins, 1992, p. 3; she is writing about Cecil Rhodes and Southern Rhodesia). I have not yet read Duncan Kennedy, *Sexy Dressing Etc.: Essays On the Power and Politics of Cultural Identity* (Cambridge, Harvard University Press, 1993).

7. I insist upon this point, trivially but crucially true. It is so often neglected that I take the liberty of self-citation: 'The fact that socialism can never fully (adequately) succeed is what it has in common with everything. It is *after* that fact that one starts to make the choices, especially after the implosion of the Bolshevik experiment' ('Marginality in the teaching machine', in Spivak, *Outside in the Teaching Machine*, New York, Routledge, 1993, p. 68). What follows in the text about the foundation of the United States is a condensed version of the final chapter of this book. Mindful of Kathy E. Ferguson's critique of my apparent claim to authority in *The Man Question: Visions of Subjectivity in Feminist Theory* (Berkeley, University of California Press, 1993), p. 201, I controlled my habit of self-referencing for a while. Weighing this against many complaints of overburdened, cryptic, and incomprehensible writing, I have thought it best to revert to a modified version of my original practice.

8. Robin Blackburn, *The Overthrow of Colonial Slavery: 1776–1848* (London, Verso, 1988), pp. 123, 124.

9. For current straws in the wind, see note 6.

10. Joan Wallach Scott, 'The campaign against political correctness: what's really at stake?', *Change* 23:6 (November/December 1991), pp. 32–3. The passages from Mohanty and Fynsk are from pages 39 and 43 respectively.

11. Pierre Bourdieu, 'The philosophical institution', Alan Montefiore (ed.), *Philosophy in France Today* (Cambridge, Cambridge University Press, 1983), p. 2 (emphasis mine).

12. In this connection, the phrase 'colonial subject' may be misleadingly laden with pathos. In my estimation, the constitution of the so-called colonial subject can also be described as the violent and necessary constitution of an abstract subject of a limited-access civil society – the core of the colonial infrastructure. Eurocentric economic migration and its struggle for full access to civil rights accompanied by a validated if fantasmatic national cultural origin can then be seen as a document continuous with that constitution. For a Foucauldian elaboration of this theme, see Spivak, 'Narratives of multiculturalism', in Thomas W. Keenan (ed.) *Cultural Diversities* (forthcoming); for an elaboration of this in terms of the old multicultural imperial formations in Eurasia, see 'Response to Anahid Kasabian and David Kasanjian', *Armenian Review* (forthcoming).

13. Jacques Derrida, 'Force of law: the "Mystical Foundation of Authority"', in

Deconstruction and the Possibility of Justice, Cordoza Law Review XI.v-vi (July/August 1990), p. 971.

14. Some of these philosophical moves are to be found, with reference to a general social context, in the discussion of the aporia between the experience of the impossible and the possibility of the political in Jacques Derrida, *The Other Heading: Reflections on Today's Europe*, translated by Pascale-Anne Brault and Michael B. Naas (Bloomington, Indiana University Press, 1992), pp. 44–6; and with reference to the academic institutional context in Derrida, 'Mochlos; or, The Conflict of the Faculties', in Richard Rand (ed.), *Logomachia: the Conflict of the Faculties* (Lincoln, University of Nebraska Press, 1992), pp. 3–34.

15. Scott, 'Campaign', p. 43.

16. Herbert Marcuse, 'Repressive tolerance', in Robert Paul Wolff and Barrington Moore Jr (eds.), *A Critique of Pure Tolerance* (Boston, Beacon Press, 1965), p. 116.

17. Aihwa Ong, 'Colonialism and modernity: feminist re-presentations of women in non-Western societies', *Inscriptions* 3/4 (1988), p. 90. Although I have some problems with the details of Ong's argument, I am fully in accord with her general point.

18. I have attempted such a separate discussion in 'Diasporas old and new: women in the transnational world,' a paper delivered at Rutgers University in March 1994. Suffice it here to say that even within economic migration, women often remain exilic. The definition is, as usual, gender-sensitive.

19. Derrida, 'Force of law', p. 947.

20. V.I. Lenin, *Imperialism: the Highest Stage of Capitalism: a Popular Outline* (New York, International Publishers, 1939), p. 22.

21. Stanley Aronowitz, 'The situation of the left in the United States', *Socialist Review* 93:3 (January–March 1994), pp. 5–79. See also the collection of responses in the subsequent issue.

22. Immanuel Wallerstein et al., *Antisystemic Movements* (New York, Verso, 1989), pp. 32, 34–5.

23. Karl Marx, *Capital*, translated by David Fernbach (New York, Vintage, 1981), Vol. 3, pp. 1015–16.

24. For the argument that socialism and capitalism are each other's *différence*, see Spivak, 'Supplementing Marxism', in Steven Cullenberg and Bernd Magnus (eds), *Whither Marxism?* (New York, Routledge, 1995).

25. Amy Tan, *The Joy Luck Club* (New York, Ivy Books, 1989). Hereafter cited in text as T, followed by page reference. For specific criticism of this text and other 'ethnic minority' texts from the specific ethnic group, see my description of the liberal multiculturalist classroom above. By contrast, I am speaking of the text's witnessing to the US commonality of the migrant, 'the same difference'.

26. The fact that this struggle did not mean the same thing for the Jewish and the black sectors of the district brings forth both the element of competition and the pedagogically negotiable epistemic space of the old immigrants that I have touched on above. These examples make clear that abstract talk of the politics of difference and different histories do not go too far unless we consider only the 'white' as dominant. For details of the event, see Maurice R. Berube and Marilyn Gittell (eds), *Confrontation at Ocean Hill-Brownsville: the New York School Strikes of 1968* (New York, Praeger, 1969). For a testament in the continuing struggle in the field of black–Jewish unity, consider Thurgood Marshall's choice of Jack Greenberg in 1949 (Jack Greenberg, *Crusaders in the Courts: How a Dedicated Band of Lawyers Fought for the Civil Rights Revolution*, New York, Basic Books, 1994).

27. Scott, 'Campaign', p. 36.

28. For limited surveillance by the border patrol, see Michael Kearney, 'Borders and boundaries of state and self at the end of empire', *Journal of Historical Sociology* 4:1 (March 1991), pp. 52–74. Illegal immigration is so volatile a public issue in California that descriptive generalizations may become obsolete rather quickly.

29. Diaspora and transnationality are investigated, respectively, in Jose Saldivar, *The Dialectics of Our America: Genealogy, Cultural Critique, and Literary History* (Raleigh, Duke University Press, 1991) and *Border Matters* (Berkeley, University of California Press, forthcoming). For an appropriately gendered perspective, see Jean Franco, *Border Patrol* (Cambridge, Harvard University Press, forthcoming).

30. With texts such as Leslie Silko, *Almanac of the Dead* (New York, Simon and Schuster 1991) and the work of younger writers like Drew Taylor, such anguish seems slightly anachronistic as I revise, although it is still appropriate in the larger context.

31. Jack D. Forbes, *Black Africans and Native Americans: Color, Race and Caste in the Evolution of Red Black Peoples* (New York, Blackwell, 1988). Further references are included in the text as F followed by page number.

32. It would, for example, be interesting to play this narrative in counterpoint with Hortense Spillers, 'The Tragic Mulatta', in Elizabeth A. Meese and Alice Parker (eds) *The Difference Within: Feminism and Critical Theory* (Amsterdam, John Benjamin 1989), or with the more extensive Deborah E. McDowell and Arnold Rampersad (eds), *Slavery and the Literary Imagination: Selected Papers from the English Institute*, 1987 (Baltimore, Johns Hopkins University Press, 1989). Since this is a slightly idiosyncratic reading of Foucault, I am obliged to cite my own 'More on power/ knowledge', in Spivak, *Outside in the Teaching Machine* (New York, Routledge, 1993), pp. 25–95.

33. This argument is generally present in extant scholarship. For a random and superior example, I offer Russell R. Menard, 'The Africanization of the Lowcountry labor force, 1670–1730', in Winthrop D. Jordan and Sheila L. Skemp (eds), *Race and Family in the Colonial South* (Jackson, University Press of Mississippi, 1987), pp. 81–108.

34. Contrary to some established opinion, Forbes makes a convincing case that the crucial descriptive *mulat(t)o* is a displacement of the Arabic *muwallad-maula* (F141f). The importance of Islam in discussions of imperial formations is illustrated here from below as elsewhere from above. For the general reader, the source books are Samir Amin, *Unequal Development: an Essay on the Social Formations of Peripheral Capitalism*, translated by Brian Pearce (Boston, Monthly Review Press, 1976) and the last chapter of Perry Anderson, *Lineages of the Absolutist State* (London, New Left Books, 1974). To this must now be added Jan Nederveen Pieterse, *Empire and Emancipation: Power and Liberation on a World Scale* (New York, Praeger, 1989).

35. The portions on Forbes are excerpted from Spivak, 'Race before racism and the disappearance of the American', *Plantation Society* 3:2 (Summer 1993), pp. 73–91.

36. Wallerstein, *Antisystemic Movements*, p. 21. The following phrase is on p. 20.

37. Marcuse, 'Repressive tolerance', p. 91.

38. 'Lady Prisoner', by Begum Rokeya Sakhawat Hossain, *Rokeya-Rachānali* (Dhaka, Bangla Akademi, 1984), p. 473. Translation mine.

39. Paul de Man, *Allegories of Reading: Figural Language in Rouseau, Nietzsche, Rilke, and Proust* (New Haven, Yale University Press, 1979), p. 205. The following phrase is from pp. 208–9.

40. Here I refer the reader to a more extended discussion of the cultural politics

of Indian writing in English in Spivak, 'How to teach a "culturally different" book', in Peter Hulme (ed.), *Colonial Discourse/Postcolonial Theory* (Manchester, University of Manchester Press, 1994).

41. Naila Kabeer, 'The quest for national identity: women, Islam and the state in Bangladesh', in Deniz Kandiyoti, *Women, Islam and the State* (Philadelphia, Temple University Press, 1991), pp. 115–43. The quoted phrase is on p. 138.

42. For a convenient description of the qualitative change in global exploitation to manage the recession of 1973, see David Harvey, *The Condition of Postmodernity: an Enquiry into the Origins of Cultural Change* (Cambridge, Blackwell, 1989), pp. 141–72.

43. Woman's position within the patriarchal family as a feudal mode of production has been argued forcefully by Harriet Fraad et al., in *Bringing it All Back Home: Class, Gender and Power in the Household Today* (London, Pluto Press, 1994).

44. A striking exception is the poetry of Farhad Mazhar. A selection will be available in my translation, forthcoming from Third Text.

45 Spivak, 'Three women's texts and a critique of imperialism', in Henry Louis Gates Jr (ed.), *Race, Writing, and Difference* (Chicago, University of Chicago Press, 1986), p. 272.

46. Discussion with National Press Club, broadcast on CSPAN, 28 September 1991.

47. 'Process of writing', *Declaration of Comilla* (Dhaka, Ubinig, 1991), p. xiii.

48. Assia Djébar, *Fantasia: an Algerian Cavalcade*, translated by Dorothy S. Blair (New York, Quartet Books, 1985). Translation modified in all cited passages. Hereafter cited in text as D followed by page reference. This concluding passage is a modified version of the opening of 'Acting bits/identity talk,' in *Critical Inquiry*, 18: 4 (Summer 1992), pp. 770–803.

49. Frantz Fanon, *A Dying Colonialism*, translated by Haakan Chevalier (New York, Grove Weidenfeld, 1965), pp. 65–6, 67.

50. It would be interesting to work out the itinerary of Rolland's exile from the energetic analysis of 1848 by Marx, 'The Eighteenth Brumaire of Louis Bonaparte', in *Surveys from Exile*, translated by Ben Fowkes (New York, Vintage Books, 1974), pp. 143–249.

PART THREE

Global imaginaries

The emerging Metastate versus the politics of ethno-nationalist identity

Sol Yurick

One always looks for some symbolic point where one can say 'that ended and this began', even though there are no beginnings and no endings. Our climacteric is the end of the Cold War, symbolized by the tearing down of the Berlin Wall. In 1989, as the leaders of a piece of Euroasiatic territory were trying to parturate a new transnational formation, Europe 1992, the Soviet 'empire's' collapse, which had begun a long time ago, accelerated. The curtain fell on that profitable, Manichaean theatre of illusions called the Cold War, which had made many fortunes. This war had ironically not only *united* the world in a grand purpose but seemed to have speeded up the grand movement of the world towards modernization, rationalization and human secularism ... at least the 'Western' version of that movement.

The 'West' (sometimes called 'civilization') prepared to celebrate a New World Order, a turn of phrase redolent with terrible, Hitlerian associations. The ideologues of the 'West' trumpeted their victory; not only had social-ism and/or communism failed, but indeed Marxist collectivizing thought – all those dreary, Marxist–socialist, all-encompassing categories such as social-economic class (long under attack by conservatives and the 'new postmodern' movements), surplus labour value, the falling rate of profit and that much maligned, now happily discredited Agent of History, the proletariat – were dead once and for all. Like the Annunciation, the world of the free market, (putative) democracy, free speech, the primacy of the individual, free choice, etcetera, had, we were told, arrived. And if History (but whose?) was at an end (as some propose), the End of Days had not yet arrived. Perhaps the only thing that will 'end' is the millennium, but even this depends on whose calendar one uses.

But after all, if Marxism had failed as a *predictive* system, perhaps some part of that system of thought (itself split into a variety of tendencies) has not failed as a *descriptive* system. Note: the rate of profit (which is inversely proportional to the rate of inflation), which has been falling for at least thirty years, is still falling worldwide and the promised glories have not materialized. In fact they seem to be receding with the same speed that galaxies recede, as if in horror, from our own.

How shall we denote this developing, but not yet complete, 'New

World Order'? Name it the post-industrialist, postmodern, post-nationalist, post-neocolonial, post-structural, porous-bordered, cannibalistic, resource-devouring, garbage-spewing, plague-ridden, hyper-capitalist, post-materialist, hyper-polluted, universalized (Catholic-like), monocultural, ultra-techno-logized, telecommunication-and-computer-nerved, significations age. For this period becomes more and more the era of abstraction: the production, selling, consumption and trading of *things* gives way, more and more, to the production, selling, consumption and trading of *signs* of things. The signs and the speculation in signs proliferate out of proportion to the things of the material world. Dialectical materialism been replaced by *di-electrical immaterialism*.

A new form of cosmopolis seems ready to emerge; it is the age of the Metastate, in relation to which, more and more, all 'discrete' cities, states/ provinces, nations or regions, ethnicities, indeed discrete *minds*, appear as exploitable colonies. This development has terrible implications for a considerable part of the world's proliferating population. To paraphrase Dickens: it is the best of times for those who have and the worst of times for those who have not or are about not to have. Or as the Bible has it: 'To him who hath shall be given and from him who hath not shall be taken.'

Possibly this New World Order should be attended by anger, fear and resistance on the part of those billions who, if they have been invited to the feast of reason, will not be admitted to the feast of food (indeed, given the fact that reason is more and more confined to computers, there is an entrance fee). Like the witch in the ancient folktale, who was not invited to the celebratory ceremonies at the beginning of time, they should lay a curse on it. However, this orgy of harmonic unification, celebrated on the paradisiacal, *offshore*, blessed isles of finance, is counterpointed by a dangerous disharmony on the 'bottom'. Virulent nationalisms have been wakened from their long, enchanted slumber giving rise to an orgy of multi-cultural, ethno-entropic, postcolonialist politics of 'identity'. But what does 'identity' in this context mean? Certainly not the ideology of possessive individualism of the world of the free market. 'Identity', as regards nationalism, culture, ethnicism, racism, means *identification-with*, which entails a submersion of one's psychological self in some greater, mass 'self'.

As the Soviet Empire broke up and its people were 'liberated' from the yoke of political, economic and ideational tyranny, two events followed: (1) an economic disaster; the once-communist 'East' was integrated into the 'Third World' as the 'Second World' disappeared. And (2) the return of the repressed: the re-emergence of national identity, language, custom, culture and religion within the one-time Soviet orbit.

This seventy-five-year war of attrition – in which the major economic mode of production was military – finally left the Soviet Union (as it had vast sectors of the 'West') more or less bankrupt. Or should we amend that statement to say that it was the subjects, not the leaders of the US and the USSR's ruling classes, who became bankrupt? Astonishingly, the

Soviet Union had gone to, of all things, the loan sharks of the 'West'. How did it happen that the communist 'East' was able to borrow money from the 'West' while engaged in an all-or-nothing, military, intelligence, economic, cultural and ideological battle with its mortal enemies? Why did it need to borrow money? Weren't its resources enough to provide for its population? Had, in fact, the leaders of the 'East' and 'West' made financial peace while waging ideological and para-military warfare? And/ or had there, secretly, sprung up an energy/goods/money-devouring, exploitive hierarchical class society within the Soviet orbit, very much 'Western'-oriented, seduced by the 'West's' goods and styles, siphoning off 'public' money accumulated by the exploitation of its workers, what the socialist-communists of the 'East' euphemistically called *socialist* surplus labour value (exploitation with a human face)?

In short, was the Soviet Union, within its centralized, state-controlled economy, oriented (*sic*) towards a fundamental logic of the 'West', arriving at capitalism through the back door, as it were? The fact of the matter is that communism, as it was actually practised, was as much an emanation of the thought of 'Western civilization' as capitalism. Communism, in its unquestioned commitment and acceptance of some of the canonic, ancient, cultural-mathemetaphysico-logical, reality-representing assumptions that 'inspired' and drove the capitalist 'West' it contended with, had un-consciously swallowed and metabolized the *Weltanschauung* of 'Western civilization'.

To ask what these cultures are that one 'identifies' with is to ask what a culture is in distinction to a class (in the Marxist sense). Lithuanians, Estonians, Latvians, Azerbaijanis, Ukrainians, Georgians, Ossetes, Arme-nians, Bosnians, Serbs, Croats – the list is endless – clamour for, if not total independence, national 'identity', at least *cultural* independence in an *economically* interdependent world. Many are exhorted, or even coerced by bloody and politically ambitious leaders into longing for their traditional sacred lands and languages, whatever those were. They begin to dream of a return to mythic pasts. Each fanatical subunit promotes the bloody primacy of its cultural 'selfhood' and 'self'-determination. Reflexively, all cultural, national and/or religious 'others' become anathema.

To ask why the Soviet Union failed to convert all the populations under its hegemonic control to an internationalist, secular perspective is to ask why the 'West' had also failed to do so. As far as communism was concerned, what had begun as an internationalist, left-wing movement, full of hope and promise, a movement of almost religious dimension, became a repressive, corrupt, Great-Russian-dominated hegemony, whose leaders too longed for the baubles and offshore bank accounts of the 'West.'

While the Soviet-dominated 'East' existed, many intellectuals, both from inside the 'East' and from the outside, the 'West', clamoured for democracy, free speech (including the right to speak one's 'national' language) and cultural/national 'self'-determination. Yet almost none of these free-speech-seeking intellectuals ever seemed to mention food, housing and clothing. Perhaps they were afraid that such demands might smack of socialist state planning. What is free speech without food? Silence. As Brecht put it: 'Erst kommt das Fressen, dann die Moral.'

As part of the 'West's' military, intelligence and cultural war against the socialist 'East,' the propaganda and intelligence services allocated considerable funds for dissident national leaders in exile, playing the ethnic-nationalist-racist-cultural card all over the world against Soviet hegemony. 'Western' radio stations, cultural periodicals were used to penetrate what only appeared to be the hermetically sealed borders of the 'East' (as well as the porous borders of the 'underdeveloped' countries) and kept the passionate and invented memory of glorious pasts alive.

But lest it seem as if we are implying that 'indigenous' populations are mindless zombies – ready to submit their imaginations to the latest ideologue who magically pushes their mnemonic buttons, arousing memories, false or real, of a better 'past' (and all that implies) persisting in the secreted realms of consciousness, generating a longing for that which they thought, or had been persuaded to think, had been taken away – let us also observe that in every society, past or present, 'primitive' or 'modern', subsets of the population look longingly backwards to happier times precisely when things begin to change.

What is this new desire for national 'selfhood'? Why have these 'primitive,' infantile emotions continued to persist? What powerful gravitational magic is there in nationalist, ethnic, religious, frequently racist, cultural 'identities' (and any combination thereof) that makes certain populations take leave of their senses and desire to return to a hypothetical 'past' state of cultural, if not material, plenty; or to remember a litany of past hurts, as the Serbs do? Why this desire, these feelings, these compulsions to practise certain customs, to speak in a certain language, to don national costumes and dance national dances, to worship old gods, to practise the so-called ancient rites of national and cultural identity, all usually tied to certain pieces of sacred land (while longing for jeans, of course, and the monocultural pop music of the 'West' at the same time)?

And these tropisms towards the various suns of 'self'-identity are not confined to the dissolving confines of what was once the Soviet Union and its satellites. The movements towards decolonization that followed the Second World War, so-called nationalist-cultural passions, in India and Africa for example, preceded the latest break-ups into ethnocentric warlordism, tribalism, religious fundamentalism and horrendous corruption (no more corrupt, one should point out, than the 'West', however). Various forms of separatism have also sprung up in the very heartland of the so-called postindustrial empire. Consider, for instance, calls for Welsh, Basque, Breton, Scottish, Jewish, African-American, etcetera, autonomy and identity.

And, at the same time, 'nativists' residing in the 'mother' countries demand that their sacred land be purged of 'outsiders,' 'others' – one thinks of France, England and Germany – who came during the great migrations of cheap labour that followed the Second World War, and are coming, and are diluting or polluting the purity of 'national identity', a racial, ethnic purity that no one can specify although everyone feels that they instinctively 'know' what it consists of.

But when these manifold groupings began to demand that their histories and cultures be placed on the educational agenda, many intellectuals began to resist in the name of a something 'higher' than a culture, a body of thought and texts called 'Western civilization' with its gold standard of canonic landmarks, landmarks which at first glance seem to have nothing to do with political and/or economic power (the relationship between canonic cultural texts and political economy is too complicated to put on our agenda).

Let us note in passing that cultural fragmentation *seems* to be a 'natural' movement not only among mass populations but also among those professional intellectuals who traffick in ideas. Great disciplines tend to fragment into subdisciplines, which then become major disciplines in their own right. And since representational languages are generated within each and every discipline, only understood by initiates, it may also be said that each and every emerging area of thought constitutes a kind of culture which, ironically, comes at a time that physicists hunt for a Grand Unifying Theory. Nonscientific, postmodern, theoreticians with a deconstructive turn of mind attack all totalizing master theories as if they are manifestations of totalitarianism.

Cultural fragmentation

But even among those populations of nonprofessionals, there *seems* to be a natural drift towards linguistic diversity, a drift that, let us stress our qualifier, *seems* analogous to constant speciation in biological populations (is specialization speciation?). Localization, 'self'-isolation of social groups of all kinds, and the languages they speak, 'degenerates' into jargons and dialects which 'mutate' into completely new languages. 'New' customs, languages, symbol systems and discourses that constitute complete cultures spring up. And when social groups isolate themselves – one thinks of fundamentalist sects – they are on their way to becoming new 'races' because political and/or cultural and/or religious and/or nationalistic isolation tends to generate endogamous breeding practices.

Yet it should be kept in mind that every culture, each with its own set of customs – no matter how (from a 'modern', 'logical', 'rational', indeed 'scientific' perspective) 'irrational' – is related (not in any strict cause–effect way), directly or indirectly, to the inexorable logic of survival: in other words, to the production and reproduction of material life and the survival of, if not the whole human race, then at least the 'race' or 'species' one belongs to. It is in this sense that *all* cultures exhibit signs of what, to Marxists at least, are the prime components of economic class.

Perhaps every – what shall we call it, precapitalist? – cultural enclave recoils at the encroachment of the ultimate, inhuman, 'mind possessing other', the capitalist Metastate, the destroyer of all those diverse, non-capitalist cultures, languages and identities redolent with strong, emotion-wrenching, magical symbolisms as against the pale, all-devouring, all-levelling, cosmopolitan secularisms of both socialism and capitalism.

To put it another way: a technology-linked, free-market, etcetera, modernity tends toward the universal; culture tends toward the 'local'. Modernity is centripetal: it concentrates. Culture, in the sense we are talking about, is centrifugal: it scatters, fragments, entropizes. Modernity abhors boundary: it insists on free flow of goods, services, ideas and capital. Culture needs exclusion, purity to survive intact: it erects intellectual tariff boundaries: the slightest deviant thought threatens the culture's smooth mental fabric. Modernity is ultimately intellectual and calculating (although to spread its messages of reason, it will, like the Inquisition, torture and kill). Cultures are unique, essentialist, irrational, but only in relation to 'Western' rationalism. Modernity rationalizes; it hates uniqueness, for the truly singular (and a case may be made to show that everything and every person is unique) cannot be expressed in terms of some universal text or value, and thus computed. Modernity is quantity-destroying-quality. (The word 'rational' – as well as the word 'reason' – has within it the idea of ratio, of setting some set of objects or people against some standard. And all social standards, as distinct *perhaps* from the standard of science, are arbitrary and open to question. Looked at from this aspect, every society, every culture is and has been 'rational'.)

The modern, 'Western' mode of thought – long in the making – tends to be additive: it assumes that the universe is made up of equal, fundamental elements and basic forces. All things in the universe are composed of these elements, bound or repelled by the elementalized forces. The 'West's' act of faith is that all can be represented by some fundamental text out of which we build the grammar of the universe. The ever-more-complex combinations of elements and grammar forces can presumably be represented by a mathematical *text*, a text that is assigned the magical property such that to 'utter' text, like a prayer, is to alter the material world (and that text becomes powerful when it is further instrumentalized by computers). But one should bear in mind that all societies assume an instrumental relationship between text and a thing. But to 'utter' does not change the world: it changes the minds of people whose perspectives are altered which, in turn, changes their daily practices *vis-à-vis* the universe.

It is here, however, that we run into trouble. Even though the fundamental particles are presumably identical, all complex combinations, planets, stars, galaxies, oranges, apples, organic molecules, humans, can be demonstrated to have some differentiating, singular, uncalculable *quality*.

It is when all things are equalized, valued, and thus become exchangeable, that the texts that represent everything approach the mystical in daily practice. The transubstantiative, metamorphosic aspects of the texts of modern, abstractive thought rely, when it comes to capital, on the notion of stored labour value, itself not only a text but a form of *compelling* memory. How? The energies of those who work and who worked in the past, used to convert the hostile environment into a livable universe, can be *stored*, but only in the form of *textual* representations. These representations can be used to build and move machines and people to work. But how? A text is, after all, merely a text. But when all believe in that text, in the energies resident in that text, the *textualized* energies can not only be said to *live* but be wielded to energize and command. It is in this aspect that we can see that socialism as well as capitalism is a 'Western'-derived culture … a belief system. Credit is Credo. In short, in the face of the onslaught of the Metastate, all cultures, and those who identify with such deviant cultures, in fact those very cultures, devolve into theatrical games … except for those whose belief in such systems are so strong that they are willing to negate themselves and sacrifice their lives for them.

The usages of such a 'text' are on their way towards the realization of the ancient dream of alchemical power in terms of transmuting the lead of diverse experience to the gold of a monoculture. In the information age, manipulating representations – a form of knowledge – of the accumulated work energies of people, and of material reality, converts anything into anything else. This is to say that while actual things may still be traded in different parts of the world, and work energy may in some dim corners of the world reign supreme, as modernity inextricably linked to capitalism triumphs, *all* enterprise is carried out via the exchange of representations. Those who resist the onslaught of this culture must be forced to change their ways. These struggles take place not only between classes (and within classes) and diverse cultures, but within the emerging Metastate itself. Why else would there be extensive negotiations in the form of huge contracts of hundreds of pages, and accounting books which are talmudically devoted to constantly defining expense and profit, and devoted to argumentation with the representatives of various national tax bureaux? Capital must intervene to dominate and colonize, not only global and cosmological space but conceptual spaces of the imaginary.

This long, historical process/project, 'progressively' moving from the simple to the complex, from the 'primitive' and 'superstitious' to the rational, logical, 'scientifically' based view of the universe, has taken along some ghosts of the past. Lurking behind this Euro-American worldview, emerging out of the Judeo-Christian-Graeco-Roman cultural complex (there had been, to be sure, a multiplicity of cultural inputs from the Arabic, Indian – 'East' and 'West' – and African worlds) are *cultural* assumptions, that is to say, behind the emergent modern logical cast of mind are complex acts of faith. The notion of quality is being replaced by the notion that everything could be quantified (a project that goes back to at least Pythagoras, Democritus, Euclid and that Hebrew discipline called *gematria* that substitutes number for text) an idea that *may* be correct in science, but when one equalizes everything and assigns a common denominator, value, one enters the realm of cultural choice. This modern mindset not only applies to the objects of the physical universe but also to capital (and the social relations thereto attendant: which is to say theorized populations – and ultimately theory comes out of the barrel of a gun – arranged in classes, yet ultimately equatable) and the way in which these things and people are represented. Once the project of equating takes hold – things equal to the same thing are equal to one another, when, in fact, nothing is equal to anything else – quantifying everything and everyone, all can become commodified (measured-against) and for sale and/or trade.

There are problems inherent in all forms of even the most 'advanced and modern' theorizing and classification. The very notion of theory arises out of something called 'Western' thought; that is to say, the making of inclusive, bounded sets to encompass, manage and describe parts of reality. It is thought that premodern societies do not theorize. However, it should be added, in fairness, that any and every society in all climes and with all degrees of 'development' classifies and categorizes and, so, theorizes. One thinks, for instance, of the incredibly complicated systems of ordering of the ancient Maya or the Hindus. It is just that so-called primitive modes of classification are qualitatively different, and in conflict with the 'Western' mode.

In fact, the very 'Western' intellectual notion of the mode of sorting into, of constructing classes and sets into systems, in which any set of items or sets of people can be equated to any other set and assigned some value, raises questions about the whole 'Western' project of logic. Since Occam and his razor, the 'Western' project has been to simplify, aiming towards a basic logic presumably in harmony with the universe itself (Boolean operators in computers … and life). And yet, Gödel has demonstrated that in the linkage between every logical term lies a gap bridged by a leap of faith. Contrarywise, the 'primitive,' or 'pre'-modern mode proliferates categories. But after all, it is difficult to calculate on the basis of, say, totemic characteristics, or on the basis of the qualities and forces of the gods. Yet once we have looked closely at any gathered-together items that compose any set, we begin to see that *all* sets are fuzzy; *almost all* statements containing the notion of *all* are full of significant exceptions. But it is, of course, not enough that some set of people, no matter how powerful, not only decide to calculate in a certain new manner, but everyone must learn and use that discourse. It is in this sense that 'Western' thought is, in fact, imperial.

Capitalism, this transnational system – which has its own symbols, images, ideas, significations, representations of material reality – requires that all things and people already possessed by the transformative effects of a world system of production, as well as those things and people (if there will be any left) of nature still uncaptured (perhaps the very heavens itself), be baptized in the acidic ocean of monetary liquidity, dissolving all previous custom. Once immersed, the representations of all things and people emerge washed clean of the sins of the unique, the special, the sacred. And what enclaves within any nation-state, or any nation-state, can withstand this oceanic force which has rendered all borders and cultures porous?

Given the worsening and permanent global economic conditions, the increase of global pollution, what difference will it make if Latvians, Croatians, French farmers, Armenians, South African blacks, African-Americans, Palestinians, Arab and Israeli fundamentalists, northern Irish, gain their independence and/or cultural autonomy? All are going to suffer under a hegemonic, fisco-sadistic taskmaster as far away as some galaxies-distant, alien and alienating, universal god, the One who may appear in the guise of some local political deity–leader, wearing the national-ethnic costumes, seizing the opportunity to scream for independence, but who has pawned the locale's resources to the Divine IMFocrat. What good has Mobutu done for Zaire, other than to serve as a tax farmer for the 'Western' empyrean, a one-person cash laundry, siphoning off aid, loans and exploited surplus labour, depositing these gains in the Metastate's banks? What good has Daniel Arap Moi done for Kenya *as a whole*? Clearly, various regions, not only in the 'South,' but also in the 'North' have become nothing more or less than a series of banana republics vis-à-vis the emerging Metastate.

What shall one call this worldwide retrogression into frenzied global fragmentation? Lebanonization? A neo-feudalism that threatens to destroy the possibility of one world? And all at a time when, more than ever before in history, one world is needed. *But whose version?*

The emerging Metastate

What is this transnational Other, this hypertheoretical Metastate? Does such a thing even exist? We are moving closer and closer to sighting this people-, technology- and money-funnel into which the world's energy, in its capital, intelligence, information, culture and life form, is sucked and transformed.

The notion of the Metastate is analogously based on the nation-state. (But at the same time it is impossible to look at any nation-state without looking at the Metastate.) The word 'state' (or any variant that uses the word) implies the static, the frozen, a portrait taken in a slice of time. But in 'real' life a 'state' is an active, elusive dynamism: an entity composed of people, rising and falling, wielding power in temporary alliance and some-times – or even at the same time, sometimes in one place and other times in many places – in bloody contention. Indeed, the closer one looks at, and maps/charts any modern nation-state, even the most totalitarian, the more it begins to look like a composite of fighting factions. And at other times, viewed from the galactic perspective of theory, it appears like a united dynamism.

As we scan the variety and plethora of 'states' present and past, and try to define them, the difficulties grow. 'State', 'nation', 'ethnicity' (and other modes of grouping) are *intellectual* and practico-political constructs, concepts, ideas, categories, classifications and laws within whose borders certain items, such as a class of people, who seem to have similar features, who seem to be doing the same thing, reside. At the same time, at variance with all intellectual forms of fixated categorization, those 'items' are living, 'self'-defining entities (constructed from 'above,' 'below' and 'within').

Is territory the criterion? A nation-state is a bounded piece of real estate on this earthly globe. After all, the USA is 'somewhere'; France, Germany, Japan and Russia are 'somewhere'. 'Somewhere' means stretches of territory with definable, perceivable, sometimes agreed-upon, frequently fought-over, borders.

Contrarywise, the Metastate's borders are unfixable. Like an ever-shifting archipelago of islands, the Metastate manifests itself above, below, by the side of, outside of and yet in the nation-state. Its multi-allegianced members frequently sit in the highest councils of nation-states. Does it sometimes unite, sometimes divide the nation-states, as the Catholic Church (both a unity and a hodge-podge of fiefdoms) in the Middle Ages interpenetrated a confused multiplicity of 'states', interlocked in complex ways (one thinks of maps of medieval Germany)?

Shall we talk of population? What are the characteristic features of the population that inhabits the Metastate as against those who inhabit a nation-state? This (these) population(s) come from many nations. They may be Arabs, Israelis, French, Americans, Brazilians, British, Singaporeans, Russians, etcetera, joined together for certain periods of time for certain purposes. They seem to have an international discourse whose alpha-numerabet, grammar, syntax and semantics are devoted to accumulation and the conquest of nature. One could say that this international population constitutes a ruling class in classic, Marxist terms. If, in fact, it engages in class and intra-class struggles (distinguished for the time being from cultural struggles), it is not so much over shared interests as over unshared access to markets, profits and power: a way of doing things.

But if the members of this class share a discourse, one that supersedes the behaviour discourses and sacred histories of their origins – and all discourses are socially constructed – can it be said that they are consolidated into a culture? Which are they loyal to? Culture? Nation-state? Metastate? To ask this is to ask if 'rational' capitalism, if there is such a thing, and its practical, everyday practice, is, in fact, a *culture* with all the irrational features of any culture?

In contrast to the members of the Metastate, a nation-state is composed of a so-called *national* population, which is to say a group of people who have – or *seem* to have – certain irreducible characteristics in common: homogenization. The word 'nation' carries within it the idea of birth from a single source, implying the reproduction and proliferation of a people from a mythical, single source, a 'father' and/or 'mother.' Thus, nationality connotes, if it is not identical with, ethnicity. An ethnic population presumably shares 'blood', or 'genes', which reinforces that elusive concept 'self', or 'identity', almost in the sense of being part of a hive. That is to say that it is implied that an ethnicity contains some unique set of genes which, although mixed with other genes, imparts recognizable characteristics such as skin colour, 'Jewish' noses, or 'Germanic–Aryan' blond hair. But, since it has always been possible for people to mate and reproduce across 'blood', or 'genetic' lines – indeed, more than ever in this historic time of global exogamy, they cannot be stopped – this unity of 'shared blood' and/or 'genes' is problematic. What are we left with? Shared customs, language, ideas, beliefs: hypothetical, *ideational* genes. This too is usually, but not always, tied to a specific, sacred land: Israel for the Jews, Japan for the Japanese, Germany for the Germans …

But the harder, closer and more critically we scan any nation-state the more difficult it is to find any ethnically homogenous grouping. Some fundamentalists in Israel would purify their people, attempting to create a theogenetic state. Nazi Germany failed in its ideological-*cum*-blood-purification programme. Serbs seek to purify their ethnicity of a contamination of Croats and Bosnians … Slavs all. Shall we forget the Turks against the Armenians or the Kurds?

While each modern, particular regional instance is different, there is a formal similarity in the process of nation-building. The leaders of *every* nation-state have historically sought to *selectively* integrate, nationalize and tame their various ethnicities (who sometimes fight assimilation and frequently war against one another) by imposing upon them national patriotisms, customs and a homogenous, national language, not only through these leaders' public education policies but through their control of media (with the advent of radio and television, one began to see the accelerated erosion of regional dialects in the USA, if not worldwide; the international computer networks almost demand that one speak English). This policy was known as the melting-pot in the USA, determined, for the most part, at the highest levels (frequently confounded by many local conflicts over agendas, such as the tracking of different populations into different social and racial classes). In the process of integration, thousands of languages and ethnic customs are destroyed, to say nothing of the actual destruction of races, such as in the Americas.

These national processes of assimilation of deviant populations allow us to look at colonization in a new light. Colonization can be thought of not only as the control of some area *external* to the 'homeland' but as a process of *internalizing* the alienating code of the overarching nation-state's, the mass-psychological process of socially *re*constructing the minds of people by distributing and constantly repeating the myth-*cum*-ideology of ruling elites, and seeding them in the unconsciousnesses and consciousnesses of diverse populations under the nation-state's governance. It would seem that the appellation applied to the old Russian Empire, 'the prison house of nations', applies to *all* nation-states.

Supposing, in the last analysis, we approach the problematic of the nation-state from the perspective of power/governance? If one examines, for instance, the political and economic behaviour of the leaders of the

USA (or any other nation-state) in actual, day-to-day practice, one must go beyond those who can be merely listed on any *official*, government table of organization. One must consider the total structure of power/governance in action. This must include nongovernmental exercisers of influence, rule, and power, such as unelected national and international bankers, corporate directors, CEOs and investors, union leaders, nonelected political brokers, thinktank intellectuals for hire, defence and intelligence 'communities' (whose members may make secret transnational 'treaties' with one another in the name of collective security), or even 'enemies', lobbyists, bribers-of-legislators, organizations of 'criminals' (who also invest in the election or appointment of political candidates), media and press lords, and so forth, constantly bending or breaking the confining rules of their own countries to their advantage.

Primarily those, almost always academics, who have investigated and written about the emergence of the trans- and/or multi-nationals have only concerned themselves with the 'legitimate' transnationals: global companies and banks. The investigators and critics have not touched on other kinds of 'illegitimate' entities, combines, cabals and consortia (who cannot long function without the complicity of various 'legitimate' institutions). The list is endless. There are many customary, *institutional* aspects they have not touched on, for instance the role of international, borderless, 'criminal' banks, such as Banco Ambrosiano, the Nugan-Hand Bank, Bank For Commerce and Credit International, etcetera, and their roles in laundering money, financing drug and weapons deals and so forth. The boundary between the 'illegal' and the 'legal', in this age of situational and relativistic ethics, is fuzzy.

For example, in the US instance, when non-Americans, such as Israelis, North Koreans, or criminal associations such as the Mafia, exert political power through lobbies and outright bribes of US politicians, they must be seen as part of the governance structure of the United States, if only for a limited time (the role of the oil majors in world history has lasted for decades). When corporations, both domestic and multinational, directly or indirectly, contribute to the political coffers of 'domestic' electoral candidates to ensure election, they expect something for their money. When elements of the CIA protect Afghan, Pakistani, Colombian or East Asian drug dealers, when the CIA, US union leaders, and the US Department of Defense banded together to overthrow Allende in Chile, *they* become part of the governance structure of that nation and conversely (after the coup, Chicago-based, Friedmanite monetarists descended on Chile to run the Chilean economy, as they now try to run Russia's economy). When we come to consider the recent Iran–Contra–Israeli–Saudi–Nicaragua–Brunei–US global cabal in action, we should not be surprised. As we begin to fixate on these relations and actions, as we learn who talked to whom, who bribed whom, who set policy, who wrote and signed the secret treaties, who diverted and laundered monies, who sold and resold what weapons systems to whom, and so forth, this complex pastiche of actions, this montage of contacts and contracts and connections, becomes *the* provisional model for the Metastate, allowing us to make fruitful generalizations.

In the case of the USA (although one can cite similar kinds of incidents for all countries), one could sight parts of an international organism extruding within the national organism. This international organism not only made policy but 'controlled', if only for a short period of time, its larger 'host', the USA.

Now it may be objected that the Iran–Contra–etcetera matter was a special case and cannot serve as a model. That the conspirators were using non-'state', *ad hoc*, unsanctioned and illegal activities: that this was not the way things were usually done: it was an aberration. Nevertheless, in scrutinizing the behaviour of the world-spanning apparatus that constitutes these national security collectivities, and their interconnections with the so-called 'private' sector, and with the 'enemy,' one sees a historic, *institutional, systemic* mode of behaviour by certain elite *classes* of people, a behaviour hidden to their subject constituencies, open to their international peers, that *always* violates the laws, customs and cultures of their own nation-states, and what becomes apparent is that such political and economic behaviour is, in itself, a culture with ancient antecedents.

In fact, history demonstrates that this kind of double and triple agentry was practiced in that paragon of early democracy, Athens, as it led a league of city-states in its war with the Persians. No doubt there are earlier examples.

It is in fact *here*, at the 'periphery' of, 'above', or 'below' the nation that certain citizens of nation-states can also be seen to be 'citizens' of the Metastate. What does loyalty to a culture or ethnicity or patriotism mean to such people? Given the fact that those who inhabit the realm of the Metastate derive from diverse nationalities, what they have in common is the culture of wealth and power, which has its own mode of behaviour and discourse. The achievement of power has, both in the present and historically, across cultures, states and nations, exhibited similar features. But when it comes to the question of modern modes of achieving power, that is to say capitalism, we see that a certain discourse, which is understood worldwide, has emerged, springing out of science-based logical rationality, a new, computer-assisted abstractionism, a flight into text that supersedes the cultural biases of those who may have diverse and variant beliefs. The ruling, multinational elites must talk in a universal *Geltsprach* in order to exert power and influence, to set the *national* military and police to moving, not only in their own nations, of which they are subjects, but in nations of which they are not citizens.

In short, those who dwell in the Metastate must, at least while operating in this realm, share a 'culture'-superseding class mentality, in the classic, Marxist sense, as they are on their way towards constituting a world ruling class, a semi-visible government, exerting hegemonic control without a *written* constitution, but have, rather an *unwritten* contract-and-accounting-based constitution which, within certain limits, fluctuates, indeed, gets rewritten (or should one say *unrewritten*) from day to day according to the dictates of the ethics demanded by the momentary situation. Living, as they may, in at least two worlds, to which do the members of this shadow government belong, the national or the metanational? Or both? At different times or at the same time? Do they sometimes play the national, protective-tariff card (GATT notwithstanding) and at other times the metanational, free-flow-of-goods-and-ideas card? Can they use the national barrier card to profit?

What is the discourse demanded of those who permanently, or moment-arily, inhabit the Metastate? It is required that one speak in the ultimate, representational language, a discourse whose *texts* have been assigned magical, indeed alchemical power, which is given the power to reconvert not only the earth, but the entire cosmos, into an empyrean inhabited by all-powerful angels who strive to live in relative immortality: pure capital?

What are the mentalities and imaginations, the day-to-day practices, the language, logic of those who inhabit the Metastate in contradistinction to those who – living in the infernal (which is to say impoverished) realms – stupidly insist on affirming their anti-'progressive', contra-universal 'identities', their 'differences', their 'cultures'? Are they purely, in Marxist terms, a class, or do they have a *culture*, which is to say a way of life, a language assumed to have sacred properties, a set of ritualized, day-to-day practices, setting themselves apart from all others who exist, within their own sacralized, underlying essentialist, religiously based mystique of iden-tity; those who are 'culture-bound' people, counter-'Western', counter-capitalist people? But let us remember that when gain is calculated, the same mathematics is used regardless of cultural differences.

At the heart of the Metastate lies a hidden theory of sacrifices, of eating, not so much flesh and blood, but in the form of life transmuted into the representation of energy. In being accumulative and concentrative, some of its members seek the power of gods, immortality, an immortality they seek to acquire through various medical, reproductive and genetic experiments.

And even as the world on the verge of blessed unification was threat-ened by history's centrifuge, other developments (or *un*developments), what if this unrestrained, accelerating, accumulating, all-encompassing meta-national culture is destroying the world? 'In the meantime, in another part of town' as novelists put it, new spectres were simultaneously haunting the world.

Capital and culture

Item. The massive, growing, global debt (which in the fevered imagination of the creditor is not only a *living* entity, almost autonomous, but even *immortal*) reaches ever-new heights, inflating into a veritable South Sea Bubble. *Every* nation (as distinct from state) is in debt to lenders in the 'private' sector. The leaders of nations who borrowed in the name of their people (while lining their pockets) cannot pay off. It is their subject populations who will be – as they are in the USA – taxed to the point of grinding penury.

Item. This is made possible because – in the 'West' – as the age becomes more and more abstract, those doing intellectual work (a population that increases proportionately to those who do manual work) constantly change what defines the composition, structure, content and relations of what is subsumed under the rubric of value representing material reality. Material reality ironically becomes vaguer and vaguer; accounting significations (should one call them correspondence significations, or objective correlatives?) are pyramided on top of one another and approach fiction. (One development that followed from this recomputation, this *revaluation* of indicators or signifiers standing for capital – financial instruments – was the great merger and *re*merger movement in which people could invest in purchases of going enterprises with extraordinarily dubious forms of debt based on hopes for generous returns from the cornucopia of the future, leading to the jettisoning of workforces as well as an incredible number of worldwide bankruptcies. Yet, nevertheless, the holders of debt insist that they be paid off. Bankruptcy is also a form of reorganizational transubstantiation: the organization disappears from sight and is resurrected under another name.)

Item. Capital, both as concrete industrial enterprise and as thing-becoming-'paper'-becoming-evanescent-electronic-signification, is in flight from national – what was once the 'Western' industrial heartland – domination (which is to say taxes and expensive labour). Aided by the information–communication revolution, capital becomes lighter and lighter and moves faster and faster: hyperbolic capital moving through relative hyperspace. The world is shaken by an unseemly haste to turn thought, in fact life itself, over to computers with their vast vistas of virtual space.

Item. Labour evaporates in the global 'North' and rematerializes in the global 'South'. Whole factories become airborne and waltz across the waters toward the salubrious climes of miserable underdevelopment where wages are lower and the level of extractable surplus-labour-value-time-energy (what the 'West' calls profit) is higher. And when wages come down in the 'West', labour and wages, much reduced, will return like those planes awaited by the South Sea cargo cults.

Item. When factories and goods of the 'West' arrive in the under-developed world, not only are local, indigenous, self-sufficient economies, agricultures and cultures destroyed (indeed, this trend has been going on for centuries), but also the environment. The colonialists (the old as well as the neo- and postneo- variety) had long ensured that no nation, developed or underdeveloped, should be self-sufficient.

Item. Local leaders, now freed from old-time, on-site, colonial domination, compete to welcome investment, waving their own flags, donning national costumes, offering national resources at bargain prices, promising tax breaks to the new arrivals, celebrating coming wealth for their own constituencies, all the time warily banking in that Avalon called the global 'West'.

Item. If we look closely, we will see strange, 'foreign' enclaves (both concrete and conceptual) proliferating within what seem to be sovereign states: 'offshore', free-trade-zone havens: lineaments of the Metastate. These enclaves are sometimes subject to different laws than those of the surrounding territories in which they are embedded, sometimes free of them, sometimes escaping by flights of mind capital. But in the long run, since all things are concrete and material, what are we talking about? Of real people, living in, moving among certain sections of Panama, Switzerland, certain streets in New York, vacation condos in Colorado, swifting to Brussels's NATOland funhouses, making a deposit in Luxembourg, striking a deal, before moving on, in a high-rise in Lagos ... surfacing in certain parts of South Africa ... Hong Kong ... Taiwan ... and behold ... in the jungles of the Golden Triangle, a portable bank teller's counter appears ...

Item. One of the common features is that these farflung 'provinces' of the Metastate are all interconnected by telephones, satellites, airplanes and other high-tech means such as telecommunicomputational systems: whole megacities in a few megabytes of 'space'. A new trend in geography emerges: telecommunication problematizes distance, only to resolve it in a new form. For example, the 'distance' between banks in, say, Panama and Switzerland is much less than the distance between, say, a street in Brooklyn, New York, USA, and a street in Manhattan, New York, USA. Significations of value accelerate, moving through account-book hyperspace from nation to nation, but, oddly, these long-distance flights may take place in one computer. More free-trade zones, unhampered by national, governmental restrictions, are created. The notion of a nation-state becomes more and more problematical. Such free-trade zones are *outside* the nation-state, indeed sometimes even encompassing whole nation-states, yet *within* its conceptually (but not spatially) tiny borders. Such realms can, and are constructed with greater and greater ease within computers ... economic cyberspaces which have expanded into veritable financial bubble-galaxies, realms of financial imagination as *fictional* as novels or poetry, but with deleterious effects – since they are linked to each other – on the *real*, everyday world.

Item. And even as capital moves to impoverished enclaves, impoverished, panic-stricken populations migrate toward what they think are rich, 'Western' enclaves. Africans appear in Russia, Russians in the USA and Israel, Turks in Germany, Moroccans, Indonesians and Surinamese in the Netherlands, Pakistanis and Indians in England and the USA, Chinese in the USA, Koreans ... and so it goes; just as opportunity has departed.

Item. Population increases at faster and faster rates. (In the developed 'North', aged populations increase in proportion to the young: in the 'South' it is the opposite.) At the same time, fewer and fewer workers are needed as factories are automated. On the one hand these technologies prosthetically augment, if not replace, the behaviour and power of various ruling elites and on the other hand they become the cryptographed repository of the ghosts of workers, their once-lived work lives transmuted into surplus labour value from the past *and the future*, whose *essences* now man (*sic*) numerically controlled machines. All these developments are trumpeted as a boon to mankind … but to which segment of mankind? The Malthusian option reappears on the world agenda. But our issue is *not* mere population numbers but a modern, consuming population in relation to diminishing resources.

Item. World unemployment, *permanent* unemployment, grows, even in what used to be known as the 'developed' world. And, at the same time, as the 'West' demands efficiency and 'growth' (odd how that ancient agrarian metaphor persists), speedups and longer hours are instituted and wages go, and are going, down. Benefits – health, welfare, social security, and other – are taken away, moved from one side of the capitalist ledger to the other; self-enriching sleight of hand, adding to this cancerous growth-proliferation: metastasis in the Metastate! All this is to say that more and more populations will have less and less place in the New World Order. What is to be done with those who will never have a chance to earn a living at *anything*?

Item. Organized, unionized, 'Western' labour (actually a small percentage of the 'West's' workers) has, for the past twenty years, been under attack, now that it has fulfilled its historic, tactical mission of serving as the labour agency for the world's employers. Perhaps the doom for the worker was written at the point where labour's leaders opted for trade-union economism. (Then too one thinks of the 'Western' labour leadership's role as an ally in the Cold War. This 'historic compromise' came when labour leaders – of course not all of them – opted to work with the 'West's' intelligence agencies to fight the Soviet Union's oppression of workers during the Cold War.)

Item. And, as all these changes were taking place, all the old, premodern, precapitalist, precolonial customs and cultures were, and are being, eroded by the world's media. In the old days, 'Western' priests arrived in the 'South' to convert the heathen. These days the global church sends jazz, rock, *I Love Lucy* and Elvis Presley to proselytize. Perhaps, inadvertently, in the midst of calls for cultural 'identity', or 'difference' capitalism is in the process of ironically realizing the prediction of Marx and Engels in *The Communist Manifesto*, that capital would, in the future, destroy non-capitalist cultures, even at this historic moment when identity politics has emerged with new vigour. Humanity slowly appears to become mono-acculturated, which is to say 'Westernized', as cultural diversity is eroded. But if a world monoculture is to come, then political-economic-social *class*, indeed in the Marxian sense, will triumph over the politics of cultural, racial and gender difference and/or even personal identity, in fact fulfilling what Marx saw coming.

Item. Some intellectuals, given to optimistic hyperbole, feel that these technological developments will lead to something known as the 'global village'. They praise the liberatory possibilities in what are nothing more than networks of ingenious and speedy adding machines designed to imperfectly mimic reality, a reality converted to digital. They feel that if we are all connected by a world's prosthetic neural network, we will speak the same language. And, if we speak the same language, it will lead to a universally shared monoculture. And if we few, we happy few, live in this monoculture, we will *understand* (and thus sympathize with) one another, and all conflict will evaporate.

Item. As the ideologues of the open and free society celebrate the triumph of free speech, of knowledge, more and more becomes expropriated, copyrighted and priced property, and thus scarcer. Some of these developments were foreseen, for instance, in Marx's *Capital*, Volume I, in which he saw that, first, productive knowledge was expropriated from craftspeople and concentrated in the hands of those who ruled. In a tradeoff exchange, ignorance, that is to say forgetfulness, was distributed to the masses. But, more important, he saw that, second, knowledge/ information/communication, at a certain stage, becomes equivalent to population, which is to say capital-as-text replacing living people. For those of us with grosser sensibilities, financial (virtual) space is metaphysical. To the financial archons, people and the very earth itself becomes metaphysical. As for those who died producing the material world ... their souls have been expro-resurrected into the empyrean of surplus value, perhaps to constitute the celebrated *Weltgeist* who resides in cyberspace.

Item. Health services (practically nonexistent in the 'underdeveloped' world) are industrialized, placed under the stringent aegises of the gods of Efficiency, Productivity, and Growth. Consequently, health care for the many is degraded, if not abandoned, in the over-'developed' 'West'. The charnelhouses return. Old plagues, their microscopic populations mutated and reinvigorated, return with new virulence. New plagues arise: global AIDS (which proves, cultural differences notwithstanding, that all humans are brothers and sisters).

Item. This econo-techno-cultural-information-communication-political global change in the thinking of the leaders of societies has led to the development of a prosthetic nervous system, binding the farflung elements of the Metastate, drawing them closer, relative to those cultural and political entities that are not so linked. As a result, the world's financial market seems to be on its way towards a kind of massified, autonomous, ever-accelerated, uncontrolled, ever-expanding, *infla-nertic* life of its own (what human can keep up with the twenty-four-hour financial trading markets?) in which the *representations* of material life, and their relational forces, begin to achieve a state of auto-dynamization. Actual people buying and selling financial instruments begin to be replaced by 'expert systems'. (Consider the reasons the stock market crashed (*sic*) in 1987: programmed trading.) But also, given the fact that many of these representations are projections of pure, intellectual imagination, representing everything and new worlds of *nothing* given value, at any given moment in the day, given the volume and velocity of instrumental (monetary) flows, there is at least one major financial institution that is bankrupt – sometimes for nanoseconds, other times for hours – lending or borrowing monies that are sheer fictional inventions. One can only view the conceptual pyramid, the very fragility of the world's banking systems, with horror and wait for collapse, already foreshadowed in the US savings and loan scandals.

Item. In addition, because of this technology, it has become easier to track and spy on populations.

Item. (There are, of course, in progress other scientific-technocultural revolutions with social and economic effects. Biogenetics, for one. But there is no room here to discuss these developments at length other than to consider biogenetics an ongoing immortality – and concurrent death – project. And yet, because these projects are generated by those with a sociobiological cast of mind (every psychological and social manifestation is caused by a gene), this new determinism has a bearing on ethnic strife.

Item. One could see, alas too late, an acceleration of the ongoing, long-term privatization of public resources (although the question of what constitutes the 'private' as distinct from the 'public' sector is problematical: compare comments about the 'state' below), a frenzied selling off, at bargain prices, of government-owned institutions such as the state-run telecommunications and postal systems in the UK, Japan and the USA, or the state-run enterprises of the now-defunct Soviet Union, even as the infrastructures of many advanced states decay.

Item. The educational systems of the 'West', which were made available to more people than ever following the Second World War, are being abandoned or priced out of reach of the masses. But then, in its postwar/Cold War profligacy, capitalism had overproduced intellectuals.

Item. And, as always in history, when things grow worse, criminality (or what the leaders of various nation-states define as criminal) proliferates: one thinks of the Latin American drug warlords (able to contend with their own states), the various ethnic 'mafias' within (and outside) the borders of what used to be the Soviet Union … etcetera. These local warlords, emerging onto the global scene, look more and more like those early feudal lords of old who began their careers as bandits.

Item. And even as no nation-state can control its own economic borders, no nation-state can control the 'free flow' of pollution, which spreads like – if not with the ease of – money. Toxic chemical and nuclear waste continues to proliferate. Garbage dumps are rented by the world's 'North' in the world's 'South' (one thinks of Somalia). The oceans are polluted. The climate warms. The seas rise. The ozone layer looks like Swiss cheese. These too are the results of the unplanned, global, resource-devouring omnivorism of the free market. The world's people are exhorted to control their waste emissions and garbage but no such restriction is asked of the greatest producers of pollution: capital. *Perhaps the possible end of – if not all of, then at least a significant part of – the human race looms on the* Weltgeist's *agenda. This should perhaps be our major consideration.*

This leaves us with the issue of what to do in relation to the destruction of the global environment in the context of accelerated consumption and the depletion of resources. The world, including the 'developed' world, stands on the brink not only of a superdepression, but of an ecological disaster that capital-intensive technology, indeed modern science itself, as it is now constituted, cannot, absolutely cannot, solve. Furthermore, the splitting into ethnicities–nationalites in fact *accelerates* demand. It must be fought on a global level, which is to say that many must give up not only their growing expectations but also their way of living, their cultures. All cultures can no longer be contained within small, geographic enclaves; 'small' appetites have global-economic consequences. Brazilians, for instance, cannot be allowed to have any say on a local level since their actions in burning down 'their' rainforests affect all humanity. After all, 'development' of the 'underdeveloped', *as it is now constituted*, must be stopped.

Of the world's populations, who will be called on to give up their goods and their way of living? The deprived or the globally wealthy, who are the world's capital-intensive polluters, which in turn is a function of their system of production and consumption?

Briefly sketched, three draconian solutions come to mind. First, from the capitalist perspective: unnecessary populations should be eliminated in order to preserve the structures, as they are presently constituted, of capital and technological concentration. But what this implies, with the diminution of consumption, which also of course involves production, is, within the present context, that the *rate* and *velocity* of consumption, and the *price* must be increased. On the other hand, the 'overdeveloped' must be selectively 'underdeveloped'. There cannot be some five and a half billion automobiles, nor is it possible to deliver five and a half billion computers to the world's population. Some 'Western' thinkers have asserted that we should ideally be looking at a world population of perhaps *some* three hundred million people. Since there cannot continue to be, considering even such a small population, the levels of consumption of today and the intensity and mass of such consumption, what this means is that fewer and fewer people must circulate capital (in all of its forms) at greater and greater masses and velocities, spending more and more for less and less. But isn't capitalism a system based on the sacrosanctity of hierarchical scarcity?

Second and in conflict with the above, from a socialistic, population-preserving perspective: if an attempt is made to save *the whole world's population* as it now stands in such a way that everyone can enjoy some more than mere survival-value existence, some modicum of goods, democracy and, of course, dignity, there must be a revolution in production and distribution, a retreat from many current forms of modern technology.

Third, this implies that it is time to rewrite the world's capitalist texts, which, among other things, involves the forgiveness–elimination of all great debts. Why not? They are fictions anyway.

But, in either case, since this is a world project, it follows that there must be a world monoculture in the sense we have been talking about. Everyone must give up something, which includes certain hitherto unquestioned ways of doing things, that is to say their cultures, and there must be a total rethinking of how technology is used, even a selective return to less capital-intensive technology.

The self wandering between cultural localization and globalization

Susantha Goonatilake

Culture, the content of humans' minds, is a historically derived social construct, forming a continuum from the past through the present to the future (Wertsch 1985). Social science (which is historically a largely Eurocentric enterprise) has treated cultures of non-European lands through a variety of broad sensitizing metaphors.

In the first, colonial–imperial phases, the time of European cultures' rise to hegemony, these non-Western cultures were mostly cognitively invisible or described in comparison with those of Europe, as the implict standard by which cultures were judged. These descriptions varied from at times a grudging cognition of civilizational entities such as those of East, South and West Asia, the subject matter of various orientalist discourses, to the studies of the 'primitive' and 'the savage' in the form of classical anthropology.

With the political emancipation of subject peoples in the mid-twentieth century, the political economy of social science began to change. Europe's others began to be cognized in different ways. The anthropological subject's culture began to be viewed by some as consisting of a 'little' tradition in relation to a 'great' tradition. Later, various anticolonial tracts placed the social science disciplines themselves as part of the colonial enterprise. And, consequently, from the sixties to the eighties one saw various perspectives on the colonial and neocolonial divisions in the global cultural landscape.

By the late eighties, however, nearly two generations after decolonization, major changes emerged not only in these classical divisions derived from colonialism but also in certain macroeconomic and social characteristics in the world, particularly in modes of production and exchange. At the end of the millennium we are therefore seeing at one level a demise of the economic and political hegemony of the European heartland and its settler bastions. We are also seeing today, in the field of culture, two contradictory though intertwined historical processes that are operating simultaneously: a globalizing tendency, where the economies and cultures around the world are being embedded increasingly in more and more pervasive global webs; and a localizing tendency, expressed in its extreme form by a number of insurgencies on the basis of ethnic, religious and other local identities.

Adding to the complexity of the situation is the emergence, as part of global exchanges, of an exponentially growing information system based on electronic storage, processing and communication. This information system is in effect also becoming a significant cultural 'other' to humans. Increasingly, humans are mediating their actions and interacting with cultural data in electronic form, bringing an entirely new qualitative dimension to cultural interactions.

How these different tendencies will interact can be seen only by examining their respective dynamics. A fresh perspective on cultural dynamics around the world is required. A new sensitizing metaphor, that cognizes directly the reality of localizing and globalizing processes, has now to be used to map cultural relations.

Localization

There has always been, even with the same technological and economic givens, a large multiplicity of historically derived cultures across the globe. Many contemporary societies carry elements of the structural manifestations drawn from this variety of historical–technological unfoldings. These various cleavages of culture built up historically across the world provide potential fault lines for acrimony based on new cultural assertions or new reactions to perceived or actual discrimination.

Mobilization on the basis of local identities occurs on cleavages of religion, race, tribe, language, or, in the case of India, caste. It also includes in the context of Marxism-Leninism a 'separatism' based on class and 'socialism in one country', a principle that is now largely receding.

In a large entity like India, many of these fault lines exist. Thus, India has all the major religions in the world represented in sizeable numbers: Hindus, Muslims, Buddhists, Jains, Zoroastrians, Sikhs, and Christians. Her languages belong to several major families, with nearly two dozen major languages and over five hundred dialects. In addition, because she possesses all the major modern industries and forms of industrial ownership, she has all the major professional and class cleavages of the industrial world.

Divisive tendencies based on these social fault lines, especially ethnicity and religion, have today reached a dramatic form globally, illustrated by the number of non-interstate armed conflicts. Consequently, in large parts of the world, major social fault lines are opening up, whilst in others they remain dormant.

Globalization

The expression of an opposite though related trend is seen in the integrating and globalizing tendencies in the political, economic, cultural, religious and technological spheres. These tendencies are much more pervasive than the hegemonizing tendencies of empires of yore, the present cultural globalization often being a stronger superimposition on the regional cultural hegemonies wrought by these past empires.

Global integration of culture is brought about by people sharing their thoughts, actions, ideas, in short, their culture, across vast distances. Trade and financial links and telecommunications increase this shared universe. Common institutions help bring about this shared world which takes the form of larger social entities, political organizations and common administrative systems, divisions of social labour, common laws, widespread media networks and communication links (Pelton 1982). Other potential integrating factors include increased physical travel of people as well as common learning systems resulting in a common core knowledge. Mass travel and tourism, although limited to the inhabitants of developed countries and the elites of the developing world, is, partially, a form of cross-border cultural traffic. This is augmented by more permanent migratory trends such as those of migratory workers and refugees. A dominant vector in global economic changes is the transnational corporation, making for the globalization of social relations and putting pressure on both national and international state structures (Picciotto 1991). Changes in technology and the economy have led to states becoming, in one formulation, 'servants' of multinational corporations (Petrella 1989). Production, distribution and consumption tend to be partially organized on a global basis, pushed by the growing integration of economic sectors and technologies.

If the companies of the colonial period were associated with a single parent nation, multinational corporations have been increasingly traded publicly and across borders. It has become increasingly difficult to identify multinational companies with one geographic location as their ownership is being moulded by joint ventures and cross-border alliances.

The search for profit maximization of these large economic entities has also led to symbiotic relationships with smaller economic entities in the developing world, covering not only trade, but also technology and manufacturing capacity. Recent studies of such economic relationships suggest that they have led not only to a search for cheap labour, the initial logic of relocation, but also to a transfer of significant research and development facilities (Henderson 1989). Capital, technology, knowledge and, to a lesser extent, labour have become much more mobile in the new emerging global order.

Electronically linked financial and currency trade links, especially, have been girdling the globe and growing rapidly. At the end of 1992 the international daily traffic of currency trading was estimated at one trillion US dollars, having increased by 50 per cent over the three years up to 1992. This has limited the ability of individual countries to control their internal financial domains, even to defend them in times of crisis. The foreign exchange held by all the world's central banks is estimated as only one trillion US dollars, the same amount traded daily. This means that today no single government, even the USA, Japan or any individual member of the Organization for Economic Cooperation and Development (OECD), can by itself defend its financial borders (Greenhouse 1992).

This financial globalization is intimately linked to the new information and communications technologies. These have added new integrating technological links to the earlier technologies of power, irrigation, roads and rail systems that had increasingly crisscrossed the world. The world telecommunication system is today being integrated with that of computer devices. The rapidly developing pervasive communication network (Pelet 1987) has been giving rise to a vast network of data girdling the world (Miles et al. 1988) growing at an exponential rate (Kobayashi 1983).

The ensuing transborder computerized data flows ignore and bypass local and national decision making (Schiller 1981), which raises questions of privacy, sovereignty, cultural identity and vulnerability of countries that have no control over their data flows (UNCTC 1983). The communication girdle also leads to an emerging global redivision of labour, relocating certain brain work, parallel to the relocation of brawn work of the last two decades, leading to a new type of global worker, an 'electronic immigrant' (Pelton 1989). Their precursors have already been seen in the relatively unskilled activity of data entry workers in developing countries who key in data for firms in developed countries. Already, telemarketing in the USA has occurred from Jamaican soil while insurance claims have been processed in Ireland (*International Herald Tribune*, 7 October 1991). The new type of professional worker, 'telecommuting' over thousands of miles, would span a spectrum of similar skills. Some of this network already exists when currency traders, including those in most developing countries, buy and sell currencies worldwide. Other examples include software exports in developing countries such as India, which have been growing rapidly over the last few years (*India Abroad*, 17 July 1991).

Telecommunication links have not yet penetrated developing countries extensively. But those few in developing countries who have telecommunication links are those who influence decisions in their countries and in turn are affected by global trends. It is through them that global financial transactions and telecommuting decisions take place.

As part of this hegemonic blanket, new technologies have an impact on regional religions and are, for example, reintroducing Christianity as an important global cultural actor. US religious radio and television broadcasters have been developing a global presence, spreading across the globe the strong role that Christian broadcasting has in US culture (Hadden 1990).

Cultural globalizing tendencies are most evident in the common core syllabuses that have spread across the globe. Schoolchildren, whether they be in Islamic Iran, Croatia, or the Basque Country, learn to master the same basic mathematics, physics, chemistry and biology. As an orientation to the world, this common global socialization provides strong constitutive elements for a core commonality. Further, this type of scientific knowledge is today growing exponentially and feeds into an ever-widening web of scientific and technological practitioners around the world (Price 1963). Although this knowledge is still created and distributed unequally in the world, its web is expanding and drawing key segments of the world together in a common discourse. There are, however, less universal cultural packages being pushed by advertising and media, often projecting Eurocentric commercial and other messages as universal ones. National media culture is thus partly subsumed under transnational corporate interests (Schiller 1991).

These ongoing processes of cultural globalization are tending to wipe out local cultural identities. As a result, a vast reservoir of culturally learned responses of humankind, built up over thousands of years, is being threatened, a parallel – one should note – to the loss of genetic diversity in the biological world.

Communities: face to face, cross-border, and virtual

What are the key dynamic relationships between these two contradictory processes, globalization and localization, and hence the future directions in culture that these dynamics suggest? To reach an acceptable frame of discourse, one has to raise some basic questions regarding culture.

How are different cultures kept together, how do they break down, how are they drawn into a larger whole? Cultures, one should note, are knit together by communication between their members, and they break down or grow into larger wholes when these links and patterns of communication change. It is in the links between these different cultural worlds that one has to see the future of the interplay between globalizing and localizing tendencies.

Thus, there are several types of cultural communities in the world today. The information contents of these cultural communities inhabit the constituent members' minds and it is the exchange of these contents that binds them together.

First, there are communities that inhabit the same geographical space with the potential for face-to-face contact with each other. Next are members of this same community who are in different geographical locations, including through migration to other countries. These communities can be based on criteria of religion, race or ethnicity but transcend national boundaries. Thus over 25 per cent of Sikhs in India live outside the Punjab, as do over 50 per cent of Sri Lankan Tamils outside their traditional areas. In addition, significant segments of these and other communities live in foreign countries.

To the class of transborder communities increasingly belong also professional callings. The modern physicist, doctor or engineer finds his overseas compatriots talking a near-identical language and existing in a common universe of discourse. They are bound together by their disciplines, their practices and professional norms. Their subject matter changes every few years, and the links across borders are vital for the lateral exchange of knowledge essential to the discipline. The employees of transnational corporations who exchange lateral information, especially at the professional level, also belong to this category of transborder community.

In the same category, though to a lesser extent, are the auxiliary staff and skilled workers associated with these professions, such as, say, technicians, nurses or skilled workers. The knowledge of these groups changes too and requires lateral cross-border communication to constantly upgrade them. But some of that new information can, of course, come diachronically from professionals in their own territories who have been exposed to newer transborder professional knowledge.

Less influenced by transborder contacts are traditional craftsmen such as carpenters and masons, who earlier lived professional lives in which information was largely handed down from generation to generation within a nation, with little or no knowledge transmitted laterally across borders, because new developments were few and far between.

In addition to these communities, there is another transborder set of communities that is increasingly being linked on a daily basis by the global chains of electronic media. These include bankers, and traders of currency and stocks, who are bound together by the common electronic transborder data flows that have been described earlier. They exchange information very rapidly across borders and have a sense of immediacy as they communicate and compete electronically with foreign-based colleagues.

Transborder communities of a less universal kind such as those of religion and ethnicity are also being connected through the expanding telecommunication links. Thus, segments of the population of areas of ethnic tension, living outside their territory, both nationally and internationally, increasingly communicate electronically. The localization tendency in this sense is helped by telecommunications across the localizing group. In fact, these telelinks often provide some of the most vital avenues for both information gathering and propaganda for the militant operations of these communities. But these 'local' electronic communities are intimately embedded within the larger electronic community, including the latter's massive technology support group.

These electronic communities generally constitute what have been termed 'virtual communities'. The dynamics of these communities have been studied in some detail in one special setting, in the case of virtual classrooms that are linked electronically with each other (Riel and Levin 1991). These studies indicate several facets that are common to many virtual communities of telecommuters. The process of acquiring information in such settings, although removed in space, is consistent with that of the social psychologist Vygotsky's 'zone of proximal development' through which a child uses the assistance of other close members of society for acquiring knowledge (Spencer 1988). Persons linked to such a system share their experiences and receive new information (Stuve 1991).

Dynamics of interpenetrating communities

How do these different communities, face-to-face, crossborder, and virtual, interact? One individual self, it should be noted, could today live in several of these cultural worlds. Earlier, when communities were simple and relatively isolated, a person generally had one cultural realm which he or she occupied. This was the role to which he or she was inducted, largely through primary socialization. By and large, s/he lived throughout her/his life within this cultural identity, although with some few changes as s/he crossed different age boundaries. But at any given time s/he had a single cultural identity. These cultural identities were, in simpler societies, common to the whole community, a person being socialized to almost all the group's activities.

With increased differentiation of society, cultural cleavages arose on the basis of class, profession and craft groups. But, within broad limits, a cultural identity once acquired remained. With increased social and geographical mobility, specially after the onset of industrialization, these cultural certainties began to shift somewhat, a person in his lifetime being able to occupy one or more cultural identities.

The conventional view of a nation is a group of individuals inhabiting a common territory with common cultural and racial backgrounds, shared values, customs and traditions, including those of religion and language (Anderson 1983; Hobsbawm 1990). But with modern changes in global cultural processes, through economic transformations, communications, travel and migration, these constituents have split up so that they tend not to coincide today in one territory. Different cultural communities spread their tentacles across geographical areas and draw their members together through multiple cross-boundary links, giving rise to several geographically separated subcultures such as those based on ethnic, religious, class or electronic links.

Thus one may be born in country A, get primary socialization through a religion B, secondary socialization through predominantly European science C, military training D on Chinese military strategy, work in country E, have as employer an internationally traded company F, upgrade or change the profession through a new training G, receive a transnational global cultural package H through radio and television, and travel in country J. Today's self is encroached upon dynamically by many shifting cultures.

It is in the above shifting subcultures that the drama of globalization and localization is being played out. Although cultures exist in different social groups, their contents are physically located in different human minds. It is in minds that cultural residues collect, accommodating and jostling with each other. It is in these mental reservoirs that the various urges for, as well as the human results of, globalization and localization occur.

If we are to answer the questions of the 'ultimate' effects of the interplay between the two, it is in this internal mental jostling that the drama will be played out. Societies may be the larger arena of social analysis, but it is in human minds that the cultural struggle ultimately takes place. Now, how are these cultural residues that would battle with each other, formed and contained within the mind?

An individual could today generally be a member of his face-to-face community, his transborder expatriate community or his virtual electronic community. Each of these communities could also have different subgroups within them. The contents of a citizen's mind are thus increasingly composed of elements not exclusive to a country, ethnic group or religion. Thus no firm separatism within the internal cultural world of an individual, is objectively possible, or viable in a real sense in today's world. A cultural 'Lebanonization' of the mind occurs, with multiple frames of reference for action, corresponding to each subculture. In fact, such multiple frames have been shown to occur in studies of industrial organizations of developing countries in rapid transformation, even before the advent of electronic communities (Goonatilake 1972).

The community that struggles for ethnic, political or religious purity and separation, based on fresh cultural assertions, real or imagined historical slights, and achieves it, realizes therefore only a partial and perhaps phyrric victory. Even the victory itself is achieved by transgressing pure cultural identities. To achieve his liberation, the separatist for an ethnic, class or religious cause has to operate in the world of overlapping cultures and overlapping selves.

To obtain arms and communication equipment, to launch propaganda, to master the modern arts of technological war and of battlefield medicine, one has to be a member of the many cultural worlds outside the single cultural identity for which the struggle is carried out. In the act of 'freeing' oneself from the enemy, one has to draw on common discourses in which one's greatest antagonist is also enmeshed. Thus Serbs and Croats, and Serbian and Muslim Bosnians, are implicated in the same cultural realms of military hardware, communication technology, and use the same global circuits for propaganda. A Khomeini could use a Sony tape recorder as a tool for disseminating his message; but behind every Sony and its tape there is a world of technical and economic culture which provides the technicians as well as laymen amongst Khomeni's flock with a different set of cultural messages. Khomeini's message becomes only the surface culture resting on the deeper structure of a technological culture.

In this sense, unlike in the past, searches for absolute fundamentalist sovereignty are doomed. Today, one cannot without contradictions build 'socialism in one country' or a regime of pure Islam. Eastern Europe, China and Cambodia all have in this sense imploded from their earlier searches for purity, because of the dynamics of multiple identities. The enemy is no longer across the border but within, part of oneself.

Separatist struggles for cultural purity today, whether based on ethnicity, religion or class, ultimately lead only to partial and phyrric cultural victories. For some time, the victorious separatist unit could exist isolated in its collective, conscious imagination, savouring the pride of pure cultural assertion or redressing perceived or real historical wrongs. But in its unconscious psyche, the 'enemy' is regrouping within, re-establishing tentacles across mental boundaries, tentacles that reach within the inner individual soul.

More important, in immediate cross-border disputes, where the enemy is one's neighbour, as in many of today's armed conflicts, integrating links of roads, electricity, telephone, travel and face-to-face interaction will be restored – maybe in years, maybe in decades – once the state of warfare and siege is removed. In addition, the vast links of finance and tele-communications that straddle the globe are re-established. In fact, several such severed links were restored because of economic and technical necessity in the two separate entities of former Czechoslovakia barely a few months after their separation (*New York Times* 27 October 1992).

As technological and other links with neighbours intensify because of obvious technological and economic advantage, cross-border interactions between communities increase. It is possible that a repressive purist regime could survive for some time without any of these links. But given the integrating nature of the economic and cultural worlds, it would be an isolated existence of relative material and cultural poverty. Albania is not a possible long-term economic option today. The 'liberated' zone is soon drawn within the larger cultural world once again, perhaps in a less intertwined form than earlier on, and with some filters for cross-border interactions. Sovereignty inevitably becomes limited.

It is very possible, and in some cases probable, that the localization wars now being waged would achieve liberation. But once the new flag is hoisted, the anthem adopted and the UN seat allotted, the external world inevitably closes in once again, on somewhat renegotiated terms, but not on the basis of an absolutist separation or purity. The concept of 'self-determination' of yesteryear, of an identification of certain cultural attrib-utes with a sovereign nation, now appears quaint in a world where cultural identities have spilled over national boundaries.

If affiliations of, and interactions within, the mind are considered a measure of the degree of sovereign cultural separation corresponding to religion, ethnicity or class, then one gets a still clearer view. In a full sovereign cultural state, one's mind is only imbued with the single culture of the particular community one has been struggling for. But in today's world, multiple selves and multiple identities are necessary to function in any viable society, including one that has declared sovereign separation. No single subculture has exclusive access to an individual mind, no one culture owns it exclusively. Different socialization packages, which are transmitted lifelong, are carried through school, travel and electronic and other media and continuously shape and mould the individual. This is the contemporary modern self, a very different modern self from the exclusive Eurocentric one that recent commentators have tried to describe (Taylor 1989).

If one were to view the mind as a vessel with different layers of cultural packages stored in it, one would get a measure of the relative importance of these multiple cultural contents. One can get such a measure by considering the rates of growth of knowledge and the length of socialization in the several domains. The relative rates of growth in this multilayered cultural system are not all equal. Revealed religion or strongly held political positions are, by their very definition, sacred to varying degrees and so not subject to much change. But other contents change very rapidly. The contents of the scientific professions double according to some estimates every ten years or so (Price 1963). The electronic globalizing processes change this knowledge much more rapidly, so much so that keeping up with it now becomes as difficult as 'drinking water from a fire hose' (Waldrop 1990).

The relative contents of the separatist's self are thus constantly changing very profoundly. The static purist core increasingly becomes a smaller and smaller residue, as the accelerated growth in the other cultural packages continues.

The relative 'amounts' of the different cultural contents are also indicated by the length of time required to acquire them. In simpler societies, where the total knowledge held by society is small, there is a simple division of labour and all individuals share a large amount of knowledge in common (Berger and Luckmann 1967). In classical preindustrial societies with a relatively low division of labour, the individual learns within a few years, mostly by participation in the family, at work and in religious worship, in temple or church. Sometimes, as in the case of craftsmen or religious occupations, a longer apprenticeship is required for socialization. In industrial society, to instruct a person, eleven to sixteen years of formal full-time instruction is necessary (Worsley 1970: 163). For more exacting roles, this period of training both within the formal education system, such as school or university, as well as at the workplace, could be extended up to another ten years. And in the last decade or so, there have been calls for lifelong learning, a demand now more urgent because of the rapid growth of new knowledge. The relative lengths of socialization, as information increases, must by its very nature in the long run increasingly push the purist culture to a relatively smaller part.

Yet one should note that this small purist core can, at times of felt insecurity and need to assert, steer some of the other larger cultural agendas of society. It can attempt an Islamic science, in which Islamic values can presumably attempt to regulate science. But such attempts at steering cannot replace in sheer size the larger, rapidly increasing elements.

The question that now has to be raised is, are these processes in one sense, leading to an inevitable domination of a unipolar world? Would cultural and political liberation struggles not only become unfashionable, but also ultimately impossible? The answer to this has to be approached indirectly.

The present hegemonic structures are very different from the earlier global ones. Thus the Christianization after the mercantile explorations of Latin America was a crude, one-way imposition. A single religion dominated. In the cultural colonization of the industrial era, of the nineteenth and early twentieth centuries, the imposition was a larger package of culture, less virulent than the religious fanaticism of the sixteenth century, but still beholden generally to one mother country, say Britain or France.

The contents of the present global information network are, partially, the local parochialism of the dominant countries writ large, and what had emerged from the internal cultural dynamics of these countries. This increasing global system is mapped atop of past continents of regional culture, say of religion and language. Yet increasingly there is no single dominant locus to the globalizing culture. The USA for the present still predominates, and a group of industrialized countries, such as the OECD, collectively has a greater influence. Yet the globalization process is trading currencies, ownership and also, partially, identities across the entire global system. Multinationals increasingly indulge in cross-marriages, still arranged among the dominant group but no longer within one territory. No single player dominates absolutely in that sense, like a Sun King. The whole is increasingly becoming greater than any single constituent, as the current difficulties of central banks in controlling their currencies illustrate. And even the poorest country, although drawn into an unequal relationship, has its weak voice registered in the globe-girdling electronic babble. This includes the possibility, as countries become more porous to financial transactions, and shares are increasingly traded across all national boundaries, of some elements of the remotest country owning some part of the global economic girdle.

As a precursor to how such a global system would (on occasion) work, we can take past examples of cases of cultural elements of the periphery that emerged as an influential cultural force. Depending on context, a Gandhi in political culture or a Ramanujan in mathematics could thus emerge. One example of a class of cultural elements, which could be a paradigm for the future of such processes, has been the growth of jazz, and related music of the ex-slaves of America, to become a dominant musical form in many parts of the world. This was the result of a variety of complex social and cultural factors including powerful commercial forces that identified important market opportunities. Another emerging example of the cultural knowledge of the weakest cultures becoming in some ways global, is the knowledge of plants and animals held by the smallest social groupings in the world. These are being sought after by biotechnology companies to be incorporated in the latest technology. This is a process done under unequal criteria and the subject of much contentious debate in the field of intellectual property rights, yet it illustrates the possibilities in the globalization of local cultural elements (Juma 1988).

Studies of examples such as these could yield vital clues to how the world would evolve culturally in a future torn between the twin tensions of localization and globalization. One can see pointers to aspects of such a global society in two national examples: India and the USA. Both have their problems and have had persistent inequalities. Yet both have accommodated to varying degrees a very strong mix of subcultures. Although India has several insurgencies now, it should be remembered that her large cities have always been bustling cosmopolitan mixtures. In the same locality, there have been overlapping universes of culture and of structures of meaning, drawn from language, caste, class and religion. They constitute a cultural babble of the means to cope with the world, a veritable 'speaking tree' (Lannoy 1971).

The USA has been one of the world's worst examples of race relations, and has not been a melting pot. Yet, it too possesses examples of the same jostling, viable multiple cultures. In many cities such as New York, communities from different parts of the world exist side by side. In one part of New York, Elmhurst, over one hundred and thirty nationalities exist in an area of half a square mile and live culturally overlapping and relatively accommodating lives (*New York Times* 24 January 1993). These overlaps in the case of a developed country like the USA extend beyond the ethnic group, to the profession, to electronic virtual communities. The selves here are multidimensional, and in that sense, a potential precursor of the emergent global future.

But so, increasingly, is India such a precursor. In addition to the cultural mosaic derived from earlier times, it is today crisscrossed by cultural domains of the new professions as well as of increasing pockets of electronic virtual communities. Several years ago, India was one of the first countries to experiment with the uses of satellites for village education, and today, in the form of software exports, she is a developing country pioneer in electronic telecommuting.

The present tensions between localizing and globalizing tendencies are symptomatic of a deeper, largely unconscious drama. It is not in the macrosocial structures of globalization and localization that one has to search for clues to some of the most interesting outcomes of the drama, but in the interactions on the individual self. It is here that the essential dynamics are played out and the different social tendencies impinge, fracturing and reassembling a wandering self. The self as it navigates today's interpersonal and physical space becomes a new type of wanderer torn from its original moorings.

Now, these processes impacting on the self through the globalization and localization processes are occurring while major changes in the mode of cultural exchange are taking place. Specifically, cultures both at the local and global levels are increasingly mediated through electronic means. The twin processes of localization and globalization are in fact occurring in two realms of information; one set is cultural information and the other set although cultural in origin, resides in machines. The Internet, which by the mid-1990s was connecting together at least 20 million computers, is an important global electronic system, though not the only one. Although space does not permit a detailed treatment, it is useful at least to sketch some of the broad outlines of the implications of such machine-held information for the future of culture.

In the first set of information, the information is human thoughts as they are transmitted from person to person, thereby building up a community. This set may originate as part of cultural information of a very localized region. But in today's migratory world even these local groups would increasingly be spreading themselves and their culture as smaller or larger social islands across the globe in one process of globalization. Thus, in the world of human-held information, there are both pockets as well as larger global entities.

In the electronic 'cyberspace' too, a similar situation of pockets and larger entities exists. There are local information islands, located in one machine or in a local interconnected system. In addition, there are more global interconnected systems through which global currents of machine-based information circulate. These islands as well as the global system exchange information, change their internal states and then transmit the changed states to the human thought realm. It is the latter, human thoughts, one should note, that was in the first place mapped as electronic information. But now the realm of human thought is a recipient of information that has been electronically transformed. And this transformed information becomes in essence, for the human receiving it, novel information. The human thought system imbibes this, and itself thereby becomes changed.

The electronic information system thus constitutes, to the human one, a 'significant other'. That is, for many purposes it interacts for the human recipient as if it were another human sending information. But this information is not just of an individual 'other', it is a collective other. It interacts in a similar manner with a human group as would another interacting social group, because the electronic system itself is often organized as collectivities of information processing and exchange.

Several sets of islands of information therefore are interacting with each other. Islands of human culture interact with each other, say, on a face-to-face basis. Human islands of information interact with electronic ones. In turn, different islands of electronic information also interact with each other. So, the significant other to a cultural island of information can be another cultural island of information or an electronic one. And conversely, for an electronic island, the significant other could be another electronic island or a human one. The result is a richly interacting, dynamic whole of human cultural and electronic islands exchanging information and changing their respective internal states.

The ensuing dynamic play of information as it shifts between human domain and human domain, between electronic domain and electronic domain, between human domain and electronic domain, between one island and another, is very rich. If the totality of life on earth can be considered as some sort of 'Gaia', a total whole, greater than the sum of its constituent parts, then the emerging information system operating at the cultural and electronic, local and global levels is also one such totality, with a 'life' of its own.

The metaphor of the future cultural system is biological, a jungle of information fields, of information systems responding to a changing social and technological environment, in which a continously dissembled and reassembled self navigates.

References

Anderson, B. 1983 *Imagined Communities: Reflections on the Origin and Spread of Nationalism* London, Verso.

Berger, P.L. and Luckmann, T. 1967 *The Social Construction of Reality: a Treatise in the Sociology of Knowledge* New York, Doubleday.

Goonatilake, Susantha 1972 'Environmental influence on an industrial organization in Ceylon', *Modern Ceylon Studies* 3(1).

Greenhouse, Steven 1992 'Greenspan sees risks globally', *New York Times* 14 October.

Hadden, Jeffrey K. 1990 'Precursors to the globalization of American televangelism', *Social Compass* 37(1): 161–7.

Henderson J. 1989 *The Globalization of High Technology Production* London, Routledge.

Hobsbawm, E.J. 1990 *Nations and Nationalism since 1780* Cambridge, Cambridge University Press.

Juma, Calestous 1988 *The Gene Hunters* London and Princeton, Zed Books and Princeton University Press.

Kobayashi, Koji 1983 'Integration of computers and communications, C + C: the influence of space technology', *Interdisciplinary Science Reviews* 8(1).

Lannoy, Richard 1971 *The Speaking Tree: a Study of Indian Culture and Society* London, Oxford University Press.

Miles, Ian, R. Muskens and W. Grupelaan 1988 *Global Telecommunications Networks/ Strategic Considerations* Dordrecht, Kluwer.

New York Times 24 January 1993 'No aardvark or zebra in Queens alphabet soup'.

Pelet, Abraham 1987 'The next computer revolution', *Scientific American* 257(4).

Pelton, J.N. 1982 'Global talk and the world of telecommuterenergetics', in Howard F. Didsbury (ed.) *In Communication and the Future: Prospects, Promises and Problems* Bethesda, World Future Society.

Pelton, J.N. 1989 'Telepower: the emerging global brain', *The Futurist* September/ October.

Petrella, Riccardo 1989 'The globalization of technology and the economy: a prospective thesis', *Futuribles* 135: 3–25.

Picciotto, Sol 1991 'The internationalization of the state', *Capital and Class* 43: 43–63.

Price, D.J. de Solla 1963 *Little Science, Big Science* London, Macmillan.

Riel, M.M. and Levin, J.A. 1991 'Building electronic communities: successes and failure in computer networking', *Instructional Science* 19: 145–69.

Schiller, H.I. 1981 *Who Knows: Information in the Age of the Fortune 500* Norwood, Ablex.

Schiller, H.I. 1991 'Not yet the post-imperialist era', *Critical Studies in Mass Communication* 8(1): 13–28.

Spencer, K. 1988 *The Psychology of Educational and Instructional Media* London, Routledge.

Stuve, Matthew J. 1991 'Exploring virtual classrooms: network communication in a cross-cultural context', *Intelligent Tutoring Media* 2(2).

Taylor, Charles 1989 *Sources of the Self: the Making of the Modern Identity* Boston, MA, Harvard University Press.

UNCTC 1983 *Transborder Data Flows: Access to the International On-line Data Base Market* New York.

Waldrop, M. Mitchell 1990, 'Learning to drink from a fire hose', *Science* 248: 674–5.

Wertsch, J.V. 1985 *Vygotsky and the Social Formation of Mind* Moscow, Voprosyfilosafi.

Worsley, Peter 1970 *Introducing Sociology* Harmondsworth, Penguin.

Index